Jane Addams

Founder of Hull-House in Chicago, first president of the Women's International League for Peace and Freedom, and co-winner of the Nobel Peace Prize for 1931, Jane Addams was a crusader for social justice, a dedicated American who devoted her life to caring for the underprivileged and the oppressed and to fighting for the rights of workers, women, and children. She was born on September 6, 1860 at Cedarville, Illinois. After receiving her A.B. degree from Rockford College in 1882, she entered The Woman's Medical College of Philadelphia. Illness compelled her to give up her studies. In 1887, on one of her many trips to Europe, she observed the social experimentations at Toynbee Hall in London; this led to her decision to establish a similar center in Chicago, where she could put her social principles into action. Her tireless work with reform groups resulted in improved housing, education, and working conditions—in a better way of life for her Chicago neighbors and for people all across the land. A delegate to the first national convention of the Progressive Party in 1912, Jane Addams gave campaign speeches on the social justice planks of the platform, and seconded the nomination of Theodore Roosevelt as presidential candidate. In 1915 she founded The Women's International League for Peace and Freedom. Jane Addams's concern for humanity is reflected in her writings: *Democracy and Social Ethics* (1902), *Newer Ideals of Peace* (1907), *Twenty Years at Hull-House* (1910), *The Second Twenty Years at Hull-House* (1930), *The Excellent Becomes the Permanent* (1932). In 1931 Miss Addams was co-winner of the Nobel Peace Prize, and characteristically enough she donated the prize money to the Women's Peace Party. She died in Chicago on May 21, 1935.

Twenty YEARS *at* HULL-HOUSE

WITH AUTOBIOGRAPHICAL NOTES

by JANE ADDAMS

With a Foreword by
HENRY STEELE COMMAGER

Drawings by
NORAH HAMILTON

A SIGNET CLASSIC from
NEW AMERICAN LIBRARY
TIMES MIRROR
New York and Scarborough, Ontario
The New English Library Limited, London

CONTENTS

To the Memory of
MY FATHER

FOREWORD

Even as a little girl in the pastoral community of Cedarville, in northern Illinois, Jane Addams was—as she herself tells us—"busy with the old question eternally suggested by the inequalities of the human lot." There were not many inequalities in Cedarville, but even there were poverty and frustration: the war widows, the forlorn old couple who had lost all five of their sons, the farmers who were victims of the postwar depression, and the newcomers who could never really get started. And when she visited the neighboring town—was it Freeport?—she was shocked by the "horrid little houses" and, characteristically, wondered what could be done to make them less horrid. She could sympathize with the misfits and the victims of society for she was herself a misfit—so she felt anyway—"an ugly, pigeon-toed little girl whose crooked back obliged her to walk with her head held very much upon one side," who was constantly afraid that she might embarrass the handsome father she adored.

At nearby Rockford Seminary, too—it was not yet a college—the air was heavy with a sense of responsibility —moral, cultural, and even social. Here the girls, most of them deeply religious, encountered a strong missionary tradition, and here too a compelling sense of the obligation of women to prove themselves in what was still a man's world. It was all very Victorian: the passion for Culture, the passion for Good Works. Miss Addams's Greek oration on Bellerophon and his fight with the Chimera "contended that social evils could be overcome by him who soared above them into idealism"—not precisely the doctrine that she later espoused.

There was a brief effort to study medicine—still a bit daring in the eighties—then a breakdown, and after that a long visit to Europe. She was sent abroad to drink up the culture of the Old World, like any Daisy Miller (Henry James was a fellow passenger), but she would have none of it. She wrote later, and bitterly, of "the sweet dessert in the morning, and the assumption that the sheltered, educated girl has nothing to do with the bitter poverty and the social maladjustment which is all about her, and which, after all, cannot be concealed, for it breaks through poetry and literature in a burning tide which overwhelms her; it peers at her in the form of the heavy-laden market women and underpaid street laborers, gibing her with a sense of her own uselessness."

This assumption was valid enough for most of the girls who made the Grand Tour in the comfortable eighties, but not for Jane Addams nor for her friend Ellen Starr, who was her companion. Miss Addams's travels on the Continent and in Britain merely strengthened and deepened her already lively concern for the welfare of those whom Jacob Riis was to call "the other half." What she visited was not cathedrals and galleries, but factories and slums. It was on one of these visits in London's East End that she found herself looking at the spectacle of hunger and want through the eyes of literature, instead of the thing itself, and concluded even then that "lumbering our minds with literature only served to cloud the really vital situation." She had already visited Toynbee Hall, which applied Christian Socialism to the needs of the London poor, and she saw that if she would be true to herself she would have to cast her own lot in with the poor and the neglected, with those whom Theodore Parker called "the dangerous and perishing classes." She too would open a settlement house—not another Toynbee Hall, for it could not be religious or even give the appearance of a gesture of *noblesse oblige*. With Ellen Starr she returned to Chicago, and on that long *via dolorosa*, Halsted Street, found a decayed mansion that had been built by a merchant, Charles Hull, and now belonged to the ever-generous Helen Culver. On September 18, 1889—a day that Chicago should commemorate—Hull-House opened its doors to those who cared to enter. Jane Addams liked to remember that her father had never locked his doors; the doors of Hull-House were always open to the world.

As Miss Addams saw it, there was nothing dramatic about the opening of Hull-House; yet it was a historic event. For here was the beginning of what was to be one of the great social movements in modern America—the Settlement House movement; here, in a way, was the beginning of social work. As yet there was no organized social work in the United States—the beneficent program of Mary Richmond was still in the future—and as yet there was not even any formal study of sociology. It was no accident that the new University of Chicago, which was founded just a few years after Hull-House, came to be the center of sociological study in America, and that so many of its professors were intimately associated with Hull-House—Albion Small and John Dewey and the wonderful Miss Breckenridge and the two famous Abbott sisters, Edith and Grace, and thereafter two generations of academic reformers.

The time was ripe and the place logical. By 1890, just a hundred years after the founding of the Republic, the "Promise of American Life" was becoming an illusion. The extremes of wealth and poverty were as great as those in the Old World. Millions of immigrants crowded into the slums of American cities, constituting a proletariat not only impoverished but alien: these newcomers were the first immigrants who had not been absorbed. The Negro had achieved his freedom, but as yet not acceptance or recognition. Unemployment plagued the land, organized labor was in retreat, farmers were becoming peasants. As Woodrow Wilson was to say in his First Inaugural Address, we were in a hurry to be great and did not stop "to count the cost of lives snuffed out, of energies overtaxed and broken, the fearful physical and spiritual cost of the men and women and children upon whom the dead weight and burden of it all has fallen pitilessly the years through." It was an America familiar to us in the novels of Theodore Dreiser and Upton Sinclair, an America that accepted uncritically the grim doctrines of Social Darwinism that promised success to the strong and the ruthless, and remorselessly condemned the weak and the helpless to defeat. The welfare state was as yet unknown and almost unimagined; even social legislation was a thing of the future. Men worked twelve or fourteen hours a day, and thought themselves lucky to have work. Women toiled long hours at night as well as day; even little children of five or six were unprotected by enforceable legislation. Slums grew apace, and with them disease and crime and vice. Business and government combined to smash strikes, break unions, silence critics, and jail agitators who disturbed their peace.

As for Chicago, all the evils and vices of American life seemed to be exaggerated there. It was, wrote Lincoln Steffens at this time, "first in violence, deepest in dirt; loud, lawless, unlovely, ill-smelling, new; an overgrown gawk of a village, the teeming tough among cities. Criminally it was wide open; commercially it was brazen; and socially it was thoughtless and raw." Happily, it had other qualities, too—the qualities that built the University of Chicago, established the Art Museum and maintained the great symphony orchestra, laid out a network of parks and boulevards, and responded to the challenge that young Jane Addams flung before it.

If there was one part of Chicago that dramatized all its problems more than any other, it was the five miles of Halsted Street from the Chicago River to the stockyards—the great street teeming with Irish and Germans and Russians and Italians and Poles, lined with dingy saloons, pawnshops, and—on the side streets— houses of prostitution. It was Halsted Street that Jane Addams came, and Ellen Starr, and soon the indefatigable Julia Lathrop and the remarkable Florence Kelley and the wonderful Dr. Alice Hamilton, and a score of other intrepid women, and men, to inaugurate what was to be a great experiment in social service.

A great experiment. They thought of it as a simple matter of neighborliness. "It is natural to feed the hungry and care for the sick," wrote Jane Addams. "It is certainly natural to give pleasure to the young, comfort the aged, and to minister to the deep-seated craving for social intercourse that all men feel." That is what they proposed to do and that is what they did.

The "first resident" was an old lady who had lived at Brook Farm and had known Emerson and Bronson Alcott and that pioneer of social reform, Theodore Parker. Soon men and women and children of all ages

thronged through the hospitable doors of the old mansion
now reborn to new life; before long 2,000 people crossed
its portals every day. Hull-House caught the imagination of Chicago—as it was to catch the imagination of
the whole nation. There were gifts of buildings and of
land from the ever-benevolent Miss Culver and eventually of money from many others. Hull-House grew and
spread until in time it came to be a kind of community
center for the whole of Chicago: a boys' club, an art
museum, a theater, a music school, a gymnasium, and a
dozen other buildings, all in use from morning until late
into the night. Children came to play; the young to act
or to draw or to dance; girls in trouble who had been
turned out of their homes; men out of work, or on the
run; the sick and the tired and the frightened and the
lonely, and along with them scholars from universities
like John R. Commons and E. A. Ross, down from
nearby Madison, or John Dewey, or young Robert
Morss Lovett. And along with them came the leaders
of Chicago society, for Hull-House had become fash-
ionable.

Calm and serene and authoritative, Jane Addams presided over it all. She took care of babies, even acting as
midwife—had she not planned to be a doctor? She
supervised all the varied activities of the sprawling community, kept the accounts, dealt with the scores of visitors, found work for the eager assistants and even trained
them; she lectured, she wrote articles and books; she
carried on a tremendous correspondence with social
workers throughout the country, she served on committees and pleaded with legislatures and won over
governors. Nothing was too difficult for her, and nothing
too simple. She tells us of the tasks that fell to her in
the early weeks—and that continued to make demands
upon her:

For six weeks after an operation we kept in one of our
three bedrooms a forlorn little baby who, because he
was born with a cleft palate, was most unwelcome even
to his mother, and we were horrified when he died of
neglect a week after he was returned to his home; a little
Italian bride of fifteen sought shelter with us one November
evening to escape her husband, who had beaten her every
night for a week when he returned from work because she

had lost her wedding ring; two of us officiated quite alone at the birth of an illegitimate child because the doctor was late in arriving, and none of the honest Irish matrons would "touch the likes of her"; we ministered at the deathbed of a young man who, during a long illness of tuberculosis, had received so many bottles of whisky through the mistaken kindness of his friends that the cumulative effect produced wild periods of exultation, in one of which he died.

Over the years Jane Addams built a bridge between the immigrants and the old-stock Americans, between the working classes and the immigrants, between the amateur reformers and the professional politicians, even between private philanthropy and government. She made Hull-House a clearinghouse for every kind of social service, an experimental laboratory in social reform, in art and music and drama and education as well; she made it a school of citizenship and a university of social service.

It was all done so simply and so naturally, so much as part of the day by day housekeeping, that contemporaries did not always realize that was a product of head as well as of heart. Miss Addams knew what she was about; she has told us that

The Settlement then, is an experimental effort to aid in the solution of the social and industrial problems which are engendered by the modern conditions of life in a great city. It insists that these problems are not confined to any one portion of a city. It is an attempt to relieve, at the same time, the overaccumulation at one end of society and the destitution at the other. . . . The one thing to be dreaded in the Settlement is that it lose its flexibility, its power of quick adaptation, its readiness to change its methods as its environment may demand. It must be open to conviction and must have a deep and abiding sense of tolerance. It must be hospitable and ready for experiment. It should demand from its residents a scientific patience in the accumulation of facts and the steady holding of their sympathies as one of the best instruments for that accumulation. It must be grounded in a philosophy whose foundation is on the solidarity of the human race, a philosophy which will not waver when the race happens to be represented by a drunken woman or an idiot boy. Its residents must be emptied of all conceit of opinion and all self-assertion, and ready to arouse and interpret the public opinion of their neighborhood.

Jane Addams had many talents, but none more remarkable than her ability to work from the immediate to the general, from practical problems to philosophy, and even from the local to the national and the international. She always began with the job at hand, no matter how elementary or undignified; she took on the job of inspector of garbage removal for her ward to show how it should be done—and did it so well that the boss had to abolish the job itself in order to protect those collectors who held their jobs as sinecures; she went to the Illinois legislature with case histories of working women to push through labor legislation—legislation struck down by the courts. What she saw of youth on the city streets ended up as a program of school playgrounds; what she learned of children in trouble with the law ended as the first juvenile courts in the nation.

She had another genius, too. "You utter instinctively the truths we others vainly seek," William James wrote her. Yet it was not really instinct, but experience and wisdom—experience so full and wisdom so deep that they functioned like a second nature. Long before Lincoln Steffens she learned that corruption in politics was not the exclusive privilege of the wicked but stemmed from the respectable as well, and she learned, too, that it was possible to win politicians and spoilsmen to your side. *Democracy and Social Ethics* anticipated E. A. Ross's penetrating discovery that personal virtue was not enough—that social virtue was necessary to triumph over social sin. Her essay on the Pullman strike, "A Modern King Lear," saw the problem of capital and labor not so much in moral as in psychological terms, and she anticipated scholars like Frank Tannenbaum in seeking the deep social conservatism of the labor movement. And in her appreciation of art as experience, her realization that "life consists of processes . . ." and that "democracy is that which affords a rule of living as well as a test of faith," she both anticipated and influenced John Dewey.

Yet to what end all of these melioristic activities? "In the face of desperate hunger and need," Jane Addams wrote in 1894, the depth of the worst of our depressions, "these activities could not but seem futile and superficial." More and more she came to feel like Alice with the Red Queen: no matter how fast she ran, she was still in the same place; the poverty, the slums, the crime and vice, the misgovernment, the illiteracy, the exploitation, the inhumanity of man to man—all these were still there. How futile to bind up wounds that should never have been inflicted; to put together parts of lives that should never have been shattered; to rescue girls from city streets when fair wages would have kept them safely at home in the first place; to give children a chance to play in the late hours of the evening when the whole day should belong to them; to provide emergency nursing for diseases that should never have infected their victims. How futile was the cure, how imperative was prevention!

One of the many merits of *Twenty Years* is that it dramatizes to us that lesson which every generation has to learn anew if it is to achieve understanding of either past or present: that those who stand at the levers of control, whether they are Southern slaveholders in the 1850's, or industrial barons in the 1890's, or labor bosses in the 1950's, tend to use power ruthlessly, and that there seems to be a close correlation between the social respectability of power and the ruthlessness. Certainly no farmer or labor organization in our history ever displayed the contempt for law, the brutality toward women and children, the prejudice against aliens, the ferocity toward those who stood in their way, that corporate wealth displayed in the Chicago, and in the Illinois, that Miss Addams describes in these tragic pages.

Very early Miss Addams and her Hull-House associates found that they had to move into the political arena. They helped push through labor legislation, set up juvenile courts, provided school playgrounds, worked for adequate enforcement of housing and sanitation laws, improved the school system, agitated for broader participation in politics—including woman suffrage—called for legal protection for immigrants, served as an embryonic Civil Liberties Union to preserve due process. They turned first to the municipal government, then at the very apex of corruption; then to Springfield, which was not much better. Eventually they looked to Congress

and the President for national action. By the end of the
first twenty years so lovingly chronicled in these pages
Jane Addams was ready for a national crusade for social justice—a crusade to be waged in politics. Another
five or six years and the World War launched her on an
international crusade: the last years of her life were
dedicated to the cause of peace, and the little girl from
Cedarville who had always walked a few steps behind
her father ended up by organizing the women of Austria
and Italy, Japan and India, for world peace. She became
the first woman to win the Nobel Peace Prize. That is
the story of the Second Twenty Years.

Yet, of course, Hull-House remained the center of
her interest, and indeed of her world, and when she
came to record the later years and the larger crusades
she called the story, quite appropriately, *The Second
Twenty Years at Hull-House*. There it was, growing,
flourishing, spreading its influence throughout the city,
the state, the nation, the entire world. It was, in all these
years, a Settlement House, a cultural center, a social
service training school, a university, and almost a church.
An institution, it has been said, is the lengthened shadow
of one man. Hull-House is more than the shadow of
Jane Addams; it is the very substance.

Miss Addam's earlier activities on behalf of labor
laws and slum clearance and the rights of the poor and
the despised had earned her the suspicion and hostility
of some businessmen and of some conservative politicians; her later activities on behalf of what we would call
the welfare state, and the cause of peace, won for her
the hatred and contumely of the professional patriots.
The American Legion denounced her as un-American,
and the Daughters of the American Revolution stigma-
tized her as "a factor in a movement to destroy civilization and Christianity." She was used to these pin pricks;
she had fought stouter opponents most of her life.
Nor did she ever allow her serenity to be ruffled by
attack, or her judgment to be warped by bitterness.

In time, of course, she weathered all attacks; in time,
the querulous dissents were drowned out by a ground
swell of acclamation and affection. She had long been the
first citizen of Chicago; by the second decade of the new
century she was widely regarded as the first citizen of

the nation, and she came in time to occupy something of the place in the affection and admiration of the world that Eleanor Roosevelt holds today.

Jane Addams had many talents; not the least of them, and not the least astonishing, was her literary talent. She wrote for the best of reasons, because she had something that very much needed to be said. She wrote with the best of styles—direct, lucid, and simple. She knew by instinct what the great encyclopaedist Jean D'Alembert taught: "Have lofty sentiments and your manner of writing will be noble." Miss Addams did not consciously entertain lofty sentiments, but her whole character was noble, and so too her style. She never thought of herself; even her autobiography is the story of Hull-House. Was there ever a more impersonal autobiography? Henry Adams pretended to impersonality by using the third person, but it is Adams, Adams, all the way, and in the end the cosmos is invoked to explain the Adams family. Miss Addams does not ask us to consider her, but only the society she served; yet how luminously her character shines through: firm, just, gentle, efficient, tenacious, upright, and endlessly compassionate.

She was, the British labor leader John Burns said, "the only saint America had produced." It was as Saint Jane that she was known to millions around the earth and none now will challenge her right to that name.

—HENRY STEELE COMMAGER

Amherst, Mass.

PREFACE

EVERY preface is, I imagine, written after the book has been completed, and now that I have finished this volume I will state several difficulties which may put the reader upon his guard unless he too postpones the preface to the very last.

Many times during the writing of these reminiscences, I have become convinced that the task was undertaken all too soon. One's fiftieth year is indeed an impressive milestone at which one may well pause to take an accounting, but the people with whom I have so long journeyed have become so intimate a part of my lot that they cannot be written of either in praise or blame; the public movements and causes with which I am still identified have become so endeared, some of them through their very struggles and failures, that it is difficult to discuss them.

It has also been hard to determine what incidents and experiences should be selected for recital, and I have found that I might give an accurate report of each isolated event and yet give a totally misleading impression of the whole, solely by the selection of the incidents. For these reasons and many others I have found it difficult to make a faithful record of the years since the autumn of 1889 when without any preconceived social theories or economic views, I came to live in an industrial district of Chicago.

If the reader should inquire why the book was ever undertaken in the face of so many difficulties, in reply I could instance two purposes, only one of which in the language of organized charity, is "worthy." Because Settlements have multiplied so easily in the United States I hoped that a simple statement of an earlier effort, including the stress and storm, might be of value in their interpretation and possibly clear them of a certain charge of superficiality. The unworthy motive was a desire to start a "backfire," as it were, to extinguish two biographies of myself, one of which had been submitted to me in outline, that made life in a Settlement all too smooth and charming.

The earlier chapters present influences and personal motives with a detail which will be quite unpardonable if they fail to make clear the personality upon whom various social and industrial movements in Chicago reacted during a period of twenty years. No effort is made in the recital to separate my own history from that of Hull-House during the years when I was "launched deep into the stormy intercourse of human life" for, so far as a mind is pliant under the pressure of events and experiences, it becomes hard to detach it.

It has unfortunately been necessary to abandon the chronological order in favor of the topical, for during the early years at Hull-House, time seemed to afford a mere framework for certain lines of activity and I have found in writing this book, that after these activities have been recorded, I can scarcely recall the scaffolding.

More than a third of the material in the book has appeared in *The American Magazine*, one chapter of it in *McClure's Magazine,* and earlier statements of the Settlement motive, published years ago, have been utilized in chronological order because it seemed impossible to reproduce their enthusiasm.

It is a matter of gratification to me that the book is illustrated from drawings made by Miss Norah Hamilton of Hull-House, and the cover designed by another resident, Mr. Frank Hazenplug. I am indebted for the making of the index and for many other services to Miss Clara Landsberg, also of Hull-House.

If the conclusions of the whole matter are similar to those I have already published at intervals during the twenty years at Hull-House, I can only make the defense that each of the earlier books was an attempt to set forth a thesis supported by experience, whereas this volume endeavors to trace the experiences through which various conclusions were forced upon me.

🌸 🌸 *Chapter* I

EARLIEST IMPRESSIONS

ON the theory that our genuine impulses may be connected with our childish experiences, that one's bent may be tracked back to that "No-Man's Land" where character is formless but nevertheless settling into definite lines of future development, I begin this record with some impressions of my childhood.

All of these are directly connected with my father, although of course I recall many experiences apart from him. I was one of the younger members of a large family and an eager participant in the village life, but because my father was so distinctly the dominant influence and because it is quite impossible to set forth all of one's early impressions, it has seemed simpler to string these first memories on that single cord. Moreover, it was this cord which not only held fast my supreme affection, but also first drew me into the moral concerns of life, and later afforded a clue there to which I somewhat wistfully clung in the intricacy of its mazes.

It must have been from a very early period that I recall "horrid nights" when I tossed about in my bed because I had told a lie. I was held in the grip of a miserable dread of death, a double fear, first, that I myself should die in my sins and go straight to that fiery Hell which was never mentioned at home, but which I had heard all about from other children, and, second, that my father—representing the entire adult world which I had basely deceived—should himself die before I had time to tell him. My only method of obtaining relief was to go downstairs to my father's room and make full confession. The high resolve to do this would push me out of bed and carry me down the stairs without a touch of fear. But at the foot of the stairs I would be faced by the awful necessity of passing the front door—which my father, because of his Quaker tendencies, did not lock—and of crossing the wide and black expanse of the living room in order to reach his door. I would invariably cling to the newel post while I contemplated the perils of the situation, complicated by the fact that the literal first step meant putting my bare foot upon a piece of oilcloth in front of the door, only a few inches wide, but lying straight in my path. I would finally reach my father's bedside perfectly breathless and, having panted out the history of my sin, invariably received the same assurance that if he "had a little girl who told lies," he was very glad that she "felt too bad to go to sleep afterward." No absolution was asked for or received, but apparently the sense that the knowledge of my wickedness was shared, or an obscure understanding of the affection which underlay the grave statement, was sufficient, for I always went back to bed as bold as a lion, and slept, if not the sleep of the just, at least that of the comforted.

I recall an incident which must have occurred before I was seven years old, for the mill in which my father transacted his business that day was closed in 1867. The mill stood in the neighboring town adjacent to its poorest quarter. Before then I had always seen the little city of ten thousand people with the admiring eyes of a country child, and it had never occurred to me that all its streets were not as bewilderingly attractive as the one which contained the glittering toyshop and the confectioner. On that day I had my first sight of the poverty which implies squalor, and felt the curious distinction between the ruddy poverty of the country and that which even a small city presents in its shabbiest streets. I remember launching at my father the pertinent inquiry why people lived in such horrid little houses so close together, and that after receiving his explanation I declared with much firmness when I grew up I should, of course, have a large house,

Homestead at Cedarville

but it would not be built among the other large houses, but right in the midst of horrid little houses like these.

That curious sense of responsibility for carrying on the world's affairs which little children often exhibit because "the old man clogs our earliest years" I remember in myself in a very absurd manifestation. I dreamed night after night that everyone in the world was dead excepting myself, and that upon me rested the responsibility of making a wagon wheel. The village street remained as usual, the village blacksmith shop was "all there," even a glowing fire upon the forge and the anvil in its customary place near the door, but no human being was within sight. They had all gone around the edge of the hill to the village cemetery, and I alone remained alive in the deserted world. I always stood in the same spot in the blacksmith shop, darkly pondering as to how to begin, and never once did I know how, although I fully realized that the affairs of the world could not be resumed until at least one wheel should be made and something started. Every victim of nightmare is, I imagine, overwhelmed by an excessive sense of responsibility and the consciousness of a fearful handicap in the effort to perform what is required; but perhaps never were the odds more heavily against "a warder of the world" than in these reiterated dreams of mine, doubtless compounded in equal parts of a childish version of Robinson Crusoe and of the end-of-the-world predictions of the Second Adventists, a few of whom were found in the village. The next morning would often find me, a delicate little girl of six, with the further disability of a curved spine, standing in the doorway of the village blacksmith shop, anxiously watching the burly, red-shirted figure at work. I would store my mind with such details of the process of making wheels as I could observe, and sometimes I plucked up courage to ask for more. "Do you always have to sizzle the iron in water?" I would ask, thinking how horrid it would be to do. "Sure!" the good-natured blacksmith would reply, "that makes the iron hard." I would sigh heavily and walk away, bearing my responsibility as best I could, and this of course I confided to no one, for there is something too mysterious in the burden of "the winds that come from the fields of sleep" to be communicated, although it is at the same time too heavy a burden to be borne alone.

My great veneration and pride in my father manifested itself in curious ways. On several Sundays, doubtless occurring in two or three different years, the Union Sunday

School of the village was visited by strangers, some of those "strange people" who live outside a child's realm, yet constantly thrill it by their close approach. My father taught the large Bible class in the lefthand corner of the church next to the pulpit, and to my eyes at least, was a most imposing figure in his Sunday frock coat, his fine head rising high above all the others. I imagined that the strangers were filled with admiration for this dignified person, and I prayed with all my heart that the ugly, pigeon-toed little girl, whose crooked back obliged her to walk with her head held very much upon one side, would never be pointed out to these visitors as the daughter of this fine man. In order to lessen the possibility of a connection being made, on these particular Sundays I did not walk beside my father, although this walk was the great event of the week, but attached myself firmly to the side

Jane Addams, aged Seven, from a Photograph of 1867

of my Uncle James Addams, in the hope that I should be mistaken for his child, or at least that I should not remain so conspicuously unattached that troublesome questions might identify an Ugly Duckling with·her imposing parent. My uncle, who had many children of his own, must have been mildly surprised at this unwonted attention, but he would look down kindly at me, and say, "So you are going to walk with me today?" "Yes, please, Uncle James," would be my meek reply. He fortunately never explored my motives, nor do I remember that my father ever did, so that in all probability my machinations have been safe from public knowledge until this hour.

It is hard to account for the manifestations of a child's adoring affection, so emotional, so irrational, so tangled with the affairs of the imagination. I simply could not endure the thought that "strange people" should know that my handsome father owned this homely little girl. But even in my chivalric desire to protect him from his fate, I was not quite easy in the sacrifice of my uncle, although I quieted my scruples with the reflection that the contrast was less marked and that, anyway, his own little girl "was not so very pretty." I do not know that I commonly dwelt much upon my personal appearance, save as it thrust itself as an incongruity into my father's life, and in spite of unending evidence to the contrary, there were even black moments when I allowed myself to speculate as· to whether he might not share the feeling. Happily, however, this specter was laid before it had time to grow into a morbid familiar by a very trifling incident. One day I met my father coming out of his bank on the main street of the neighboring city, which seemed to me a veritable whirlpool of society and commerce. With a playful touch of exaggeration, he lifted his high and shining silk hat and made me an imposing bow. This distinguished public recognition, this totally unnecessary identification among a mass of "strange people" who couldn't possibly know unless he himself made the sign, suddenly filled me with a sense of the absurdity of the entire feeling. It may not even then have seemed as absurd as it really was, but at least it seemed enough so to collapse or to pass into the limbo of forgotten specters.

I made still other almost equally grotesque attempts to express this doglike affection. The house at the end of the village in which I was born, and which was my home until

I moved to Hull-House, in my earliest childhood had opposite to it—only across the road and then across a little stretch of greensward—two mills belonging to my father; one flour mill, to which the various grains were brought by the neighboring farmers, and one sawmill, in which the logs of the native timber were sawed into lumber. The latter offered the great excitement of sitting on a log while it slowly approached the buzzing saw which was cutting it into slabs, and of getting off just in time to escape a sudden and gory death. But the flouring mill was much more beloved. It was full of dusky, floury places which we adored, of empty bins in which we might play house; it had a basement with piles of bran and shorts which were almost as good as sand to play in, whenever the miller let us wet the edges of the pile with water brought in his sprinkling pot from the mill-race.

In addition to these fascinations was the association of the mill with my father's activities, for doubtless at that time I centered upon him all that careful imitation which a little girl ordinarily gives to her mother's ways and habits. My mother had died when I was a baby and my father's second marriage did not occur until my eighth year.

I had a consuming ambition to possess a miller's thumb, and would sit contentedly for a long time rubbing between my thumb and fingers the ground wheat as it fell from between the millstones, before it was taken up on an endless chain of mysterious little buckets to be bolted into flour. I believe I have never since wanted anything more desperately than I wanted my right thumb to be flattened, as my father's had become, during his earlier years of a miller's life. Somewhat discouraged by the slow process of structural modification, I also took measures to secure on the backs of my hands the tiny purple and red spots which are always found on the hands of the miller who dresses millstones. The marks on my father's hands had grown faint, but were quite visible when looked for, and seemed to me so desirable that they must be procured at all costs. Even when playing in our house or yard, I could always tell when the millstones were being dressed, because the rumbling of the mill then stopped, and there were few pleasures I would not instantly forego, rushing at once to the mill, that I might spread out my hands near the millstones in the hope that the little hard flints flying from the miller's chisel would light upon their backs and make the longed-for marks. I used hotly to accuse the German miller, my dear friend Ferdinand, "of trying not to hit my hands," but he scornfully replied that he could not hit them if he did try, and that they were too little to be of use in a mill anyway. Although I hated his teasing, I never had the courage to confess my real purpose.

This sincere tribute of imitation, which affection offers its adored object, had later, I hope, subtler manifestations, but certainly these first ones were altogether genuine. In this case, too, I doubtless contributed my share to that stream of admiration which our generation so generously poured forth for the self-made man. I was consumed by a wistful desire to apprehend the hardships of my father's earlier life in that faraway time when he had been a miller's apprentice. I knew that he still woke up punctually at three o'clock because for so many years he had taken his turn at the mill in the early morning, and if by chance I awoke at the same hour, as curiously enough I often did, I imagined him in the early dawn in my uncle's old mill reading through the entire village library, book after book, beginning with the lives of the signers of the Declaration of Independence. Copies of the same books, mostly bound in calfskin, were to be found in the library below, and I courageously resolved that I too would read them all and try to understand life as he did. I did in fact later begin a course of reading in the early morning hours, but I was caught by some fantastic notion of chronological order and early legendary form. Pope's translation of the *Iliad,* even followed by Dryden's *Virgil,* did not leave behind the residuum of wisdom for which I longed, and I finally gave them up for a thick book entitled *The History of the World* as affording a shorter and an easier path.

Although I constantly confided my sins and perplexities to my father, there are only a few occasions on which I remember having received direct advice or admonition; it may easily be true, however, that I have forgotten the latter, in the manner of many seekers after advice who enjoyably set forth their situation but do not really listen to the advice itself. I can remember an admonition on one occasion, however, when, as a little girl of eight years, arrayed in a new cloak, gorgeous beyond anything I had ever worn before, I stood before my father for his approval. I was much chagrined by his remark that it was a very pretty cloak—in fact so much prettier than any cloak the other little girls in the Sunday School had that he would advise me to wear my old cloak, which would keep me quite as warm, with the added advantage of not making the other little girls feel bad. I complied with the request but I fear without inner consent, and I certainly was quite without the joy of self-sacrifice as I walked soberly through the village street by the side of my counselor. My mind was busy, however, with the old question eternally suggested by the inequalities of the human lot. Only as we neared the church door did I venture to ask what could be done about it, receiving the reply that it might never be righted so far as clothes went, but that people might be equal in things that mattered much more than clothes, the affairs of education and religion, for instance, which we attended to when we went to school and church, and that it was very stupid to wear the sort of clothes that made it harder to have equality even there.

It must have been a little later when I held a conversation with my father upon the doctrine of foreordination, which at one time very much perplexed my childish mind. After setting the difficulty before him and complaining that I could not make it out, although my best friend "understood it perfectly," I settled down to hear his argument, having no doubt that he could make it quite clear. To my delighted surprise, for any intimation that our minds were on an equality lifted me high indeed, he said that he feared that he and I did not have the kind of mind that would ever understand foreordination very well and advised me not to give too much time to it; but he then proceeded to say other things of which the final impression left upon my mind was that it did not matter much whether one understood foreordination or not, but that it was very important not to pretend to understand what you didn't understand and that you must always be honest with yourself inside, whatever happened. Perhaps on the whole as valuable a lesson as the shorter catechism itself contains.

My memory merges this early conversation on religious doctrine into one which took place years later when I put before my father the situation in which I found myself at boarding school when under great evangelical pressure, and once again I heard his testimony in favor of "mental integrity above everything else."

At the time we were driving through a piece of timber in which the wood choppers had been at work during the winter, and so earnestly were we talking that he suddenly drew up the horses to find that he did not know where he was. We were both entertained by the incident, I that my father had been "lost in his own timber" so that various cords of wood must have escaped his practiced eye, and he on his side that he should have become so absorbed in this maze of youthful speculation. We were in high spirits as we emerged from the tender green of the spring woods into the clear light of day, and as we came back into the main road I categorically asked him:

"What are you? What do you say when people ask you?"

His eyes twinkled a little as he soberly replied:

"I am a Quaker."

"But that isn't enough to say," I urged.

"Very well," he added, "to people who insist upon details, as someone is doing now, I add that I am a Hicksite Quaker"; and not another word on the weighty subject could I induce him to utter.

These early recollections are set in a scene of rural beauty, unusual at least for Illinois. The prairie around the village was broken into hills, one of them crowned by pine woods, grown up from a bagful of Norway pine seeds sown by my father in 1844, the very year he came to Illinois, a testimony perhaps that the most vigorous pioneers gave at least an occasional thought to beauty. The banks of the mill stream rose into high bluffs too perpendicular to be climbed without skill, and containing caves of which one at least was so black that it could not be explored without the aid of a candle; and there was a deserted limekiln which became associated in my mind with the unpardonable sin of Hawthorne's "Lime-Burner." My stepbrother and I carried on games and crusades which lasted week after week, and even summer after summer, as only free-ranging country children can do. It may be in contrast to this that one of the most piteous aspects in the life of city children, as I have seen it in the neighborhood of Hull-House, is the constant interruption to their play which is inevitable on the streets, so that it can never have any continuity—the most elaborate "plan or chart" or "fragment from their dream of human life" is sure to be rudely destroyed by the passing traffic. Although they start over and over again, even the most vivacious become worn out at last and take to that passive "standing 'round" varied by rude horseplay, which in time becomes so characteristic of city children.

We had of course our favorite places and trees and birds and flowers. It is hard to reproduce the companionship which children establish with nature, but certainly it is much too unconscious and intimate to come under the head of æsthetic appreciation or anything of the sort. When we said that the purple wind-flowers—the anemone patens—"looked as if the winds had made them," we thought much more of the fact that they were wind-born than that they were beautiful: we clapped our hands in sudden joy over the soft radiance of the rainbow, but its enchantment lay in our half-belief that a pot of gold was to be found at its farther end; we yielded to a soft melancholy when we heard the whippoorwill in the early twilight but while he aroused in us vague longings of which we spoke solemnly, we felt no beauty in his call.

We erected an altar beside the stream, to which for several years we brought all the snakes we killed during our excursions, no matter how long the toilsome journey which we had to make with a limp snake dangling between two sticks. I remember rather vaguely the ceremonial performed upon this altar one autumn day, when we brought as further tribute one out of every hundred of the black walnuts which we had gathered, and then poured over the whole a pitcher full of cider, fresh from the cider mill on the barn floor. I think we had also burned a favorite book or two upon this pyre of stones. The entire affair carried on with such solemnity was probably the result of one of those imperative impulses under whose compulsion children seek a ceremonial which shall express their sense of identification with man's primitive life and their familiar kinship with the remotest past.

Long before we had begun the study of Latin at the village school, my brother and I had learned the Lord's Prayer in Latin out of an old copy of the Vulgate, and gravely repeated it every night in an execrable pronunciation because it seemed to us more religious than "plain English."

When, however, I really prayed, what I saw before my eyes was a most outrageous picture which adorned a song-book used in Sunday School, portraying the Lord upon His throne surrounded by tiers and tiers of saints and angels all in a blur of yellow. I am ashamed to tell how old I was when that picture ceased to appear before my eyes, especially when moments of terror compelled me to ask protection from the heavenly powers.

I recall with great distinctness my first direct contact with death when I was fifteen years old: Polly was an old nurse who had taken care of my mother and had followed her to frontier Illinois to help rear a second generation of children. She had always lived in our house, but made annual visits to her cousins on a farm a few miles north of the village. During one of these visits, word came to us one Sunday evening that Polly was dying, and for a number of reasons I was the only person able to go to her. I left the lamplit, warm house to be driven four miles through a blinding storm which every minute added more snow to the already high drifts, with a sense of starting upon a fateful errand. An hour after my arrival all of the cousin's family went downstairs to supper, and I was left alone to watch with Polly. The square, old-fashioned chamber in the lonely farmhouse was very cold and still, with nothing to be heard but the storm outside. Suddenly the great change came. I heard a feeble call of "Sarah," my mother's name, as the dying eyes were turned upon me, followed by a curious breathing and in place of the face familiar from my earliest childhood and associated with homely household cares, there lay upon the pillow strange, august features, stern and withdrawn from all the small affairs of life. That sense of solitude, of being unsheltered in a wide world of relentless and elemental forces which is at the basis of childhood's timidity and which is far from outgrown at fifteen, seized me irresistibly before

I could reach the narrow stairs and summon the family from below.

As I was driven home in the winter storm, the wind through the trees seemed laden with a passing soul and the riddle of life and death pressed hard; once to be young, to grow old and to die, everything came to that, and then a mysterious journey out into the Unknown. Did she mind faring forth alone? Would the journey perhaps end in something as familiar and natural to the aged and dying as life is to the young and living? Through all the drive and indeed throughout the night these thoughts were pierced by sharp worry, a sense of faithlessness because I had forgotten the text Polly had confided to me long before as the one from which she wished her funeral sermon to be preached. My comfort as usual finally came from my father, who pointed out what was essential and what was of little avail even in such a moment as this, and while he was much too wise to grow dogmatic upon the great theme of death, I felt a new fellowship with him because we had discussed it together.

Perhaps I may record here my protest against the efforts, so often made, to shield children and young people from all that has to do with death and sorrow, to give them a good time at all hazards on the assumption that the ills of life will come soon enough. Young people themselves often resent this attitude on the part of their elders; they feel set aside and belittled as if they were denied the common human experiences. They too wish to climb steep stairs and to eat their bread with tears, and they imagine that the problems of existence which so press upon them in pensive moments would be less insoluble in the light of these great happenings.

An incident which stands out clearly in my mind as an exciting suggestion of the great world of moral enterprise and serious undertakings must have occurred earlier than this, for in 1872, when I was not yet twelve years old, I came into my father's room one morning to find him sitting beside the fire with a newspaper in his hand, looking very solemn; and upon my eager inquiry what had happened, he told me that Joseph Mazzini was dead. I had never even heard Mazzini's name, and after being told about him I was inclined to grow argumentative, asserting that my father did not know him, that he was not an American, and that I could not understand why we should be expected to feel badly about him. It is impossible to recall the conversation with the complete breakdown of my cheap arguments, but in the end I obtained that which I have ever regarded as a valuable possession, a sense of the genuine relationship which may exist between men who share large hopes and like desires, even though they differ in nationality, language, and creed; that those things count for absolutely nothing between groups of men who are trying to abolish slavery in America or to throw off Hapsburg oppression in Italy. At any rate, I was heartily ashamed of my meager notion of patriotism, and I came out of the room exhilarated with the consciousness that impersonal and international relations are actual facts and not mere phrases. I was filled with pride that I knew a man who held converse with great minds and who really sorrowed and rejoiced over happenings across the sea. I never recall those early conversations with my father, nor a score of others like them, but there comes into my mind a line from Mrs. Browning in which a daughter describes her relations with her father:

> He wrapt me in his large
> Man's doublet, careless did it fit or no.

꧁꧂ *Chapter* 2

INFLUENCE OF LINCOLN

I suppose all the children who were born about the
time of the Civil War have recollections quite unlike those
of the children who are living now. Although I was but
four and a half years old when Lincoln died, I distinctly
remember the day when I found on our two white gateposts American flags companioned with black. I tumbled
down on the harsh gravel walk in my eager rush into the
house to inquire what they were "there for." To my
amazement I found my father in tears, something that I
had never seen before, having assumed, as all children do,
that grown-up people never cried. The two flags, my father's tears, and his impressive statement that the greatest
man in the world had died, constituted my initiation, my
baptism, as it were, into the thrilling and solemn interests
of a world lying quite outside the two white gateposts. The
great war touched children in many ways: I remember an
engraved roster of names, headed by the words "Addams'
Guard," and the whole surmounted by the insignia of the
American eagle clutching many flags, which always hung
in the family living room. As children we used to read this
list of names again and again. We could reach it only by
dint of putting the family Bible on a chair and piling the

dictionary on top of it; using the Bible to stand on was
always accompanied by a little thrill of superstitious awe,
although we carefully put the dictionary above that our
profane feet might touch it alone. Having brought the roster within reach of our eager fingers,—fortunately it was
glazed,—we would pick out the names of those who "had
fallen on the field" from those who "had come back from
the war," and from among the latter those whose children were our schoolmates. When drives were planned,
we would say, "Let us take this road," that we might pass
the farm where a soldier had once lived; if flowers from
the garden were to be given away, we would want them to
go to the mother of one of those heroes whose names we
knew from the "Addams' Guard." If a guest should become interested in the roster on the wall, he was at once
led by the eager children to a small picture of Colonel
Davis which hung next the opposite window, that he might
see the brave Colonel of the Regiment. The introduction
to the picture of the one-armed man seemed to us a very
solemn ceremony, and long after the guest was tired of
listening, we would tell each other all about the local hero,
who at the head of his troops had suffered wounds unto
death. We liked very much to talk to a gentle old lady
who lived in a white farmhouse a mile north of the
village. She was the mother of the village hero, Tommy,
and used to tell us of her long anxiety during the spring
of '62; how she waited day after day for the hospital to
surrender up her son, each morning airing the white homespun sheets and holding the little bedroom in immaculate
readiness. It was after the battle of Fort Donelson that
Tommy was wounded and had been taken to the hospital
at Springfield; his father went down to him and saw him
getting worse each week, until it was clear that he was
going to die; but there was so much red tape about the
department, and affairs were so confused, that his discharge could not be procured. At last the hospital surgeon
intimated to his father that he should quietly take him
away; a man as sick as that, it would be all right; but when
they told Tommy, weak as he was, his eyes flashed, and he
said, "No, sir; I will go out of the front door or I'll die
here." Of course after that every man in the hospital
worked for it, and in two weeks he was honorably dis-

charged. When he came home at last, his mother's heart
was broken to see him so wan and changed. She would
tell us of the long quiet days that followed his return,
with the windows open that the dying eyes might look over
the orchard slope to the meadow beyond where the younger brothers were mowing the early hay. She told us of
those days when his school friends from the Academy
flocked in to see him, their old acknowledged leader, and
of the burning words of earnest patriotism spoken in the
crowded little room, so that in three months the Academy
was almost deserted and the new Company who marched
away in the autumn took as drummer boy Tommy's third
brother, who was only seventeen and too young for a
regular. She remembered the still darker days that followed, when the bright drummer boy was in Andersonville
prison, and little by little she learned to be reconciled that
Tommy was safe in the peaceful home graveyard.

However much we were given to talk of war heroes,
we always fell silent as we approached an isolated farmhouse in which two old people lived alone. Five of their
sons had enlisted in the Civil War, and only the youngest
had returned alive in the spring of 1865. In the autumn of
the same year, when he was hunting for wild ducks in a
swamp on the rough little farm itself, he was accidentally
shot and killed, and the old people were left alone to
struggle with the half-cleared land as best they might.
When we were driven past this forlorn little farm our
childish voices always dropped into speculative whisper-
ings as to how the accident could have happened to this
remaining son out of all the men in the world, to him who
had escaped so many chances of death! Our young hearts
swelled in first rebellion against that which Walter Pater
calls "the inexplicable shortcoming or misadventure on
the part of life itself"; we were overwhelmingly oppressed
by that grief of things as they are, so much more mysterious and intolerable than those griefs which we think
dimly to trace to man's own wrongdoing.

It was well perhaps that life thus early gave me a hint
of one of her most obstinate and insoluble riddles, for I
have sorely needed the sense of universality thus imparted
to that mysterious injustice, the burden of which we are

all forced to bear and with which I have become only too
familiar.

My childish admiration for Lincoln is closely associated
with a visit made to the war eagle, Old Abe, who, as we
children well knew, lived in the state capitol of Wisconsin,
only sixty-five miles north of our house, really no farther
than an eagle could easily fly! He had been carried by the
Eighth Wisconsin Regiment through the entire war, and
now dwelt an honored pensioner in the state building itself.

Many times, standing in the north end of our orchard,
which was only twelve miles from that mysterious line
which divided Illinois from Wisconsin, we anxiously
scanned the deep sky, hoping to see Old Abe fly south-
ward right over our apple trees, for it was clearly possible
that he might at any moment escape from his keeper, who,
although he had been a soldier and a sentinel, would have
to sleep sometimes. We gazed with thrilled interest at one
speck after another in the flawless sky, but although Old
Abe never came to see us, a much more incredible thing
happened, for we were at last taken to see him.

We started one golden summer's day, two happy children in the family carriage, with my father and mother
and an older sister to whom, because she was just home
from boarding school, we confidently appealed whenever
we needed information. We were driven northward hour
after hour, past harvest fields in which the stubble glinted
from bronze to gold and the heavy-headed grain rested
luxuriously in rounded shocks, until we reached that beautiful region of hills and lakes which surrounds the capital
city of Wisconsin.

But although Old Abe, sitting sedately upon his high
perch, was sufficiently like an uplifted ensign to remind us
of a Roman eagle, and although his veteran keeper, clad
in an old army coat, was ready to answer all our questions
and to tell us of the thirty-six battles and skirmishes
which Old Abe had passed unscathed, the crowning moment of the impressive journey came to me later, illus-
trating once more that children are as quick to catch the
meaning of a symbol as they are unaccountably slow to
understand the real world about them.

The entire journey to the veteran war eagle had itself
symbolized that search for the heroic and perfect which

so persistently haunts the young; and as I stood under the great white dome of Old Abe's stately home, for one brief moment the search was rewarded. I dimly caught a hint of what men have tried to say in their world-old effort to imprison a space in so divine a line that it shall hold only yearning devotion and high-hearted hopes. Certainly the utmost rim of my first dome was filled with the tumultuous impression of soldiers marching to death for freedom's sake, of pioneers streaming westward to establish self-government in yet another sovereign state. Only the great dome of St. Peter's itself has ever clutched my heart as did that modest curve which had sequestered from infinitude, in a place small enough for my child's mind, the courage and endurance which I could not comprehend so long as it was lost in "the void of unresponsible space" under the vaulting sky itself. But through all my vivid sensations there persisted the image of the eagle in the corridor below and Lincoln himself as an epitome of all that was great and good. I dimly caught the notion of the martyred President as the standard bearer to the conscience of his countrymen, as the eagle had been the ensign of courage to the soldiers of the Wisconsin regiment.

Thirty-five years later, as I stood on the hill campus of the University of Wisconsin with a commanding view of the capitol building a mile directly across the city, I saw again the dome which had so uplifted my childish spirit. The University, which was celebrating its fiftieth anniversary, had honored me with a doctor's degree, and in the midst of the academic pomp and the rejoicing, the dome again appeared to me as a fitting symbol of a state's aspiration even in its high mission of universal education.

Thousands of children in the sixties and seventies, in the simplicity which is given to the understanding of a child, caught a notion of imperishable heroism when they were told that brave men had lost their lives that the slaves might be free. At any moment the conversation of our elders might turn upon these heroic events; there were redletter days, when a certain general came to see my father, and again when Governor Oglesby, whom all Illinois children called "Uncle Dick," spent a Sunday under the pine trees in our front yard. We felt on those days a connection with the great world so much more heroic than the village world which surrounded us through all the other days. My father was a member of the state senate for the sixteen years between 1854 and 1870, and even as a little child I was dimly conscious of the grave march of public affairs in his comings and goings at the state capital.

He was much too occupied to allow time for reminiscence, but I remember overhearing a conversation between a visitor and himself concerning the stirring days before the war, when it was by no means certain that the Union men in the legislature would always have enough votes to keep Illinois from seceding. I heard with breathless interest my father's account of the trip a majority of the legislators had made one dark day to St. Louis, that there might not be enough men for a quorum, and so no vote could be taken on the momentous question until the Union men could rally their forces.

My father always spoke of the martyred President as Mr. Lincoln, and I never heard the great name without a thrill. I remember the day—it must have been one of comparative leisure, perhaps a Sunday—when at my request my father took out of his desk a thin packet marked "Mr. Lincoln's Letters," the shortest one of which bore unmistakable traces of that remarkable personality. These letters began, "My dear Double-D'ed Addams," and to the inquiry as to how the person thus addressed was about to vote on a certain measure then before the legislature, was added the assurance that he knew that this Addams "would vote according to his conscience," but he begged to know in which direction the same conscience "was pointing." As my father folded up the bits of paper I fairly held my breath in my desire that he should go on with the reminiscence of this wonderful man, whom he had known in his comparative obscurity, or better still, that he should be moved to tell some of the exciting incidents of the Lincoln-Douglas debates. There were at least two pictures of Lincoln that always hung in my father's room, and one in our old-fashioned upstairs parlor, of Lincoln with little Tad. For one or all of these reasons I always tend to associate Lincoln with the tenderest thoughts of my father.

I recall a time of great perplexity in the summer of 1894, when Chicago was filled with federal troops sent there by the President of the United States, and their presence was resented by the governor of the state, that I walked the wearisome way from Hull-House to Lincoln Park—for no cars were running regularly at that moment of sympathetic strikes—in order to look at and gain magnanimous counsel, if I might, from the marvelous St. Gaudens statue which had been but recently placed at the entrance of the park. Some of Lincoln's immortal words were cut into the stone at his feet, and never did a distracted town more sorely need the healing of "with charity towards all" than did Chicago at that moment, and the tolerance of the man who had won charity for those on both sides of "an irrepressible conflict."

Of the many things written of my father in that sad August in 1881, when he died, the one I cared for most was written by an old political friend of his who was then editor of a great Chicago daily. He wrote that while there were doubtless many members of the Illinois legislature who during the great contracts of the wartime and the demoralizing reconstruction days that followed, had never accepted a bribe, he wished to bear testimony that he personally had known but this one man who had never been offered a bribe because bad men were instinctively afraid of him.

I feel now the hot chagrin with which I recalled this statement during those early efforts of Illinois in which Hull-House joined, to secure the passage of the first factory legislation. I was told by the representatives of an informal association of manufacturers that if the residents of Hull-House would drop this nonsense about a sweatshop bill, of which they knew nothing, certain businessmen would agree to give fifty thousand dollars within two years to be used for any of the philanthropic activities of the Settlement. As the fact broke upon me that I was being offered a bribe, the shame was enormously increased by the memory of this statement. What had befallen the daughter of my father that such a thing could happen to her? The salutary reflection that it could not have occurred unless a weakness in myself had permitted it, withheld me at least from an heroic display of indignation before the two men making the offer, and I explained as gently as I could that we had no ambition to make Hull-

House "the largest institution on the West Side," but that we were much concerned that our neighbors should be protected from untoward conditions of work, and—so much heroics, youth must permit itself—if to accomplish this the destruction of Hull-House was necessary, that we would cheerfully sing a Te Deum on its ruins. The good friend who had invited me to lunch at the Union League Club to meet two of his friends who wanted to talk over the sweatshop bill here kindly intervened, and we all hastened to cover the awkward situation by that scurrying away from ugly morality which seems to be an obligation of social intercouse.

Of the many old friends of my father who kindly came to look up his daughter in the first days of Hull-House, I recall none with more pleasure than Lyman Trumbull, whom we used to point out to the members of the Young Citizens' Club as the man who had for days held in his keeping the Proclamation of Emancipation until his friend President Lincoln was ready to issue it. I remember the talk he gave at Hull-House on one of our early celebrations of Lincoln's birthday, his assertion that Lincoln was no cheap popular hero, that the "common people" would have to make an effort if they would understand his greatness, as Lincoln painstakingly made a long effort to understand the greatness of the people. There was something in the admiration of Lincoln's contemporaries, or at least of those men who had known him personally, which was quite unlike even the best of the devotion and reverent understanding which has developed since. In the first place, they had so large a fund of common experience; they too had pioneered in a western country, and had urged the development of canals and railroads in order that the raw prairie crops might be transported to market; they too had realized that if this last tremendous experiment in self-government failed here, it would be the disappointment of the centuries and that upon their ability to organize self-government in state, county, and town depended the verdict of history. These men also knew, as Lincoln himself did, that if this tremendous experiment was to come to fruition, it must be brought about by the people themselves; that there was no other capital fund upon which to draw. I remember an incident occurring

when I was about fifteen years old, in which the conviction was driven into my mind that the people themselves
were the great resource of the country. My father had
made a little address of reminiscence at a meeting of "the
old settlers of Stephenson County," which was held every
summer in the grove beside the mill, relating his experiences in inducing the farmers of the county to subscribe
for stock in the Northwestern Railroad, which was the
first to penetrate the county and to make a connection
with the Great Lakes at Chicago. Many of the Pennsyl-
vania German farmers doubted the value of "the whole
new-fangled business," and had no use for any railroad,
much less for one in which they were asked to risk their
hard-earned savings. My father told of his despair in one
farmers' community dominated by such prejudice which
did not in the least give way under his argument, but finally
melted under the enthusiasm of a high-spirited German
matron who took a share to be paid for "out of butter and
egg money." As he related his admiration of her, an old
woman's piping voice in the audience called out: "I'm
here today, Mr. Addams, and I'd do it again if you asked
me." The old woman, bent and broken by her seventy
years of toilsome life, was brought to the platform and
I was much impressed by my father's grave presentation
of her as "one of the public-spirited pioneers to whose
heroic fortitude we are indebted for the development of this
country." I remember that I was at that time reading with
great enthusiasm Carlyle's *Heroes and Hero Worship,* but
on the evening of "Old-Settlers' Day," to my surprise, I
found it difficult to go on. Its sonorous sentences and exal-
tation of the man who "can" suddenly ceased to be convincing. I had already written down in my commonplace
book a resolution to give at least twenty-five copies of this
book each year to noble young people of my acquaintance.
It is perhaps fitting to record in this chapter that the very
first Christmas we spent at Hull-House, in spite of exigent
demands upon my slender purse for candy and shoes, I
gave to a club of boys twenty-five copies of the then new
Carl Schurz's "Appreciation of Abraham Lincoln."

In our early effort at Hull-House to hand on to our
neighbors whatever of help we had found for ourselves,

we made much of Lincoln. We were often distressed by
the children of immigrant parents who were ashamed of
the pit whence they were digged, who repudiated the language and customs of their elders, and counted themselves
successful as they were able to ignore the past. Whenever I held up Lincoln for their admiration as the greatest
American, I invariably pointed out his marvelous power
to retain and utilize past experiences; that he never forgot
how the plain people in Sangamon County thought and felt
when he himself had moved to town; that this habit was
the foundation for his marvelous capacity for growth; that
during those distracting years in Washington it enabled
him to make clear beyond denial to the American people
themselves, the goal toward which they were moving. I
was sometimes bold enough to add that proficiency in the
art of recognition and comprehension did not come without effort, and that certainly its attainment was necessary
for any successful career in our conglomerate America.

An instance of the invigorating and clarifying power of
Lincoln's influence came to me many years ago in England. I had spent two days in Oxford under the guidance
of Arnold Toynbee's old friend Sidney Ball of St. John's
College, who was closely associated with that group of
scholars we all identify with the beginnings of the Settlement movement. It was easy to claim the philosophy of
Thomas Hill Green, the road-building episode of Ruskin,
the experimental living in the east end by Frederick
Maurice, the London Workingmen's College of Edward
Dennison, as foundations laid by university men for the
establishment of Toynbee Hall. I was naturally much interested in the beginnings of a movement whose slogan
was "Back to the People," and which could doubtless claim
the Settlement as one of its manifestations. Nevertheless
the processes by which so simple a conclusion as residence among the poor in East London was reached seemed
to me very involved and roundabout. However inevitable
these processes might be for class-conscious Englishmen,
they could not but seem artificial to a western American
who had been born in a rural community where the early
pioneer life had made social distinctions impossible. Always on the alert lest American Settlements should become

mere echoes and imitations of the English movement, I found myself assenting to what was shown me only with that part of my consciousness which had been formed by reading of English social movements, while at the same time the rustic American inside looked on in detached comment.

Why should an American be lost in admiration of a group of Oxford students because they went out to mend a disused road, inspired thereto by Ruskin's teaching for the bettering of the common life, when all the country roads in America were mended each spring by self-respecting citizens, who were thus carrying out the simple method devised by a democratic government for providing highways. No humor penetrated my high mood even as I somewhat uneasily recalled certain spring thaws when I had been mired in roads provided by the American citizen. I continued to fumble for a synthesis which I was unable to make until I developed that uncomfortable sense of playing two roles at once. It was therefore almost with a dual consciousness that I was ushered, during the last afternoon of my Oxford stay, into the drawingroom of the Master of Balliol. Edward Caird's *Evolution of Religion,* which I had read but a year or two before, had been of unspeakable comfort to me in the labyrinth of differing ethical teachings and religious creeds which the many immigrant colonies of our neighborhood presented. I remember that I wanted very much to ask the author himself how far it was reasonable to expect the same quality of virtue and a similar standard of conduct from these divers people. I was timidly trying to apply his method of study to those groups of homesick immigrants huddled together in strange tenement houses, among whom I seemed to detect the beginnings of a secular religion or at least of a wide humanitarianism evolved out of the various exigencies of the situation; somewhat as a household of children, whose mother is dead, out of their sudden necessity perform unaccustomed offices for each other and awkwardly exchange consolations, as children in happier households never dream of doing. Perhaps Mr. Caird could tell me whether there was any religious content in this

> Faith to each other; this fidelity
> Of fellow wanderers in a desert place.

But when tea was over and my opportunity came for a talk with my host, I suddenly remembered, to the exclusion of all other associations, only Mr. Caird's fine analysis of Abraham Lincoln, delivered in a lecture two years before.

The memory of Lincoln, the mention of his name, came like a refreshing breeze from off the prairie, blowing aside all the scholarly implications in which I had become so reluctantly involved, and as the philosopher spoke of the great American "who was content merely to dig the channels through which the moral life of his countrymen might flow," I was gradually able to make a natural connection between this intellectual penetration at Oxford and the moral perception which is always necessary for the discovery of new methods by which to minister to human needs. In the unceasing ebb and flow of justice and oppression we must all dig channels as best we may, that at the propitious moment somewhat of the swelling tide may be conducted to the barren places of life.

Gradually a healing sense of well-being enveloped me and a quick remorse for my blindness, as I realized that no one among his own countrymen had been able to interpret Lincoln's greatness more nobly than this Oxford scholar had done, and that vision and wisdom as well as high motives must lie behind every effective stroke in the continuous labor for human equality; I remembered that another Master of Balliol, Jowett himself, had said that it was fortunate for society that every age possessed at least a few minds which, like Arnold Toynbee's, were "perpetually disturbed over the apparent inequalities of mankind." Certainly both the English and American settlements could unite in confessing to that disturbance of mind.

Traces of this Oxford visit are curiously reflected in a paper I wrote soon after my return at the request of the American Academy of Political and Social Science. It begins as follows:

> The word "settlement," which we have borrowed from London, is apt to grate a little upon American ears. It is not, after all, so long ago that Americans who settled were those who had adventured into a new country, where they were pioneers in the midst of difficult surroundings. The

word still implies migrating from one condition of life to another totally unlike it, and against this implication the resident of an American settlement takes alarm.

We do not like to acknowledge that Americans are divided into two nations, as her prime minister once admitted of England. We are not willing, openly and professedly, to assume that American citizens are broken up into classes, even if we make that assumption the preface to a plea that the superior class has duties to the inferior. Our democracy is still our most precious possession, and we do well to resent any inroads upon it, even though they may be made in the name of philanthropy.

Is it not Abraham Lincoln who has cleared the title to our democracy? He made plain, once for all, that democratic government, associated as it is with all the mistakes and shortcomings of the common people, still remains the most valuable contribution America has made to the moral life of the world.

Chapter 3

BOARDING-SCHOOL IDEALS

As MY three older sisters had already attended the seminary at Rockford, of which my father was trustee, without any question I entered there at seventeen, with such meager preparation in Latin and algebra as the village school had afforded. I was very ambitious to go to Smith College, although I well knew that my father's theory in regard to the education of his daughters implied a school as near at home as possible, to be followed by travel abroad in lieu of the wider advantages which an eastern college is supposed to afford. I was much impressed by the recent return of my sister from a year in Europe, yet I was greatly disappointed at the moment of starting to humdrum Rockford. After the first weeks of homesickness were over, however, I became very much absorbed in the little world which the boarding school in any form always offers to its students.

The school at Rockford in 1877 had not changed its name from seminary to college, although it numbered, on its faculty and among its alumnæ, college women who were most eager that this should be done, and who really accomplished it during the next five years. The school was one of the earliest efforts for women's higher education in

46

the Mississippi Valley, and from the beginning was called "The Mount Holyoke of the West." It reflected much of the missionary spirit of that pioneer institution, and the proportion of missionaries among its early graduates was almost as large as Mount Holyoke's own. In addition there had been thrown about the founders of the early western school the glamour of frontier privations, and the first students, conscious of the heroic self-sacrifice made in their behalf, felt that each minute of the time thus dearly bought must be conscientiously used. This inevitably fostered an atmosphere of intensity, a fever of preparation which continued long after the direct making of it had ceased, and which the later girls accepted, as they did the campus and the buildings, without knowing that it could have been otherwise.

There was, moreover, always present in the school a larger or smaller group of girls who consciously accepted this heritage and persistently endeavoured to fulfill its obligation. We worked in those early years as if we really believed the portentous statement from Aristotle which we found quoted in Boswell's Johnson and with which we illuminated the wall of the room occupied by our Chess Club; it remained there for months, solely out of reverence, let us hope, for the two ponderous names associated with it; at least I have enough confidence in human nature to assert that we never really believed that "There is the same difference between the learned and the unlearned as there is between the living and the dead." We were also too fond of quoting Carlyle to the effect, " 'Tis not to taste sweet things, but to do noble and true things that the poorest son of Adam dimly longs."

As I attempt to reconstruct the spirit of my contemporary group by looking over many documents, I find nothing more amusing than a plaint registered against life's indistinctness, which I imagine more or less reflected the sentiments of all of us. At any rate here it is for the entertainment of the reader if not for his edification: "So much of our time is spent in preparation, so much in routine, and so much in sleep, we find it difficult to have any experience at all." We did not, however, tamely accept such a state of affairs, for we made various and restless attempts to break through this dull obtuseness.

At one time five of us tried to understand De Quincey's marvelous *Dreams* more sympathetically, by drugging ourselves with opium. We solemnly consumed small white powders at intervals during an entire long holiday, but no mental reorientation took place, and the suspense and excitement did not even permit us to grow sleepy. About four o'clock on the weird afternoon, the young teacher whom we had been obliged to take into our confidence grew alarmed over the whole performance, took away our De Quincey and all the remaining powders, administered an emetic to each of the five aspirants for sympathetic understanding of all human experience, and sent us to our separate rooms with a stern command to appear at family worship after supper "whether we were able to or not."

Whenever we had chances to write, we took, of course, large themes, usually from the Greek because they were the most stirring to the imagination. The Greek oration I gave at our Junior Exhibition was written with infinite pains and taken to the Greek professor in Beloit College that there might be no mistakes, even after the Rockford College teacher and the most scholarly clergyman in town had both passed upon it. The oration upon Bellerophon and his successful fight with the Chimera contended that social evils could only be overcome by him who soared above them into idealism, as Bellerophon, mounted upon the winged horse Pegasus, had slain the earthy dragon.

There were practically no economics taught in women's colleges—at least in the fresh-water ones—thirty years ago, although we painstakingly studied "Mental" and "Moral" Philosophy, which, though far from dry in the classroom, became the subject of more spirited discussion outside, and gave us a clue for animated rummaging in the little college library. Of course we read a great deal of Ruskin and Browning, and liked the most abstruse parts the best; but like the famous gentleman who talked prose without knowing it, we never dreamed of connecting them with our philosophy. My genuine interest was history, partly because of a superior teacher, and partly because my father had always insisted upon a certain amount of historic reading ever since he had paid me, as a little girl, five cents a "Life" for each Plutarch hero I could intelligently report to him, and twenty-five cents for every volume of Irving's *Life of Washington*.

When we started for the long vacations, a little group of five would vow that during the summer we would read all of Motley's *Dutch Republic* or, more ambitious still, all of Gibbon's *Decline and Fall of the Roman Empire*. When we returned at the opening of school and three of us announced we had finished the latter, each became skeptical of the other two. We fell upon each other with a sort of rough-and-tumble examination, in which no quarter was given or received; but the suspicion was finally removed that anyone had skipped. We took for a class motto the early Saxon word for lady, translated into bread-giver, and we took for our class color the poppy, because poppies grew among the wheat, as if Nature knew that wherever there was hunger that needed food there would be pain that needed relief. We must have found the sentiment in a book somewhere, but we used it so much that it finally seemed like an idea of our own, although of course none of us had ever seen a European field, the only page upon which Nature has written this particular message.

That this group of ardent girls, who discussed everything under the sun with such unabated interest, did not take it all out in talk may be demonstrated by the fact that one of the class who married a missionary founded a very successful school in Japan for the children of the English and Americans living there; another of the class became a medical missionary to Korea, and because of her successful treatment of the Queen, was made court physician at a time when the opening was considered of importance in the diplomatic as well as in the missionary world; still another became an unusually skilled teacher of the blind; and one of them a pioneer librarian in that early effort to bring "books to the people."

Perhaps this early companionship showed me how essentially similar are the various forms of social effort, and curiously enough, the actual activities of a missionary school are not unlike many that are carried on in a Settlement situated in a foreign quarter. Certainly the most sympathetic and comprehending visitors we have ever had at Hull-House have been returned missionaries; among them two elderly ladies, who had lived for years in India and who had been homesick and bewildered since their return, declared that the fortnight at Hull-House had been the happiest and most familiar they had had in America.

Of course in such an atmosphere a girl like myself, of serious not to say priggish tendency, did not escape a concerted pressure to push her into the "missionary field." During the four years it was inevitable that every sort of evangelical appeal should have been made to reach the comparatively few "unconverted" girls in the school. We were the subject of prayer at the daily chapel exercise and the weekly prayer meeting, attendance upon which was obligatory.

I was singularly unresponsive to all these forms of emotional appeal, although I became unspeakably embarrassed when they were presented to me at close range by a teacher during the "silent hour," which we were all required to observe every evening and which was never broken into, even by a member of the faculty, unless the errand was one of grave import. I found these occasional interviews on the part of one of the more serious young teachers, of whom I was extremely fond, hard to endure, as was a long series of conversations in my senior year conducted by one of the most enthusiastic members of the faculty, in which the desirability of Turkey as a field for missionary labor was enticingly put before me. I suppose I held myself aloof from all these influences, partly owing to the fact that my father was not a communicant of any church, and I tremendously admired his scrupulous morality and sense of honor in all matters of personal and public conduct, and also because the little group to which I have referred was much given to a sort of rationalism, doubtless founded upon an early reading of Emerson. In this connection, when Bronson Alcott came to lecture at the school, we all vied with each other for a chance to do him a personal service because he had been a friend of Emerson, and we were inexpressibly scornful of our younger fellow students who cared for him merely on the basis of his grandfatherly relation to *Little Women*. I recall cleaning the clay of the unpaved streets off his heavy cloth overshoes in a state of ecstatic energy.

But I think in my case there were other factors as well

that contributed to my unresponsiveness to the evangelical appeal. A curious course of reading I had marked out for myself in medieval history seems to have left me fascinated by an ideal of mingled learning, piety, and physical labor, more nearly exemplified by the Port Royalists than by any others.

The only moments in which I seem to have approximated in my own experience to a faint realization of the "beauty of holiness," as I conceived it, was each Sunday morning between the hours of nine and ten, when I went into the exquisitely neat room of the teacher of Greek and read with her from a Greek testament. We did this every Sunday morning for two years. It was not exactly a lesson, for I never prepared for it, and while I was held within reasonable bounds of syntax, I was allowed much more freedom in translation than was permitted the next morning when I read Homer; neither did we discuss doctrines, for although it was with this same teacher that in our junior year we studied Paul's Epistle to the Hebrews, committing all of it to memory and analyzing and reducing it to doctrines within an inch of our lives, we never allowed an echo of this exercise to appear at these blessed Sunday morning readings. It was as if the disputatious Paul had not yet been, for we always read from the Gospels. The regime of Rockford Seminary was still very simple in the 70's. Each student made her own fire and kept her own room in order. Sunday morning was a great clearing up day, and the sense of having made immaculate my own immediate surroundings, the consciousness of clean linen, said to be close to the consciousness of a clean conscience, always mingles in my mind with these early readings. I certainly bore away with me a lifelong enthusiasm for reading the Gospels in bulk, a whole one at a time, and an insurmountable distaste for having them cut up into chapter and verse, or for hearing the incidents in that wonderful Life thus referred to as if it were merely a record.

My copy of the Greek testament had been presented to me by the brother of our Greek teacher, Professor Blaisdell of Beloit College, a true scholar in "Christian Ethics," as his department was called. I recall that one day in the summer after I left college—one of the black days which followed the death of my father—this kindly scholar came to see me in order to bring such comfort as he might and to inquire how far I had found solace in the little book he had given me so long before. When I suddenly recall the village in which I was born, its steeples and roofs look as they did that day from the hilltop where we talked together, the familiar details smoothed out and merging, as it were, into that wide conception of the universe, which for the moment swallowed up my personal grief or at least assuaged it with a realization that it was but a drop in that "torrent of sorrow and anguish and terror which flows under all the footsteps of man." This realization of sorrow as the common lot, of death as the universal experience, was the first comfort which my bruised spirit had received. In reply to my impatience with the Christian doctrine of "resignation," that it implied that you thought of your sorrow only in its effect upon you and were disloyal to the affection itself, I remember how quietly the Christian scholar changed his phraseology, saying that sometimes consolation came to us better in the words of Plato, and, as nearly as I can remember, that was the first time I had ever heard Plato's sonorous argument for the permanence of the excellent.

When Professor Blaisdell returned to his college, he left in my hands a small copy of *The Crito*. The Greek was too hard for me, and I was speedily driven to Jowett's translation. That old-fashioned habit of presenting favorite books to eager young people, although it degenerated into the absurdity of "friendship's offerings," had much to be said for it, when it indicated the wellsprings of literature from which the donor himself had drawn waters of healing and inspiration.

Throughout our school years we were always keenly conscious of the growing development of Rockford Seminary into a college. The opportunity for our Alma Mater to take her place in the new movement of full college education for women filled us with enthusiasm, and it became a driving ambition with the undergraduates to share in this new and glorious undertaking. We gravely decided that it was important that some of the students should be ready to receive the bachelor's degree the very first moment that the charter of the school should secure the right to confer it. Two of us, therefore, took a course in mathematics, advanced beyond anything previously given in the school, from one of those early young women working for a Ph.D., who was temporarily teaching in Rockford that she might study more mathematics in Leipzig.

My companion in all these arduous labors has since accomplished more than any of us in the effort to procure the franchise for women, for even then we all took for granted the righteousness of that cause into which I at least had merely followed my father's conviction. In the old-fashioned spirit of that cause I might cite the career of this companion as an illustration of the efficacy of higher mathematics for women, for she possesses singular ability to convince even the densest legislators of their legal right to define their own electorate, even when they quote against her the dustiest of state constitutions or city charters.

In line with this policy of placing a woman's college on an equality with the other colleges of the state, we applied for an opportunity to compete in the intercollegiate oratorical contest of Illinois, and we succeeded in having Rockford admitted as the first woman's college. When I was finally selected as the orator, I was somewhat dismayed to find that, representing not only one school but college women in general, I could not resent the brutal frankness with which my oratorical possibilities were discussed by the enthusiastic group who would allow no personal feeling to stand in the way of progress, especially the progress of Woman's Cause. I was told among other things that I had an intolerable habit of dropping my voice at the end of a sentence in the most feminine, apologetic and even deprecatory manner which would probably lose Woman the first place.

Woman certainly did lose the first place and stood fifth, exactly in the dreary middle, but the ignominious position may not have been solely due to bad mannerisms, for a prior place was easily accorded to William Jennings Bryan, who not only thrilled his auditors with an almost prophetic anticipation of the cross of gold, but with a moral earnestness which we had mistakenly assumed would be the unique possession of the feminine orator. I so heartily concurred with the decision of the judges of the contest that it was with a carefree mind that I induced my colleague and alternate to remain long enough in "The Athens of Illinois," in which the successful college was situated, to visit the state institutions, one for the Blind and one for the Deaf and Dumb. Doctor Gillette was at that time head of the latter institution; his scholarly explanation of the method of teaching, his concern for his charges, this sudden demonstration of the care the state bestowed upon its most unfortunate children, filled me with grave speculations in which the first, the fifth, or the ninth place in an oratorical contest seemed of little moment.

However, this brief delay between our field of Waterloo and our arrival at our aspiring college turned out to be most unfortunate, for we found the ardent group not only exhausted by the premature preparations for the return of a successful orator, but naturally much irritated as they contemplated their garlands drooping disconsolately in tubs and bowls of water. They did not fail to make me realize that I had dealt the cause of woman's advancement a staggering blow, and all my explanations of the fifth place were haughtily considered insufficient before that golden Bar of Youth, so absurdly inflexible!

To return to my last year at school, it was inevitable that the pressure toward religious profession should increase as graduating day approached. So curious, however, are the paths of moral development that several times during subsequent experiences have I felt that this passive resistance of mine, this clinging to an individual conviction, was the best moral training I received at Rockford College. During the first decade of Hull-House, it was felt by propagandists of diverse social theories that the new Settlement would be a fine coign of vantage from which to propagate social faiths, and that a mere preliminary step would be the conversion of the founders; hence I have been reasoned with hours at a time, and I recall at least three occasions when this was followed by actual prayer. In the first instance, the honest exhorter who fell upon his knees before my astonished eyes, was an advocate of single tax upon land values. He begged, in that indirect phraseology which is deemed appropriate for prayer, that "the sister might see the beneficent results it would bring to the poor who live in the awful congested districts around this very house."

The early socialists used every method of attack,—a favorite one being the statement, doubtless sometimes honestly made, that I really was a socialist, but "too much of a coward to say so." I remember one socialist who habitually opened a very telling address he was in the habit of giving upon the street corners, by holding me up as an awful example to his fellow socialists, as one of their number "who had been caught in the toils of capitalism." He always added as a final clinching of the statement that he knew what he was talking about because he was a member of the Hull-House Men's Club. When I ventured to say to him that not all of the thousands of people who belong to a class or club at Hull-House could possibly know my personal opinions, and to mildly inquire upon what he founded his assertions, he triumphantly replied that I had once admitted to him that I had read Sombart and Loria, and that anyone of sound mind must see the inevitable conclusions of such master reasonings.

I could multiply these two instances a hundredfold, and possibly nothing aided me to stand on my own feet and to select what seemed reasonable from this wilderness of dogma, so much as my early encounter with genuine zeal and affectionate solicitude, associated with what I could not accept as the whole truth.

I do not wish to take callow writing too seriously, but I reproduce from an oratorical contest the following bit of premature pragmatism, doubtless due much more to temperament than to perception, because I am still ready to subscribe to it, although the grandiloquent style is, I hope, a thing of the past: "Those who believe that Justice is but a poetical longing within us, the enthusiast who thinks it will come in the form of a millennium, those who see it established by the strong arm of a hero, are not those who have comprehended the vast truths of life. The actual Justice must come by trained intelligence, by broadened sympathies toward the individual man or woman who crosses our path; one item added to another is the only method by which to build up a conception lofty enough to be of use in the world."

This schoolgirl recipe has been tested in many later

experiences, the most dramatic of which came when I was called upon by a manufacturing company to act as one of three arbitrators in a perplexing struggle between themselves, a group of trades-unionists and a nonunion employee of their establishment. The nonunion man who was the cause of the difficulty had ten years before sided with his employers in a prolonged strike and had bitterly fought the union. He had been so badly injured at that time, that in spite of long months of hospital care he had never afterward been able to do a full day's work, although his employers had retained him for a decade at full pay in recognition of his loyalty. At the end of ten years the once defeated union was strong enough to enforce its demands for a union shop, and in spite of the distaste of the firm for the arrangement, no obstacle to harmonious relations with the union remained but the refusal of the trades-unionists to receive as one of their members the old crippled employee, whose spirit was broken at last and who was now willing to join the union and to stand with his old enemies for the sake of retaining his place.

But the union men would not receive "a traitor," the firm flatly refused to dismiss so faithful an employee, the busy season was upon them, and everyone concerned had finally agreed to abide without appeal by the decision of the three arbitrators. The chairman of our little arbitration committee, a venerable judge, quickly demonstrated that it was impossible to collect trustworthy evidence in regard to the events already ten years old which lay at the bottom of this bitterness, and we soon therefore ceased to interview the conflicting witnesses; the second member of the committee sternly bade the men remember that the most ancient Hebraic authority gave no sanction for holding even a just resentment for more than seven years, and at last we all settled down to that wearisome effort to secure the inner consent of all concerned, upon which alone the "mystery of justice" as Maeterlinck has told us, ultimately depends. I am not quite sure that in the end we administered justice, but certainly employers, trades-unionists, and arbitrators were all convinced that justice will have to be established in industrial affairs with the same care and patience which has been necessary for centuries in order to institute it in men's civic relationships, although as the judge remarked the search must be conducted without much help from precedent. The conviction remained with me, that however long a time might be required to establish justice in the new relationships of our raw industrialism, it would never be stable until it had received the sanction of those upon whom the present situation presses so harshly.

Toward the end of our four years' course we debated much as to what we were to be, and long before the end of my schooldays it was quite settled in my mind that I should study medicine and "live with the poor." This conclusion of course was the result of many things, perhaps epitomized in my graduating essay on "Cassandra" and her tragic fate "always to be in the right, and always to be disbelieved and rejected."

This state of affairs, it may readily be guessed, the essay held to be an example of the feminine trait of mind called intuition, "an accurate perception of Truth and Justice, which rests contented in itself and will make no effort to confirm itself or to organize through existing knowledge." The essay then proceeds—I am forced to admit, with overmuch conviction—with the statement that woman can only "grow accurate and intelligible by the thorough study of at least one branch of physical science, for only with eyes thus accustomed to the search for truth can she detect all self-deceit and fancy in herself and learn to express herself without dogmatism." So much for the first part of the thesis. Having thus "gained accuracy, would woman bring this force to bear throughout morals and justice, then she must find in active labor the promptings and inspirations that come from growing insight." I was quite certain that by following these directions carefully, in the end the contemporary woman would find "her faculties clear and acute from the study of science, and her hand upon the magnetic chain of humanity."

This veneration for science portrayed in my final essay was doubtless the result of the statements the textbooks were then making of what was called the theory of evolution, the acceptance of which even thirty years after the publication of Darwin's *Origin of Species* had about it a touch of intellectual adventure. We knew, for instance, that our science teacher had accepted this theory, but we had a strong suspicion that the teacher of Butler's *Analogy* had not. We chafed at the meagerness of the college library in this direction, and I used to bring back in my handbag books belonging to an advanced brother-in-law who had studied medicine in Germany and who therefore was quite emancipated. The first gift I made when I came into possession of my small estate the year after I left school was a thousand dollars to the library of Rockford College, with the stipulation that it be spent for scientific books. In the long vacations I pressed plants, stuffed birds, and pounded rocks in some vague belief that I was approximating the new method, and yet when my stepbrother who was becoming a real scientist, tried to carry me along with him into the merest outskirts of the methods of research, it at once became evident that I had no aptitude and was unable to follow intelligently Darwin's careful observations on the earthworm. I made a heroic effort, although candor compels me to state that I never would have finished if I had not been pulled and pushed by my really ardent companion, who in addition to a multitude of earthworms and a fine microscope, possessed untiring tact with one of flagging zeal.

As our boarding-school days neared the end, in the consciousness of approaching separation we vowed eternal allegiance to our "early ideals," and promised each other we would "never abandon them without conscious justification," and we often warned each other of "the perils of self-tradition."

We believed, in our sublime self-conceit, that the difficulty of life would lie solely in the direction of losing these precious ideals of ours, of failing to follow the way of martyrdom and high purpose we had marked out for ourselves, and we had no notion of the obscure paths of tolerance, just allowance, and self-blame wherein, if we held our minds open, we might learn something of the mystery and complexity of life's purposes.

The year after I had left college I came back, with a classmate, to receive the degree we had so eagerly anticipated. Two of the graduating class were also ready and four of us were dubbed B.A. on the very day that Rockford Seminary was declared a college in the midst of tumultuous anticipations. Having had a year outside of college walls in that trying land between vague hope and definite attainment, I had become very much sobered in my desire for a degree, and was already beginning to emerge from that rose-colored mist with which the dream of youth so readily envelops the future.

Whatever may have been the perils of self-tradition, I certainly did not escape them, for it required eight years—from the time I left Rockford in the summer of 1881 until Hull-House was opened in the autumn of 1889—to formulate my convictions even in the least satisfactory manner, much less to reduce them to a plan for action. During most of that time I was absolutely at sea so far as any moral purpose was concerned, clinging only to the desire to live in a really living world and refusing to be content with a shadowy intellectual or æsthetic reflection of it.

🎋🎋 *Chapter* 4

THE SNARE OF PREPARATION

THE winter after I left school was spent in the Woman's Medical College of Philadelphia, but the development of the spinal difficulty which had shadowed me from childhood forced me into Dr. Weir Mitchell's hospital for the late spring, and the next winter I was literally bound to a bed in my sister's house for six months. In spite of its tedium, the long winter had its mitigations, for after the first few weeks I was able to read with a luxurious consciousness of leisure, and I remember opening the first volume of Carlyle's *Frederick the Great* with a lively sense of gratitude that it was not Gray's *Anatomy,* having found, like many another, that general culture is a much easier undertaking than professional study. The long illness inevitably put aside the immediate prosecution of a medical course, and although I had passed my examinations creditably enough in the required subjects for the first year, I was very glad to have a physician's sanction for giving up clinics and dissecting rooms and to follow his prescription of spending the next two years in Europe.

Before I returned to America I had discovered that there were other genuine reasons for living among the poor than that of practicing medicine upon them, and my brief foray into the profession was never resumed.

The long illness left me in a state of nervous exhaustion with which I struggled for years, traces of it remaining long after Hull-House was opened in 1889. At the best it allowed me but a limited amount of energy, so that doubtless there was much nervous depression at the foundation of the spiritual struggles which this chapter is forced to record. However, it could not have been all due to my health, for as my wise little notebook sententiously remarked, "In his own way each man must struggle, lest the moral law become a far-off abstraction utterly separated from his active life."

It would, of course, be impossible to remember that some of these struggles ever took place at all, were it not for these selfsame notebooks, in which, however, I no longer wrote in moments of high resolve, but judging from the internal evidence afforded by the books themselves, only in moments of deep depression when overwhelmed by a sense of failure.

One of the most poignant of these experiences, which occurred during the first few months after our landing upon the other side of the Atlantic, was on a Saturday night, when I received an ineradicable impression of the wretchedness of East London, and also saw for the first time the overcrowded quarters of a great city at midnight. A small party of tourists were taken to the East End by a city missionary to witness the Saturday night sale of decaying vegetables and fruit, which, owing to the Sunday laws in London, could not be sold until Monday, and, as they were beyond safe keeping, were disposed of at auction as late as possible on Saturday night. On Mile End Road, from the top of an omnibus which paused at the end of a dingy street lighted by only occasional flares of gas, we saw two huge masses of ill-clad people clamoring around two hucksters' carts. They were bidding their farthings and ha'pennies for a vegetable held up by the auctioneer, which he at last scornfully flung, with a gibe for its cheapness, to the successful bidder. In the momentary pause only one man detached himself from the groups. He had bidden in a cabbage, and when it struck his hand, he instantly sat down on the curb, tore it with his teeth, and hastily devoured it, unwashed and uncooked as it was. He and his fellows were types of the "submerged tenth," as our missionary guide told us, with some little satisfaction in the then new phrase, and he further added that so many of them could scarcely be seen in one spot save at this Saturday night auction, the desire for cheap food being apparently the one thing which could move them simultaneously. They were huddled into ill-fitting, cast-off clothing, the ragged finery which one sees only in East London. Their pale faces were dominated by that most unlovely of human expressions, the cunning and shrewdness of the bargain-hunter who starves if he cannot make a successful trade, and yet the final impression was not of ragged, tawdry clothing nor of pinched and sallow faces, but of myriads of hands, empty, pathetic, nerveless and workworn, showing white in the uncertain light of the street, and clutching forward for food which was already unfit to eat.

Perhaps nothing is so fraught with significance as the human hand, this oldest tool with which man has dug his way from savagery, and with which he is constantly groping forward. I have never since been able to see a number of hands held upward, even when they are moving rhythmically in a calisthenic exercise, or when they belong to a class of chubby children who wave them in eager response to a teacher's query, without a certain revival of this memory, a clutching at the heart reminiscent of the despair and resentment which seized me then.

For the following weeks I went about London almost furtively, afraid to look down narrow streets and alleys lest they disclose again this hideous human need and suffering. I carried with me for days at a time that curious surprise we experience when we first come back into the streets after days given over to sorrow and death; we are bewildered that the world should be going on as usual and unable to determine which is real, the inner pang or the outward seeming. In time all huge London came to seem unreal save the poverty in its East End. During the following two years on the Continent, while I was irresistibly drawn to the poorer quarters of each city, nothing among the beggars of South Italy nor among the salt miners of Austria carried with it the same conviction of human wretchedness which was conveyed by this momentary glimpse of an East London street. It was, of course, a most fragmentary and lurid view of the poverty of East London, and quite unfair. I should have been shown either less or more, for I went away with no notion of the hundreds of men and women who had gallantly identified their fortunes with these empty-handed people, and who, in church and chapel, "relief works," and charities, were at least making an effort toward its mitigation.

Our visit was made in November, 1883, the very year when the *Pall Mall Gazette* exposure started "The Bitter Cry of Outcast London," and the conscience of England was stirred as never before over this joyless city in the East End of its capital. Even then, vigorous and drastic plans were being discussed, and a splendid program of municipal reforms was already dimly outlined. Of all these, however, I had heard nothing but the vaguest rumor.

No comfort came to me then from any source,—and the painful impression was increased because at the very moment of looking down the East London street from the top of the omnibus, I had been sharply and painfully reminded of "The Vision of Sudden Death" which had confronted De Quincey one summer's night as he was being driven through rural England on a high mail coach. Two absorbed lovers suddenly appear between the narrow, blossoming hedgerows in the direct path of the huge vehicle which is sure to crush them to their death. De Quincey tries to send them a warning shout, but finds himself unable to make a sound because his mind is hopelessly entangled in an endeavor to recall the exact lines from the *Iliad* which describe the great cry with which Achilles alarmed all Asia militant. Only after his memory responds is his will released from its momentary paralysis, and he rides on through the fragrant night with the horror of the escaped calamity thick upon him, but he also bears with him the consciousness that he had given himself over so many years to classic learning—that when suddenly called upon for a quick decision in the world of life and death, he had been able to act only through a literary suggestion.

This is what we were all doing, lumbering our minds with literature that only served to cloud the really vital situation spread before our eyes. It seemed to me too

preposterous that in my first view of the horror of East
London I should have recalled De Quincey's literary description of the literary suggestion which had once para-
lyzed him. In my disgust it all appeared a hateful, vicious
circle which even the apostles of culture themselves admitted, for had not one of the greatest among the moderns
plainly said that "conduct, and not culture is three fourths
of human life."

For two years in the midst of my distress over the poverty which, thus suddenly driven into my consciousness,
had become to me the "Weltschmerz," there was mingled
a sense of futility, of misdirected energy, the belief that
the pursuit of cultivation would not in the end bring either
solace or relief. I gradually reached a conviction that the
first generation of college women had taken their learning
too quickly, had departed too suddenly from the active,
emotional life led by their grandmothers and great-grand-
mothers that the contemporary education of young women
had developed too exclusively the power of acquiring
knowledge and of merely receiving impressions; that somewhere in the process of "being educated" they had lost
that simple and almost automatic response to the human
appeal, that old healthful reaction resulting in activity
from the mere presence of suffering or of helplessness; that
they are so sheltered and pampered they have no chance
even to make "the great refusal."

In the German and French *pensions,* which twenty-five
years ago were crowded with American mothers and their
daughters who had crossed the seas in search of culture,
one often found the mother making real connection with
the life about her, using her inadequate German with great
fluency, gaily measuring the enormous sheets or exchang-
ing recipes with the German Hausfrau, visiting impartially
the nearest kindergarten and market, making an atmosphere of her own, hearty and genuine as far as it went, in
the house and on the street. On the other hand, her daughter was critical and uncertain of her linguistic acquire-
ments, and only at ease when in the familiar receptive
attitude afforded by the art gallery and the opera house. In
the latter she was swayed and moved, appreciative of the
power and charm of the music, intelligent as to the legend
and poetry of the plot, finding use for her trained and

developed powers as she sat "being cultivated" in the familiar atmosphere of the classroom which had, as it were, become sublimated and romanticized.

I remember a happy busy mother who, complacent with the knowledge that her daughter daily devoted four hours to her music, looked up from her knitting to say, "If I had had your opportunities when I was young, my dear, I should have been a very happy girl. I always had musical talent, but such training as I had, foolish little songs and waltzes and not time for half an hour's practice a day."

The mother did not dream of the sting her words left and that the sensitive girl appreciated only too well that her opportunities were fine and unusual, but she also knew that in spite of some facility and much good teaching she had no genuine talent and never would fulfill the expectations of her friends. She looked back upon her mother's girlhood with positive envy because it was so full of happy industry and extenuating obstacles, with undisturbed opportunity to believe that her talents were unusual. The girl looked wistfully at her mother, but had not the courage to cry out what was in her heart: "I might believe I had unusual talent if I did not know what good music was; I might enjoy half an hour's practice a day if I were busy and happy the rest of the time. You do not know what life means when all the difficulties are removed! I am simply smothered and sickened with advantages. It is like eating a sweet dessert the first thing in the morning."

This, then, was the difficulty, this sweet dessert in the morning and the assumption that the sheltered, educated girl has nothing to do with the bitter poverty and the social maladjustment which is all about her, and which, after all, cannot be concealed, for it breaks through poetry and literature in a burning tide which overwhelms her; it peers at her in the form of heavy-laden market women and underpaid street laborers, gibing her with a sense of her uselessness.

I recall one snowy morning in Saxe-Coburg, looking from the window of our little hotel upon the town square, that we saw crossing and recrossing it a single file of women with semicircular, heavy, wooden tanks fastened upon their backs. They were carrying in this primitive fashion to a remote cooling room these tanks filled with a hot brew incident to one stage of beer making. The women were bent forward, not only under the weight which they were bearing, but because the tanks were so high that it would have been impossible for them to have lifted their heads. Their faces and hands, reddened in the cold morning air, showed clearly the white scars where they had previously been scalded by the hot stuff which splashed if they stumbled ever so little on their way. Stung into action by one of those sudden indignations against cruel conditions which at times fill the young with unexpected energy, I found myself across the square, in company with mine host, interviewing the phlegmatic owner of the brewery who received us with exasperating indifference, or rather received me, for the innkeeper mysteriously slunk away as soon as the great magnate of the town began to speak. I went back to a breakfast for which I had lost my appetite, as I had for Gray's *Life of Prince Albert* and his wonderful tutor, Baron Stockmar, which I had been reading late the night before. The book had lost its fascination; how could a good man, feeling so keenly his obligation "to make princely the mind of his prince," ignore such conditions of life for the multitude of humble, hard-working folk. We were spending two months in Dresden that winter, given over to much reading of *The History of Art* and to much visiting of its art gallery and opera house, and after such an experience I would invariably suffer a moral revulsion against this feverish search after culture. It was doubtless in such moods that I founded my admiration for Albrecht Dürer, taking his wonderful pictures, however, in the most unorthodox manner, merely as human documents. I was chiefly appealed to by his unwillingness to lend himself to a smooth and cultivated view of life, by his determination to record its frustrations and even the hideous forms which darken the day for our human imagination and to ignore no human complications. I believed that his canvases intimated the coming religious and social changes of the Reformation and the peasants' wars, that they were surcharged with pity for the downtrodden, that his sad knights, gravely standing guard, were longing to avert that shedding of blood which is sure to occur when

men forget how complicated life is and insist upon reducing it to logical dogmas.

The largest sum of money that I ever ventured to spend
in Europe was for an engraving of his "St. Hubert," the
background of which was said to be from an original
Dürer plate. There is little doubt, I am afraid, that the
background as well as the figures "were put in at a later
date," but the purchase at least registered the high-water
mark of my enthusiasm.

The wonder and beauty of Italy later brought healing
and some relief to the paralyzing sense of the futility of
all artistic and intellectual effort when disconnected from
the ultimate test of the conduct it inspired. The serene and
soothing touch of history also aroused old enthusiasms,
although some of their manifestations were such as one
smiles over more easily in retrospection than at the moment. I fancy that it was no smiling matter to several people in our party, whom I induced to walk for three miles
in the hot sunshine beating down upon the Roman Cam-
pagna, that we might enter the Eternal City on foot
through the Porta del Popolo, as pilgrims had done for
centuries. To be sure, we had really entered Rome the
night before, but the railroad station and the hotel might
have been anywhere else, and we had been driven beyond
the walls after breakfast and stranded at the very spot
where the pilgrims always said "Ecco Roma," as they
caught the first glimpse of St. Peter's dome. This melo-
dramatic entrance into Rome, or rather pretended entrance, was the prelude to days of enchantment, and I
returned to Europe two years later in order to spend a
winter there and to carry out a great desire to systematically study the Catacombs. In spite of my distrust of "advantages" I was apparently not yet so cured but that I
wanted more of them.

The two years which elapsed before I again found myself in Europe brought their inevitable changes. Family
arrangements had so come about that I had spent three or
four months of each of the intervening winters in Balti-
more, where I seemed to have reached the nadir of my
nervous depression and sense of maladjustment, in spite
of my interest in the fascinating lectures given there by
Lanciani of Rome, and a definite course of reading under

the guidance of a Johns Hopkins lecturer upon the United
Italy movement. In the latter I naturally encountered the
influence of Mazzini, which was a source of great comfort
to me, although perhaps I went too suddenly from a con-
templation of his wonderful ethical and philosophical appeal to the workingmen of Italy, directly to the lecture
rooms at Johns Hopkins University, for I was certainly
much disillusioned at this time as to the effect of intellectual pursuits upon moral development.

The summers were spent in the old home in northern
Illinois, and one Sunday morning I received the rite of
baptism and became a member of the Presbyterian church
in the village. At this time there was certainly no outside
pressure pushing me toward such a decision, and at twenty-
five one does not ordinarily take such a step from a
mere desire to conform. While I was not conscious of any
emotional "conversion," I took upon myself the outward
expressions of the religious life with all humility and sincerity. It was doubtless true that I was

> Weary of myself and sick of asking
> What I am and what I ought to be,

and that various cherished safeguards and claims to self-
dependence had been broken into by many piteous failures. But certainly I had been brought to the conclusion
that "sincerely to give up one's conceit or hope of being
good in one's own right is the only door to the Universe's
deeper reaches." Perhaps the young clergyman recognized
this as the test of the Christian temper—at any rate he
required little assent to dogma or miracle, and assured me
that while both the ministry and the officers of his church
were obliged to subscribe to doctrines of well-known sever-
ity, the faith required to the laity was almost early Christian in its simplicity. I was conscious of no change from
my childish acceptance of the teachings of the Gospels,
but at this moment something persuasive within made me
long for an outward symbol of fellowship, some bond of
peace, some blessed spot where unity of spirit might claim
right of way over all differences. There was also growing
within me an almost passionate devotion to the ideals of
democracy, and when in all history had these ideals been
so thrillingly expressed as when the faith of the fisherman

and the slave had been boldly opposed to the accepted moral belief that the well-being of a privileged few might justly be built upon the ignorance and sacrifice of the many? Who was I, with my dreams of universal fellowship, that I did not identify myself with the institutional state-ment of this belief, as it stood in the little village in which I was born, and without which testimony in each remote hamlet of Christendom it would be so easy for the world to slip back into the doctrines of selection and aristocracy?

In one of the intervening summers between these Eu-ropean journeys I visited a western state where I had formerly invested a sum of money in mortgages. I was much horrified by the wretched conditions among the farmers, which had resulted from a long period of drought, and one forlorn picture was fairly burned into my mind. A number of starved hogs—collateral for a promissory note—were huddled into an open pen. Their backs were humped in a curious, camel-like fashion, and they were devouring one of their own number, the latest victim of absolute starvation or possibly merely the one least able to defend himself against their voracious hunger. The farm-er's wife looked on indifferently, a picture of despair as she stood in the door of the bare, crude house, and the two children behind her, whom she vainly tried to keep out of sight, continually thrust forward their faces almost covered by masses of coarse, sunburned hair, and their little bare feet so black, so hard, the great cracks so filled with dust that they looked like flattened hoofs. The chil-dren could not be compared to anything so joyous as satyrs, although they appeared but half-human. It seemed to me quite impossible to receive interest from mortgages placed upon farms which might at any season be reduced to such conditions, and with great inconvenience to my agent and doubtless with hardship to the farmers, as speed-ily as possible I withdrew all my investment. But some-thing had to be done with the money, and in my reaction against unseen horrors I bought a farm near my native village and also a flock of innocent-looking sheep. My partner in the enterprise had not chosen the shepherd's lot as a permanent occupation, but hoped to speedily finish his college course upon half the proceeds of our venture. This pastoral enterprise still seems to me to have been essentially sound, both economically and morally, but perhaps one partner depended too much upon the impeccability of her motives and the other found himself too preoccupied with study to know that it is not a real kindness to bed a sheepfold with straw, for certainly the venture ended in a spectacle scarcely less harrowing than the memory it was designed to obliterate. At least the sight of two hundred sheep with four rotting hoofs each, was not reassuring to one whose conscience craved economic peace. A fortunate series of sales of mutton, wool, and farm enabled the partners to end the enterprise without loss, and they passed on, one to college and the other to Europe, if not wiser, certainly sadder for the experience.

It was during this second journey to Europe that I attended a meeting of the London match girls who were on strike and who met daily under the leadership of well-known labor men of London. The low wages that were reported at the meetings, the phossy jaw which was described and occasionally exhibited, the appearance of the girls themselves I did not, curiously enough, in any wise connect with what was called the labor movement, nor did I understand the efforts of the London trades-unionists, concerning whom I held the vaguest notions. But of course this impression of human misery was added to the others which were already making me so wretched. I think that up to this time I was still filled with the sense which Wells describes in one of his young characters, that somewhere in Church or State are a body of authoritative people who will put things to rights as soon as they really know what is wrong. Such a young person persistently believes that behind all suffering, behind sin and want, must lie redeeming magnanimity. He may imagine the world to be tragic and terrible, but it never for an instant occurs to him that it may be contemptible or squalid or self-seeking. Apparently I looked upon the efforts of the trades-unionists as I did upon those of Frederic Harrison and the Positivists whom I heard the next Sunday in Newton Hall, as a manifestation of "loyalty to humanity" and an attempt to aid in its progress. I was enormously interested in the Positivists during these European years; I imagined that their philosophical conception of man's religious development might include all expressions of that for which so many ages of men have struggled and aspired. I vaguely hoped for this universal comity when I stood in Stonehenge, on the Acropolis in Athens, or in the Sistine Chapel in the Vatican. But never did I so desire it as in the cathedrals of Winchester, Notre Dame, Amiens. One winter's day I traveled from Munich to Ulm because I imagined from what the art books said that the cathedral hoarded a medieval statement of the Positivists' final synthesis, prefiguring their conception of a "Supreme Humanity."

In this I was not altogether disappointed. The religious history carved on the choir stalls at Ulm contained Greek philosophers as well as Hebrew prophets, and among the disciples and saints stood the discoverer of music and a builder of pagan temples. Even then I was startled, forgetting for the moment the religious revolutions of south Germany, to catch sight of a window showing Luther as he affixed his thesis on the door at Wittenberg, the picture shining clear in the midst of the older glass of saint and symbol.

My smug notebook states that all this was an admission that "the saints but embodied fine action," and it proceeds at some length to set forth my hope for a "cathedral of humanity," which should be "capacious enough to house a fellowship of common purpose," and which should be "beautiful enough to persuade men to hold fast to the vision of human solidarity." It is quite impossible for me to reproduce this experience at Ulm unless I quote pages more from the notebook in which I seem to have written half the night, in a fever of composition cast in ill-digested phrases from Comte. It doubtless reflected also something of the faith of the Old Catholics, a charming group of whom I had recently met in Stuttgart, and the same mood is easily traced in my early hopes for the Settlement that it should unite in the fellowship of the deed those of widely differing religious beliefs.

The beginning of 1887 found our little party of three in very picturesque lodgings in Rome, and settled into a certain student's routine. But my study of the Catacombs was brought to an abrupt end in a fortnight by a severe attack of sciatic rheumatism, which kept me in Rome with a trained nurse during many weeks, and later sent me to the Riviera to lead an invalid's life once more. Although my Catacomb lore thus remained hopelessly superficial, it seemed to me a sufficient basis for a course of six lectures which I timidly offered to a Deaconess's Training School during my first winter in Chicago, upon the simple ground that this early interpretation of Christianity is the one which should be presented to the poor, urging that the primitive church was composed of the poor and that it was they who took the wonderful news to the more prosperous Romans. The open-minded head of the school gladly accepted the lectures, arranging that the course should be given each spring to her graduating class of Home and Foreign Missionaries, and at the end of the third year she invited me to become one of the trustees of the school. I accepted and attended one meeting of the board, but never another, because some of the older members objected to my membership on the ground that "no religious instruction was given at Hull-House." I remember my sympathy for the embarrassment in which the head of the school was placed, but if I needed comfort, a bit of it came to me on my way home from the trustees' meeting when an Italian laborer paid my street-car fare, according to the custom of our simpler neighbors. Upon my inquiry of the conductor as to whom I was indebted for the little courtesy, he replied roughly enough, "I cannot tell one dago from another when they are in a gang, but sure, any one of them would do it for you as quick as they would for the Sisters."

It is hard to tell just when the very simple plan which afterward developed into the Settlement began to form itself in my mind. It may have been even before I went to Europe for the second time, but I gradually became convinced that it would be a good thing to rent a house in a part of the city where many primitive and actual needs are found, in which young women who had been given over too exclusively to study might restore a balance of activity along traditional lines and learn of life from life itself; where they might try out some of the things they had been taught and put truth to "the ultimate test of the conduct it dictates or inspires." I do not remember to have mentioned this plan to anyone until we reached Madrid in April 1888.

We had been to see a bullfight rendered in the most

magnificent Spanish style, where greatly to my surprise and horror, I found that I had seen, with comparative indifference, five bulls and many more horses killed. The sense that this was the last survival of all the glories of the amphitheater, the illusion that the riders on the caparisoned horses might have been knights of a tournament, or the matador a slightly armed gladiator facing his martyrdom, and all the rest of the obscure yet vivid associations of an historic survival, had carried me beyond the endurance of any of the rest of the party. I finally met them in the foyer, stern and pale with disapproval of my brutal endurance, and but partially recovered from the faintness and disgust which the spectacle itself had produced upon them. I had no defense to offer to their reproaches save that I had not thought much about the bloodshed; but in the evening the natural and inevitable reaction came, and in deep chagrin I felt myself tried and condemned, not only by this disgusting experience but by the entire moral situation which it revealed. It was suddenly made quite clear to me that I was lulling my conscience by a dreamer's scheme, that a mere paper reform had become a defense for continued idleness, and that I was making it a *raison d'être* for going on indefinitely with study and travel. It is easy to become the dupe of a deferred purpose, of the promise the future can never keep, and I had fallen into the meanest type of self-deception in making myself believe that all this was in preparation for great things to come. Nothing less than the moral reaction following the experience at a bullfight had been able to reveal to me that so far from following in the wake of a chariot of philanthropic fire, I had been tied to the tail of the veriest ox-cart of self-seeking.

I had made up my mind that next day, whatever happened, I would begin to carry out the plan, if only by talking about it. I can well recall the stumbling and uncertainty with which I finally set it forth to Miss Starr, my old-time school friend, who was one of our party. I even dared to hope that she might join in carrying out the plan, but nevertheless I told it in the fear of that disheartening experience which is so apt to afflict our most cherished plans when they are at last divulged, when we suddenly feel that there is nothing there to talk about, and as the golden dream slips through our fingers we are left to wonder at our own fatuous belief. But gradually the comfort of Miss Starr's companionship, the vigor and enthusiasm which she brought to bear upon it, told both in the growth of the plan and upon the sense of its validity, so that by the time we had reached the enchantment of the Alhambra, the scheme had become convincing and tangible although still most hazy in detail.

A month later we parted in Paris, Miss Starr to go back to Italy, and I to journey on to London to secure as many suggestions as possible from those wonderful places of which we had heard, Toynbee Hall and the People's Palace. So that it finally came about that in June, 1888, years after my first visit in East London, I found myself at Toynbee Hall equipped not only with a letter of introduction from Canon Fremantle, but with high expectations and a certain belief that whatever perplexities and discouragement concerning the life of the poor were in store for me, I should at least know something at firsthand and have the solace of daily activity. I had confidence that although life itself might contain many difficulties, the period of mere passive receptivity had come to an end, and I had at last finished with the ever-lasting "preparation for life," however ill-prepared I might be.

It was not until years afterward that I came upon Tolstoy's phrase "the snare of preparation," which he insists we spread before the feet of young people, hopelessly entangling them in a curious inactivity at the very period of life when they are longing to construct the world anew and to conform it to their own ideals.

Chapter 5

FIRST DAYS AT HULL-HOUSE

THE next January found Miss Starr and myself in Chicago, searching for a neighborhood in which we might put our plans into execution. In our eagerness to win friends for the new undertaking, we utilized every opportunity to set forth the meaning of the Settlement as it had been embodied in Toynbee Hall, although in those days we made no appeal for money, meaning to start with our own slender resources. From the very first the plan received courteous attention, and the discussion, while often skeptical, was always friendly. Professor Swing wrote a commendatory column in the *Evening Journal,* and our early speeches were reported quite out of proportion to their worth. I recall a spirited evening at the home of Mrs. Wilmarth, which was attended by that renowned scholar, Thomas Davidson, and by a young Englishman who was a member of the then new Fabian society and to whom a peculiar glamour was attached because he had scoured knives all summer in a camp of high-minded philosophers in the Adirondacks. Our new little plan met with criticism, not to say disapproval, from Mr. Davidson, who, as nearly as I can remember, called it "one of those unnatural attempts to understand life through coöperative living."

It was in vain we asserted that the collective living was

not an essential part of the plan, that we would always scrupulously pay our own expenses, and that at any moment we might decide to scatter through the neighborhood and to live in separate tenements; he still contended that the fascination for most of those volunteering residence would lie in the collective living aspect of the Settlement. His contention was, of course, essentially sound; there is a constant tendency for the residents to "lose themselves in the cave of their own companionship," as the Toynbee Hall phrase goes, but on the other hand, it is doubtless true that the very companionship, the give and take of colleagues, is what tends to keep the Settlement normal and in touch with "the world of things as they are." I am happy to say that we never resented this nor any other difference of opinion, and that fifteen years later Professor Davidson handsomely acknowledged that the advantages of a group far outweighed the weaknesses he had early pointed out. He was at that later moment sharing with a group of young men, on the East Side of New York, his ripest conclusions in philosophy and was much touched by their intelligent interest and absorbed devotion. I think that time has also justified our early contention that the mere foothold of a house, easily accessible, ample in space, hospitable and tolerant in spirit, situated in the midst of the large foreign colonies which so easily isolate themselves in American cities, would be in itself a serviceable thing for Chicago. I am not so sure that we succeeded in our endeavors "to make social intercourse express the growing sense of the economic unity of society and to add the social function to democracy." But Hull-House was soberly opened on the theory that the dependence of classes on each other is reciprocal; and that as the social relation is essentially a reciprocal relation, it gives a form of expression that has peculiar value.

In our search for a vicinity in which to settle we went about with the officers of the compulsory education department, with city missionaries, and with the newspaper reporters whom I recall as a much older set of men than one ordinarily associates with that profession, or perhaps I was only sent out with the older ones on what they must all have considered a quixotic mission. One Sunday afternoon in the late winter a reporter took me to visit a so-called anarchist Sunday School, several of which were to be found on the northwest side of the city. The young man in charge was of the German student type, and his face flushed with enthusiasm as he led the children singing one of Koerner's poems. The newspaperman, who did not understand German, asked me what abominable stuff they were singing, but he seemed dissatisfied with my translation of the simple words and darkly intimated that they were "deep ones," and had probably "fooled" me. When I replied that Koerner was an ardent German poet whose songs inspired his countrymen to resist the aggressions of Napoleon, and that his bound poems were found in the most respectable libraries, he looked at me rather askance and I then and there had my first intimation that to treat a Chicago man, who is called an anarchist, as you would treat any other citizen, is to lay yourself open to deep suspicion.

Another Sunday afternoon in the early spring, on the way to a Bohemian mission in the carriage of one of its founders, we passed a fine old house standing well back from the street, surrounded on three sides by a broad piazza which was supported by wooden pillars of exceptionally pure Corinthian design and proportion. I was so attracted by the house that I set forth to visit it the very next day, but though I searched for it then and for several days after, I could not find it, and at length I most reluctantly gave up the search.

Three weeks later, with the advice of several of the oldest residents of Chicago, including the ex-mayor of the city, Colonel Mason, who had from the first been a warm friend to our plans, we decided upon a location somewhere near the junction of Blue Island Avenue, Halsted Street, and Harrison Street. I was surprised and overjoyed on the very first day of our search for quarters to come upon the hospitable old house, the quest for which I had so recently abandoned. The house was of course rented, the lower part of it used for offices and storerooms in connection with a factory that stood back of it. However, after some difficulties were overcome, it proved to be possible to sublet the second floor and what had been the large drawing-room on the first floor.

The house had passed through many changes since it had been built in 1856 for the homestead of one of Chicago's pioneer citizens, Mr. Charles J. Hull, and although battered by its vicissitudes, was essentially sound. Before it had been occupied by the factory, it had sheltered a second-hand furniture store, and at one time the Little Sisters of the Poor had used it for a home for the aged. It had a half-skeptical reputation for a haunted attic, so far respected by the tenants living on the second floor that they always kept a large pitcher full of water on the attic stairs. Their explanation of this custom was so incoherent that I was sure it was a survival of the belief that a ghost could not cross running water, but perhaps that interpretation was only my eagerness for finding folklore.

The fine old house responded kindly to repairs, its wide hall and open fireplaces always insuring it a gracious aspect. Its generous owner, Miss Helen Culver, in the following spring gave us a free leasehold of the entire house. Her kindness has continued through the years until the group of thirteen buildings, which at present comprises our equipment, is built largely upon land which Miss Culver has put at the service of the Settlement which bears Mr. Hull's name. In those days the house stood between an undertaking establishment and a saloon. "Knight, Death, and the Devil," the three were called by a Chicago wit, and yet any mock heroics which might be implied by comparing the Settlement to a knight quickly dropped away under the genuine kindness and hearty welcome extended to us by the families living up and down the street.

We furnished the house as we would have furnished it were it in another part of the city, with the photographs and other impedimenta we had collected in Europe, and with a few bits of family mahogany. While all the new furniture which was bought was enduring in quality, we were careful to keep it in character with the fine old residence. Probably no young matron ever placed her own things in her own house with more pleasure than that with which we first furnished Hull-House. We believed that the Settlement may logically bring to its aid all those adjuncts which the cultivated man regards as good and suggestive of the best life of the past.

On the 18th of September, 1889, Miss Starr and I moved into it, with Miss Mary Keyser, who began by performing the housework, but who quickly developed into a

Polk Street opposite Hull-House

very important factor in the life of the vicinity as well as in that of the household, and whose death five years later was most sincerely mourned by hundreds of our neighbors. In our enthusiasm over "settling," the first night we forgot not only to lock but to close a side door opening on Polk Street, and were much pleased in the morning to find that we possessed a fine illustration of the honesty and kindliness of our new neighbors.

Our first guest was an interesting young woman who lived in a neighboring tenement, whose widowed mother aided her in the support of the family by scrubbing a downtown theater every night. The mother, of English birth, was well bred and carefully educated, but was in the midst of that bitter struggle which awaits so many strangers in American cities who find that their social position tends to be measured solely by the standards of living they are able to maintain. Our guest has long since married the struggling young lawyer to whom she was then engaged, and he is now leading his profession in an eastern city: She recalls that month's experience always with a sense of amusement over the fact that the succession of visitors who came to see the new Settlement invariably questioned her most minutely concerning "these people" without once suspecting that they were talking to one who had been identified with the neighborhood from childhood. I at least was able to draw a lesson from the incident, and I never addressed a Chicago audience on the subject of the Settlement and its vicinity without inviting a neighbor to go with me, that I might curb any hasty generalization by the consciousness that I had an auditor who knew the conditions more intimately than I could hope to do.

Halsted Street has grown so familiar during twenty years of residence that it is difficult to recall its gradual

South Halsted Street opposite Hull-House

changes—the withdrawal of the more prosperous Irish and Germans, and the slow substitution of Russian Jews, Italians, and Greeks. A description of the street such as I gave in those early addresses still stands in my mind as sympathetic and correct.

Halsted Street is thirty-two miles long, and one of the great thoroughfares of Chicago; Polk Street crosses it midway between the stockyards to the south and the shipbuilding yards on the north branch of the Chicago River. For the six miles between these two industries the street is lined with shops of butchers and grocers, with dingy and gorgeous saloons, and pretentious establishments for the sale of ready-made clothing. Polk Street, running west from Halsted Street, grows rapidly more prosperous; running a mile east to State Street, it grows steadily worse, and crosses a network of vice on the corners of Clark Street and Fifth Avenue. Hull-House once stood in the suburbs, but the city has steadily grown up around it and its site now has corners on three or four foreign colonies. Between Halsted Street and the river live about ten thousand Italians—Neapolitans, Sicilians, and Calabrians, with an occasional Lombard or Venetion. To the south on Twelfth Street are many Germans, and side streets are given over almost entirely to Polish and Russian Jews. Still farther south, these Jewish colonies merge into a huge Bohemian colony, so vast that Chicago ranks as the third Bohemian city in the world. To the northwest are many Canadian-French, clannish in spite of their long residence in America, and to the north are Irish and first-generation Americans. On the streets directly west and farther north are well-to-do English-speaking families, many of whom own their houses and have lived in the neighborhood for years; one man is still living in his old farmhouse.

The policy of the public authorities of never taking an initiative, and always waiting to be urged to do their duty, is obviously fatal in a neighborhood where there is little initiative among the citizens. The idea underlying our self-government breaks down in such a ward. The streets are inexpressibly dirty, the number of schools inadequate, sanitary legislation unenforced, the street lighting bad, the paving miserable and altogether lacking in the alleys and smaller streets, and the stables foul beyond description. Hundreds of houses are unconnected with the street sewer. The older and richer inhabitants seem anxious to move away as rapidly as they can afford it. They make room for newly arrived immigrants who are densely ignorant of civic duties. This substitution of the older inhabitants is accomplished industrially also, in the south and east quarters of the ward. The Jews and Italians for the finishing for the great clothing manufacturers, formerly done by Americans, Irish, and Germans, who refused to submit to the extremely low prices to which the sweating system has reduced their successors. As the design of the sweating system is the elimination of rent from the manufacture of clothing, the "outside work" is begun after the clothing leaves the cutter. An unscrupulous contractor regards no basement as too dark, no stable loft too foul, no rear shanty too provisional, no tenement room too small for his workroom, as these conditions imply low rental. Hence these shops abound in the worst of the foreign districts where the sweater easily finds his cheap basement and his home finishers.

The houses of the ward, for the most part wooden, were originally built for the one family and are now occupied by several. They are after the type of the inconvenient frame cottages found in the poorer suburbs twenty years ago. Many of them were built where they now stand; others were brought thither on rollers, because their previous sites had been taken for factories. The fewer brick tenement buildings which are three or four stories high are comparatively new, and there are few large tenements. The little wooden houses have a temporary aspect, and for this reason, perhaps, the tenement-house legislation in Chicago is totally inadequate. Rear tenements flourish; many houses have no water supply save the faucet in the back yard, there are no fire escapes, the garbage and ashes are placed in wooden boxes which are fastened to the street pavements. One of the most discouraging features about the present system of tenement houses is that many are owned by sordid and ignorant immigrants. The theory that wealth brings responsibility, that possession entails at length education and refinement, in these cases fails utterly. The children of an Italian immigrant owner may "shine" shoes in the streets, and his wife may pick rags from the street gutter, laboriously sorting them in a dingy court. Wealth may do something for her self-complacency and feeling of consequence; it certainly does nothing for her comfort or her children's improvement nor for the cleanliness of anyone concerned. Another thing that prevents better houses in Chicago is the tentative attitude of the real estate men. Many unsavory conditions are allowed to continue which would be regarded with horror if they were considered permanent. Meanwhile, the wretched con-

ditions persist until at least two generations of children
have been born and reared in them.

In every neighborhood where poorer people live,
because rents are supposed to be cheaper there, is an element which, although uncertain in the individual, in the
aggregate can be counted upon. It is composed of people
of former education and opportunity who have cherished
ambitions and prospects, but who are caricatures of what
they meant to be—"hollow ghosts which blame the living
men." There are times in many lives when there is a
cessation of energy and loss of power. Men and women
of education and refinement come to live in a cheaper
neighborhood because they lack the ability to make money,
because of ill health, because of an unfortunate marriage,
or for other reasons which do not imply criminality or
stupidity. Among them are those who, in spite of untoward circumstances, keep up some sort of an intellectual
life; those who are "great for books," as their neighbors
say. To such the Settlement may be a genuine refuge.

In the very first weeks of our residence Miss Starr started a reading party in George Eliot's *Romola,* which was
attended by a group of young women who followed the
wonderful tale with unflagging interest. The weekly reading was held in our little upstairs dining room, and two
members of the club came to dinner each week, not only
that they might be received as guests, but that they might
help us wash the dishes afterward and so make the table
ready for the stacks of Florentine photographs.

Our "first resident," as she gaily designated herself,
was a charming old lady who gave five consecutive readings from Hawthorne to a most appreciative audience,
interspersing the magic tales most delightfully with recollections of the elusive and fascinating author. Years
before she had lived at Brook Farm as a pupil of the Rip-
leys, and she came to us for ten days because she wished to
live once more in an atmosphere where "idealism ran
high." We thus early found the type of class which through
all the years has remained most popular—a combination
of a social atmosphere with serious study.

Volunteers to the new undertaking came quickly; a
charming young girl conducted a kindergarten in the drawing room, coming regularly every morning from her home
in a distant part of the North Side of the city. Although a

tablet to her memory has stood upon a mantel shelf in Hull-House for five years, we still associate her most vividly with the play of little children, first in her kindergarten and then in her own nursery, which furnished a veritable illustration of Victor Hugo's definition of heaven—"a place where parents are always young and children always little." Her daily presence for the first two years made it quite impossible for us to become too solemn and self-conscious in our strenuous routine, for her mirth and buoyancy were irresistible and her eager desire to share the life of the neighborhood never failed, although it was often put to a severe test. One day at luncheon she gaily recited her futile attempt to impress temperance principles upon the mind of an Italian mother, to whom she had returned a small daughter of five sent to the kindergarten "in quite a horrid state of intoxication" from the wine-soaked bread upon which she had breakfasted. The mother, with the gentle courtesy of a South Italian, listened politely to her graphic portrayal of the untimely end awaiting so immature a wine bibber; but long before the lecture was finished quite unconscious of the incongruity, she hospitably set forth her best wines, and when her baffled guest refused one after the other, she disappeared, only to quickly return with a small dark glass of whisky, saying reassuringly, "See, I have brought you the true American drink." The recital ended in seriocomic despair, with the rueful statement that "the impression I probably made upon her darkened mind was that it is the American custom to breakfast children on bread soaked in whisky instead of light Italian wine."

That first kindergarten was a constant source of education to us. We were much surprised to find social distinctions even among its lambs, although greatly amused with the neat formulation made by the superior little Italian boy who refused to sit beside uncouth little Angelina because "we eat our macaroni this way"—imitating the movement of a fork from a plate to his mouth—"and she eat her macaroni this way," holding his hand high in the air and throwing back his head, that his wide-open mouth might receive an imaginary cascade. Angelina gravely nodded her little head in approval of this distinction between gentry and peasant. "But isn't it astonishing

that merely table manners are made such a test all the
way along?" was the comment of their democratic teacher.
Another memory which refuses to be associated with death,
which came to her all too soon, is that of the young girl
who organized our first really successful club of boys, holding their fascinated interest by the old chivalric tales, set
forth so dramatically and vividly that checkers and jack-
straws were abandoned by all the other clubs on Boys'
Day, that their members might form a listening fringe to
The Young Heroes.

I met a member of the latter club one day as he flung
himself out of the House in the rage by which an emotional boy hopes to keep from shedding tears. "There is
no use coming here any more, Prince Roland is dead," he
gruffly explained as we passed. We encouraged the younger
boys in tournaments and dramatics of all sorts, and we
somewhat fatuously believed that boys who were early
interested in adventurers or explorers might later want to
know the lives of living statesmen and inventors. It is
needless to add that the boys quickly responded to such a
program, and that the only difficulty lay in finding leaders
who were able to carry it out. This difficulty has been with
us through all the years of growth and development in
the Boys' Club until now, with its five-story building, its
splendid equipment of shops, of recreation and study
rooms, that group alone is successful which commands
the services of a resourceful and devoted leader.

The dozens of younger children who from the first came
to Hull-House were organized into groups which were not
quite classes and not quite clubs. The value of these groups
consisted almost entirely in arousing a higher imagination
and in giving the children the opportunity which they could
not have in the crowded schools, for initiative and for
independent social relationships. The public schools then
contained little hand work of any sort, so that naturally
any instruction which we provided for the children took
the direction of this supplementary work. But it required
a constant effort that the pressure of poverty itself should
not defeat the educational aim. The Italian girls in the
sewing classes would count that day lost when they could
not carry home a garment, and the insistence that it should

be neatly made seemed a super-refinement to those in
dire need of clothing.

As these clubs have been continued during the twenty
years they have developed classes in the many forms of
handicraft which the newer education is so rapidly adapt-
ing for the delight of children; but they still keep their
essentially social character and still minister to that large
number of children who leave school the very week they
are fourteen years old, only too eager to close the school-
room door forever on a tiresome task that is at last well
over. It seems to us important that these children shall
find themselves permanently attached to a House that offers them evening clubs and classes with their old companions, that merges as easily as possible the school life
into the working life and does what it can to find places
for the bewildered young things looking for work. A large
proportion of the delinquent boys brought into the juvenile
court in Chicago are the oldest sons in large families whose
wages are needed at home. The grades from which many
of them leave school, as the records show, are piteously
far from the seventh and eighth where the very first instruction in manual training is given, nor have they been
caught by any other abiding interest.

In spite of these flourishing clubs for children early established at Hull-House, and the fact that our first organized undertaking was a kindergarten, we were very insistent
that the Settlement should not be primarily for the
children, and that it was absurd to suppose that grown
people would not respond to opportunities for education
and social life. Our enthusiastic kindergartner herself demonstrated this with an old woman of ninety, who, because she was left alone all day while her daughter cooked
in a restaurant, had formed such a persistent habit of pick-
ing the plaster off the walls that one landlord after another
refused to have her for a tenant. It required but a few
weeks' time to teach her to make large paper chains, and
gradually she was content to do it all day long, and in the
end took quite as much pleasure in adorning the walls as
she had formerly taken in demolishing them. Fortunately
the landlord had never heard the æsthetic principle that
the exposure of basic construction is more desirable than
gaudy decoration. In course of time it was discovered that

the old woman could speak Gælic, and when one or two grave professors came to see her, the neighborhood was filled with pride that such a wonder lived in their midst. To mitigate life for a woman of ninety was an unfailing refutation of the statement that the Settlement was designed for the young.

On our first New Year's Day at Hull-House we invited the older people in the vicinity, sending a carriage for the most feeble and announcing to all of them that we were going to organize an Old Settlers' Party.

Every New Year's Day since, older people in varying numbers have come together at Hull-House to relate early hardships and to take for the moment the place in the community to which their pioneer life entitles them. Many people who were formerly residents of the vicinity, but whom prosperity has carried into more desirable neighborhoods, come back to these meetings and often confess to each other that they have never since found such kindness as in early Chicago when all its citizens came together in mutual enterprises. Many of these pioneers, so like the men and women of my earliest childhood that I always felt comforted by their presence in the house, were very much opposed to "foreigners," whom they held responsible for a depreciation of property and a general lowering of the tone of the neighborhood. Sometimes we had a chance for championship; I recall one old man, fiercely American, who had reproached me because we had so many "foreign views" on our walls, to whom I endeavored to set forth our hope that the pictures might afford a familiar island to the immigrants in a sea of new and strange impressions. The old settler guest, taken off his guard, replied, "I see; they feel as we did when we saw a Yankee notion from down East"—thereby formulating the dim kinship between the pioneer and the immigrant, both "buffeting the waves of a new development." The older settlers as well as their children throughout the years have given genuine help to our various enterprises for neighborhood improvement, and from their own memories of earlier hardships have made many shrewd suggestions for alleviating the difficulties of that first sharp struggle with untoward conditions.

In those early days we were often asked why we had

come to live on Halsted Street when we could afford to live somewhere else. I remember one man who used to shake his head and say it was "the strangest thing he had met in his experience," but who was finally convinced that it was "not strange but natural." In time it came to seem natural to all of us that the Settlement should be there. If it is natural to feed the hungry and care for the sick, it is certainly natural to give pleasure to the young, comfort to the aged, and to minister to the deep-seated craving for social intercourse that all men feel. Whoever does it is rewarded by something which, if not gratitude, is at least spontaneous and vital and lacks that irksome sense of obligation with which a substantial benefit is too often acknowledged.

In addition to the neighbors who responded to the receptions and classes, we found those who were too battered and oppressed to care for them. To these, however, was left that susceptibility to the bare offices of humanity which raises such offices into a bond of fellowship.

From the first it seemed understood that we were ready to perform the humblest neighborhood services. We were asked to wash the newborn babies, and to prepare the dead for burial, to nurse the sick, and to "mind the children."

Occasionally these neighborly offices unexpectedly uncovered ugly human traits. For six weeks after an operation we kept in one of our three bedrooms a forlorn little baby who, because he was born with a cleft palate, was most unwelcome even to his mother, and we were horrified when he died of neglect a week after he was returned to his home; a little Italian bride of fifteen sought shelter with us one November evening, to escape her husband who had beaten her every night for a week when he returned home from work, because she had lost her wedding ring; two of us officiated quite alone at the birth of an illegitimate child because the doctor was late in arriving, and none of the honest Irish matrons would "touch the likes of her"; we ministered at the deathbed of a young man, who during a long illness of tuberculosis had received so many bottles of whisky through the mistaken kindness of his friends, that the cumulative effect produced wild periods of exultation, in one of which he died.

We were also early impressed with the curious isolation of many of the immigrants; an Italian woman once expressed her pleasure in the red roses that she saw at one of our receptions in surprise that they had been "brought so fresh all the way from Italy." She would not believe for an instant that they had been grown in America. She said that she had lived in Chicago for six years and had never seen any roses, whereas in Italy she had seen them every summer in great profusion. During all that time, of course, the woman had lived within ten blocks of a florist's window; she had not been more than a five-cent car ride away from the public parks; but she had never dreamed of faring forth for herself, and no one had taken her. Her conception of America had been the untidy street in which she lived and had made her long struggle to adapt herself to American ways.

But in spite of some untoward experiences, we were constantly impressed with the uniform kindness and courtesy we received. Perhaps these first days laid the simple human foundations which are certainly essential for continuous living among the poor: first, genuine preference for residence in an industrial quarter to any other part of the city, because it is interesting and makes the human appeal; and second, the conviction, in the words of Canon Barnett, that the things which make men alike are finer and better than the things that keep them apart, and that these basic likenesses, if they are properly accentuated, easily transcend the less essential differences of race, language, creed, and tradition.

Perhaps even in those first days we made a beginning toward that object which was afterward stated in our charter: "To provide a center for a higher civic and social life; to institute and maintain educational and philanthropic enterprises, and to investigate and improve the conditions in the industrial districts of Chicago."

Chapter 6

The Subjective Necessity for Social Settlements

THE Ethical Culture Societies held a summer school at Plymouth, Massachusetts, in 1892, to which they invited several people representing the then new Settlement movement, that they might discuss with others the general theme of Philanthropy and Social Progress.

I venture to produce here parts of a lecture I delivered in Plymouth, both because I have found it impossible to formulate with the same freshness those early motives and strivings, and because, when published with other papers given that summer, it was received by the Settlement people themselves as a satisfactory statement.

I remember one golden summer afternoon during the sessions of the summer school that several of us met on the shores of a pond in a pine wood a few miles from Plymouth, to discuss our new movement. The natural leader of the group was Robert A. Woods. He had recently returned from a residence in Toynbee Hall, London, to open Andover House in Boston, and had just issued a book, *English Social Movements,* in which he had gathered together and focused the many forms of social endeavor preceding and contemporaneous with the English

Settlements. There were Miss Vida D. Scudder and Miss Helena Dudley from the College Settlement Association, Miss Julia C. Lathrop and myself from Hull-House. Some of us had numbered our years as far as thirty, and we all carefully avoided the extravagance of statement which characterizes youth, and yet I doubt if anywhere on the continent that summer could have been found a group of people more genuinely interested in social development or more sincerely convinced that they had found a clue by which the conditions in crowded cities might be understood and the agencies for social betterment developed.

We were all careful to avoid saying that we had found a "life work," perhaps with an instinctive dread of expending all our energy in vows of constancy, as so often happens; and yet it is interesting to note that all of the people whom I have recalled as the enthusiasts at that little conference have remained attached to Settlements in actual residence for longer or shorter periods each year during the eighteen years which have elapsed since then, although they have also been closely identified as publicists or governmental officials with movements outside. It is as if they had discovered that the Settlement was too valuable as a method as a way of approach to the social question to be abandoned, although they had long since discovered that it was not a "social movement" in itself. This, however, is anticipating the future, whereas the following paper on "The Subjective Necessity for Social Settlements" should have a chance to speak for itself. It is perhaps too late in the day to express regret for its stilted title.

This paper is an attempt to analyze the motives which underlie a movement based, not only upon conviction, but upon genuine emotion, wherever educated young people are seeking an outlet for that sentiment of universal brotherhood, which the best spirit of our times is forcing from an emotion into a motive. These young people accomplish little toward the solution of this social problem, and bear the brunt of being cultivated into unnourished, oversensitive lives. They have been shut off from the common labor by which they live which is a great source of moral and physical health. They feel a fatal want of harmony between their theory and their lives, a lack of coördination between thought and action. I think it is hard for us to realize how seriously many of them are taking to the notion of human brotherhood, how eagerly they long to give tangible expression to the democratic ideal. These young men and women, longing to socialize their democracy, are animated by certain hopes which may be thus loosely formulated; that if in a democratic country nothing can be permanently achieved save through the masses of the people, it will be impossible to establish a higher political life than the people themselves crave; that it is difficult to see how the notion of a higher civic life can be fostered save through common intercourse; that the blessings which we associate with a life of refinement and cultivation can be made universal and must be made universal if they are to be permanent; that the good we secure for ourselves is precarious and uncertain, is floating in mid-air, until it is secured for all of us and incorporated into our common life. It is easier to state these hopes than to formulate the line of motives, which I believe to constitute the trend of the subjective pressure toward the Settlement. There is something primordial about these motives, but I am perhaps overbold in designating them as a great desire to share the race life. We all bear traces of the starvation struggle which for so long made up the life of the race. Our very organism holds memories and glimpses of that long life of our ancestors which still goes on among so many of our contemporaries. Nothing so deadens the sympathies and shrivels the power of enjoyment as the persistent keeping away from the great opportunities for helpfulness and a continual ignoring of the starvation struggle which makes up the life of at least half the race. To shut one's self away from that half of the race life is to shut one's self away from the most vital part of it; it is to live out but half the humanity to which we have been born heir and to use but half our faculties. We have all had longings for a fuller life which should include the use of these faculties. These longings are the physical complement of the "Intimations of Immortality," on which no ode has yet been written. To portray these would be the work of a poet, and it is hazardous for any but a poet to attempt it.

You may remember the forlorn feeling which occasionally seizes you when you arrive early in the morning a stranger in a great city: the stream of laboring people goes past you as you gaze through the plate-glass window of your hotel; you see hard workingmen lifting great burdens; you hear the driving and jostling of huge carts and your heart sinks with a sudden sense of futility. The door opens behind you and you turn to the man who brings you in your breakfast with a quick sense of human fellowship. You find yourself praying that you may never lose your hold on it all. A more poetic prayer would be that the great mother breasts of our common humanity, with its labor and suffering and its homely comforts, may never be withheld from you. You turn helplessly to the waiter and feel that it would be almost grotesque to claim from him the sympathy you crave because civilization has placed you apart, but you resent your position with a sudden sense of snobbery. Literature is full of portrayals of these glimpses: they come to shipwrecked men on rafts; they overcome the differences of an incongruous multitude when in the presence of a great danger or when moved by a common enthusiasm. They are not, however, confined to such moments, and if we were in the habit of telling them to each other, the recital would be as long as the tales of children are, when they sit down on the green grass and confide to each other how many times they have remembered that they lived once before. If these childish tales are the stirring of inherited impressions, just so surely is the other the striving of inherited powers.

"It is true that there is nothing after disease, indigence and a sense of guilt, so fatal to health and to life itself as the want of a proper outlet for active faculties." I have seen young girls suffer and grow sensibly lowered in vitality in the first years after they leave school. In our attempt then to give a girl pleasure and freedom from care we succeed, for the most part, in making her pitifully miserable. She finds "life" so different from what she expected it to be. She is besotted with innocent little ambitions, and does not understand this apparent waste of herself, this elaborate preparation, if no work is provided for her. There is a heritage of noble obligation which young people accept and long to perpetuate. The desire for action, the wish to right wrong and alleviate suffering haunts them daily. Society smiles at it indulgently instead of making it of value to itself. The wrong to them begins even farther back, when we restrain the first childish desires for "doing good" and tell them that they must wait until they are older and better fitted. We intimate that social obligation begins at a fixed date, forgetting that it begins with birth itself. We treat them as children who, with strong-growing limbs, are allowed to use their legs but not their arms, or whose legs are daily carefully exercised that after a while their arms may be put to high use. We do this in spite of the protest of the best educators, Locke and Pestalozzi. We are fortunate in the meantime if

their unused members do not weaken and disappear. They
do sometimes. There are a few girls who, by the time they
are "educated," forget their old childish desires to help the
world and to play with poor little girls "who haven't play
things." Parents are often inconsistent: they deliberately expose their daughters to knowledge of the distress in the
world; they send them to hear missionary addresses on fa-
mines in India and China; they accompany them to lectures
on the suffering in Siberia; they agitate together over the
forgotten region of East London. In addition to this, from
babyhood the altruistic tendencies of these daughters are
persistently cultivated. They are taught to be self-forgetting
and self-sacrificing, to consider the good of the whole before the good of the ego. But when all this information and
culture show results, when the daughter comes back from
college and begins to recognize her social claim to the "submerged tenth," and to evince a disposition to fulfill it, the
family claim is strenuously asserted; she is told that she is
unjustified, ill-advised in her efforts. If she persists, the family too often are injured and unhappy unless the efforts are
called missionary and the religious zeal of the family carry
them over their sense of abuse. When this zeal does not
exist, the result is perplexing. It is a curious violation of
what we would fain believe a fundamental law—that the
final return of the deed is upon the head of the doer. The
deed is that of exclusiveness and caution, but the return,
instead of falling upon the head of the exclusive and cautious, falls upon a young head full of generous and unselfish
plans. The girl loses something vital out of her life to which
she is entitled. She is restricted and unhappy; her elders,
meanwhile, are unconscious of the situation and we have
all the elements of a tragedy.

We have in America a fast-growing number of cultivated
young people who have no recognized outlet for their active
faculties. They hear constantly of the great social maladjustment, but no way is provided for them to change it,
and their uselessness hangs about them heavily. Huxley declares that the sense of usefulness is the severest shock
which the human system can sustain, and that if persistently sustained, it results in atrophy of function. These young
people have had advantages of college, of European travel,
and of economic study, but they are sustaining this shock
of inaction. They have pet phrases, and they tell you that
the things that make us all alike are stronger than the things
that make us different. They say that all men are united by
needs and sympathies far more permanent and radical than

anything that temporarily divides them and sets them in opposition to each other. If they affect art, they say that the decay in artistic expression is due to the decay in ethics, that art when shut away from the human interests and from the great mass of humanity is self-destructive. They tell their elders with all the bitterness of youth that if they expect success from them in business or politics or in whatever lines their ambition for them has run, they must let them consult all of humanity; that they must let them find out what the people want and how they want it. It is only the stronger young people, however, who formulate this. Many of them dissipate their energies in so-called enjoyment. Others not content with that, go on studying and go back to college for their second degrees; not that they are especially fond of study, but because they want something definite to do, and their powers have been trained in the direction of mental accumulation. Many are buried beneath this mental accumulation which lowered vitality and discontent. Walter Besant says they have had the vision that Peter had when he saw the great sheet let down from heaven, wherein was neither clean nor unclean. He calls it the sense of humanity. It is not philanthropy nor benevolence, but a thing fuller and wider than either of these.

This young life, so sincere in its emotion and good phrase and yet so undirected, seems to me as pitiful as the other great mass of destitute lives. One is supplementary to the other, and some method of communication can surely be devised. Mr. Barnett, who urged the first Settlement— Toynbee Hall, in East London—recognized this need of outlet for the young men of Oxford and Cambridge, and hoped that the Settlement would supply the communication. It is easy to see why the Settlement movement originated in England, where the years of education are more constrained and definite than they are here, where class distinctions are more rigid. The necessity of it was greater there, but we are fast feeling the pressure of the need and meeting the necessity for Settlements in America. Our young people feel nervously the need of putting theory into action, and respond quickly to the Settlement form of activity.

Other motives which I believe make toward the Settlement are the result of a certain renaissance going forward in Christianity. The impulse to share the lives of the poor, the desire to make social service, irrespective of propaganda, express the spirit of Christ, is as old as Christianity itself. We have no proof from the records themselves that the early Roman Christians, who strained their simple art to the point of grotesqueness in their eagerness to record a "good news" on the walls of the catacombs, considered this good news a religion. Jesus had no set of truths labeled Religious. On the contrary, his doctrine was that all truth is one, that the appropriation of it is freedom. His teaching had no dogma to mark it off from truth and action in general. He himself called it a revelation—a life. These early Roman Christians received the Gospel message, a command to love all men, with a certain joyous simplicity. The image of the Good Shepherd is blithe and gay beyond the gentlest shepherd of Greek mythology; the hart no longer pants, but rushes to the water brooks. The Christians looked for the continuous revelation, but believed what Jesus said, that this revelation, to be retained and made manifest, must be put into terms of action; that action is the only medium man has for receiving and appropriating truth; that the doctrine must be known through the will.

That Christianity has to be revealed and embodied in the line of social progress is a corollary to the simple proposition that man's action is found in his social relationships in the way in which he connects with his fellows; that his motives for action are the zeal and affection with which he regards his fellows. By this simple process was created a deep enthusiasm for humanity, which regarded man as at once the organ and the object of revelation; and by this process came about the wonderful fellowship, the true democracy of the early Church, that so captivates the imagination. The early Christians were pre-eminently nonresistant. They believed in love as a cosmic force. There was no inconoclasm during the minor peace of the Church. They did not yet denounce nor tear down temples, nor preach the end of the world. They grew to a mighty number but it never occurred to them, either in their weakness or in their strength, to regard other men for an instant as their foes or as aliens. The spectacle of the Christians loving all men was the most astounding Rome had ever seen. They were eager to sacrifice themselves for the weak, for children, and for the aged; they identified themselves with slaves and did not avoid the plague; they longed to share the common lot that they might receive the constant revelation. It was a new treasure which the early Christians added to the sum of all treasures, a joy hitherto unknown in the world—the joy of finding the Christ which lieth in each man, but which no man can unfold save in fellowship. A happiness ranging from the heroic to the pastoral enveloped them. They were to possess a revelation as long as life had new meaning to unfold, new action to propose.

I believe that there is a distinct turning among many young men and women toward this simple acceptance of Christ's message. They resent the assumption that Christianity is a set of ideas which belong to the religious consciousness, whatever that may be. They insist that it cannot be proclaimed and instituted apart from the social life of the community and that it must seek a simple and natural expression in the social organism itself. The Settlement movement is only one manifestation of that wider humanitarian movement which throughout Christendom, put pre-eminently in England, is endeavoring to embody itself, not in a sect, but in society itself.

I believe that this turning, this renaissance of the early Christian humanitarianism, is going on in America, in Chicago, if you please, without leaders who write or philosophize, without much speaking, but with a bent to express in social service and in terms of action the spirit of Christ. Certain it is that spiritual force is found in the Settlement movement, and it is also true that this force must be evoked and must be called into play before the success of any Settlement is assured. There must be the overmastering belief that all that is noblest in life is common to men as men, in order to accentuate the likenesses and ignore the differences which are found among the people whom the Settlement constantly brings into juxtaposition. It may be true, as the Positivists insist, that the very religious fervor of man can be turned into love for his race, and his desire for a future life into content to live in the echo of his deeds; Paul's formula of seeking for the Christ which lieth in each man and founding our likenesses on him, seems a simpler formula to many of us.

In a thousand voices singing the Hallelujah Chorus in Handel's "Messiah," it is possible to distinguish the leading voices, but the differences of training and cultivation between them and the voices of the chorus, are lost in the unity of purpose and in the fact that they are all human voices lifted by a high motive. This is a weak illustration of what a Settlement attempts to do. It aims, in a measure, to develop whatever of social life its neighborhood may afford, to focus and give form to that life, to bring to bear upon it the results of cultivation and training; but it receives in exchange for the music of isolated voices the volume and strength of the chorus. It is quite impossible for me to say in what proportion or degree the subjective necessity which led to the opening of Hull-House combined the three trends: first, the desire to interpret democracy in social terms; secondly, the impulse beating at the very source of our lives, urging us to aid in the race progress; and, thirdly, the Christian movement toward humanitarianism. It is difficult to analyze a living thing; the analysis is at best imperfect. Many more motives may blend with the three trends; possibly the desire for a new form of social success due to the nicety of imagination, which refuses worldly pleasures unmixed with the joys of self-sacrifice; possibly a love of approbation, so vast that it is not content with the treble clapping of delicate hands, but wishes also to hear the brass notes from toughened palms, may mingle with these.

The Settlement, then, is an experimental effort to aid in the solution of the social and industrial problems which are engendered by the modern conditions of life in a great city. It insists that these problems are not confined to any one portion of a city. It is an attempt to relieve, at the same time, the overaccumulation at one end of society and the destitution at the other; but it assumes that this overaccumulation and destitution is most sorely felt in the things that pertain to social and educational privileges. From its very nature it can stand for no political or social propaganda. It must, in a sense, give the warm welcome of an inn to all such propaganda, if perchance one of them be found an angel. The one thing to be dreaded in the Settlement is that it lose its flexibility, its power of quick adaptation, its readiness to change its methods as its environment may demand. It must be open to conviction and must have a deep and abiding sense of tolerance. It must be hospitable and ready for experiment. It should demand from its residents a scientific patience in the accumulation of facts and the steady holding of their sympathies as one of the best instruments for that accumulation. It must be grounded in a philosophy whose foundation is on the solidarity of the human race, a philosophy which will not waver when the race happens to be represented by a drunken woman or an idiot boy. Its residents must be emptied of all conceit of opinion and all self-assertion, and ready to arouse and interpret the public opinion of their neighborhood. They must be content to live quietly side by side with their neighbors, until they grow into a sense of relationship and mutual interests. Their neighbors are held apart by differences of race and language which the residents can more easily overcome. They are bound to see the needs of their neigh-

Main Entrance to Hull-House

borhood as a whole, to furnish data for legislation, and to use their influence to secure it. In short, residents are pledged to devote themselves to the duties of good citizenship and to the arousing of the social energies which too largely lie dormant in every neighborhood given over to industrialism. They are bound to regard the entire life of their city as organic, to make an effort to unify it, and to protest against its overdifferentiation.

It is always easy to make all philosophy point one particular moral and all history adorn one particular tale; but I may be forgiven the reminder that the best speculative philosophy sets forth the solidarity of the human race; that the highest moralists have taught that without the advance and improvement of the whole, no man can hope for any lasting improvement in his own moral or material individual condition; and that the subjective necessity for Social Settlements is therefore identical with that necessity, which urges us on toward social and individual salvation.

◈◈ *Chapter* 7

SOME EARLY UNDERTAKINGS

AT HULL-HOUSE

IF the early American Settlement stood for a more
exigent standard in philanthropic activities, insisting that
each new undertaking should be preceded by carefully
ascertained facts, then certainly Hull-House held to this
standard in the opening of our new coffeehouse first started as a public kitchen. An investigation of the sweatshops
had disclosed the fact that sewing women during the busy
season paid little attention to the feeding of their families,
for it was only by working steadily through the long day
that the scanty pay of five, seven, or nine cents for finishing a dozen pairs of trousers could be made into a day's
wage; and they bought from the nearest grocery the
canned goods that could be most quickly heated, or
gave a few pennies to the children with which they might
secure a lunch from a neighboring candy shop.

One of the residents made an investigation, at the instance of the United States Department of Agriculture, into
the food values of the dietaries of the various immigrants,
and this was followed by an investigation made by another resident, for the United States Department of Labor,
into the foods of the Italian colony, on the supposition

that the constant use of imported products bore a distinct relation to the cost of living. I recall an Italian who, coming into Hull-House one day as we were sitting at the dinner table, expressed great surprise that Americans ate a variety of food, because he believed that they partook only of potatoes and beer. A little inquiry showed that this conclusion was drawn from the fact that he lived next to an Irish saloon and had never seen anything but potatoes going in and beer coming out.

At that time the New England kitchen was comparatively new in Boston, and Mrs. Richards, who was largely responsible for its foundation, hoped that cheaper cuts of meat and simpler vegetables, if they were subjected to slow and thorough processes of cooking, might be made attractive and their nutritive value secured for the people who so sadly needed more nutritious food. It was felt that this could be best accomplished in public kitchens, where the advantage of scientific training and careful supervision could be secured. One of the residents went to Boston for a training under Mrs. Richards, and when the Hull-House kitchen was fitted under her guidance and direction, our hopes ran high for some modification of the food of the neighborhood. We did not reckon, however, with the wide diversity in nationality and inherited tastes, and while we sold a certain amount of the carefully prepared soups and stews in the neighboring factories—a sale which has steadily increased throughout the years—and were also patronized by a few households, perhaps the neighborhood estimate was best summed up by the woman who frankly confessed that the food was certainly nutritious, but that she didn't like to eat what was nutritious, that she liked to eat "what she'd ruther."

If the dietetics were appreciated but slowly, the social value of the coffeehouse and the gymnasium, which were in the same building, were quickly demonstrated. At that time the saloon halls were the only places in the neighborhood where the immigrant could hold his social gatherings, and where he could celebrate such innocent and legitimate occasions as weddings and christenings.

These halls were rented very cheaply with the understanding that various sums of money should be "passed across the bar," and it was considered a mean host or guest who failed to live up to this implied bargain. The consequence was that many a reputable party ended with a certain amount of disorder, due solely to the fact that the social instinct was traded upon and used as a basis for money-making by an adroit host. From the beginning the young people's clubs had asked for dancing, and nothing was more popular than the increased space for parties offered by the gymnasium, with the chance to serve refreshments in the room below. We tried experiments with every known "soft drink," from those extracted from an expensive soda water fountain to slender glasses of grape juice, but so far as drinks were concerned we never became a rival to the saloon, nor indeed did anyone imagine that we were trying to do so. I remember one man who looked about the cozy little room and said, "This would be a nice place to sit in all day if one could only have beer." But the coffeehouse gradually performed a mission of its own and became something of a social center to the neighborhood as well as a real convenience. Businessmen from the adjacent factories and school-teachers from the nearest public schools used it increasingly. The Hull-House students and club members supped together in little groups or held their reunions and social banquets, as, to a certain extent, did organizations from all parts of the town. The experience of the coffee-house taught us not to hold to preconceived ideas of what the neighborhood ought to have, but to keep ourselves in readiness to modify and adapt our undertaking as we discovered those things which the neighborhood was ready to accept.

Better food was doubtless needed, but more attractive and safer places for social gatherings were also needed, and the neighborhood was ready for one and not for the other. We had no hint then in Chicago of the small parks which were to be established fifteen years later, containing the halls for dancing and their own restaurants in buildings where the natural desire of the young for gaiety and social organization, could be safely indulged. Yet even in that early day a member of the Hull-House Men's Club who had been appointed superintendent of Douglas Park had secured there the first public swimming pool, and his fellow club members were proud of the achievement.

There was in the earliest undertakings at Hull-House a touch of the artist's enthusiasm when he translates his inner vision through his chosen material into outward form. Keenly conscious of the social confusion all about us and the hard economic struggle, we at times believed that the very struggle itself might become a source of strength. The devotion of the mothers to their children, the dread of the men lest they fail to provide for the family dependent upon their daily exertions, at moments seemed to us the secret stores of strength from which society is fed, the invisible array of passion and feeling which are the surest protectors of the world. We fatuously hoped that we might pluck from the human tragedy itself a consciousness of a common destiny which should bring its own healing, that we might extract from life's very misfortunes a power of coöperation which should be effective against them.

Of course there was always present the harrowing consciousness of the difference in economic condition between ourselves and our neighbors. Even if we had gone to live in the most wretched tenement, there would have always been an essential difference between them and ourselves, for we should have had a sense of security in regard to illness and old age and the lack of these two securities are the specters which most persistently haunt the poor. Could we, in spite of this, make their individual efforts more effective through organization and possibly complement them by small efforts of our own?

Some such vague hope was in our minds when we started the Hull-House Coöperative Coal Association, which led a vigorous life for three years, and developed a large membership under the skillful advice of its one paid officer, an English workingman who had had experience in coöperative societies at " 'ome." Some of the meetings of the association, in which people met to consider together their basic dependence upon fire and warmth, had a curious challenge of life about them. Because the coöperators knew what it meant to bring forth children in the midst of privation and to see the tiny creatures struggle for life, their recitals cut a cross section, as it were, in that world-old effort—the "dying to live" which so inevitably triumphs over poverty and suffering. And yet their very familiarity with hardship may have been responsible for that sentiment which traditionally ruins business, for a vote of the coöperators that the basket buyers be given one basket free out of every six, that the presentation of five purchase tickets should entitle the holders to a profit in coal instead of stock "because it would be a shame to keep them waiting for the dividend," was always pointed to by the conservative quarter-of-a-ton buyers as the beginning of the end. At any rate, at the close of the third winter, although the Association occupied an imposing coal yard on the southeast corner of the Hull-House block and its gross receipts were between three and four hundred dollars a day, it became evident that the concern could not remain solvent if it continued its philanthropic policy, and the experiment was terminated by the coöperators taking up their stock in the remaining coal.

Our next coöperative experiment was much more successful, perhaps because it was much more spontaneous.

At a meeting of working girls held at Hull-House during a strike in a large shoe factory, the discussions made it clear that the strikers who had been most easily frightened, and therefore first to capitulate, were naturally those girls who were paying board and were afraid of being put out if they fell too far behind. After a recital of a case of peculiar hardship one of them exclaimed: "Wouldn't it be fine if we had a boarding club of our own, and then we could stand by each other in a time like this?" After that events moved quickly. We read aloud together Beatrice Potter's little book on "Coöperation," and discussed all the difficulties and fascinations of such an undertaking, and on the first of May, 1891, two comfortable apartments near Hull-House were rented and furnished. The Settlement was responsible for the furniture and paid the first month's rent, but beyond that the members managed the club themselves. The undertaking "marched," as the French say, from the very first, and always on its own feet. Although there were difficulties, none of them proved insurmountable, which was a matter for great satisfaction in the face of a statement made by the head of the United States Department of Labor, who, on a visit to the club when it was but two years old, said that his department had investigated many coöperative undertakings, and that none founded and managed by women had ever succeeded. At the end of the third year the club occupied all of the six apartments which the original building contained, and numbered fifty members.

It was in connection with our efforts to secure a building for the Jane Club that we first found ourselves in the dilemma between the needs of our neighbors and the kind-hearted response upon which we had already come to rely for their relief. The adapted apartments in which the Jane Club was housed were inevitably more or less uncomfortable, and we felt that the success of the club justified the erection of a building for its sole use.

Up to that time, our history had been as the minor peace of the early Church. We had had the most generous interpretation of our efforts. Of course, many people were indifferent to the idea of the Settlement; others looked on with tolerant and sometimes cynical amusement which we would often encounter in a good story related at our expense; but all this was remote and unreal to us, and we were sure that if the critics could but touch "the life of the people," they would understand.

The situation changed markedly after the Pullman strike, and our efforts to secure factory legislation later brought upon us a certain amount of distrust and suspicion; until then we had been considered merely a kindly philanthropic undertaking whose new form gave us a certain idealistic glamour. But sterner tests were coming, and one of the first was in connection with the new building for the Jane Club. A trustee of Hull-House came to see us one day with the good news that a friend of his was ready to give twenty thousand dollars with which to build the desired new clubhouse. When, however, he divulged the name of his generous friend, it proved to be that of a man who was notorious for underpaying the girls in his establishment and concerning whom there were even darker stories. It seemed clearly impossible to erect a clubhouse for working girls with such money and we at once said that we must decline the offer. The trustee of Hull-House was put in the most embarrassing situation; he had, of course, induced the man to give the money and had had no thought but that it would be eagerly received; he would now be obliged to return with the astonishing, not to say insulting, news that the money was considered unfit.

In the long discussion which followed, it gradually became clear to all of us that such a refusal could be valuable only as it might reveal to the man himself and to others public opinion in regard to certain methods of money-making, but that from the very nature of the case our refusal of this money could not be made public because a representative of Hull-House had asked for it. However, the basic fact remained that we could not accept the money, and of this the trustee himself was fully convinced. This incident occurred during a period of much discussion concerning "tainted money" and is perhaps typical of the difficulty of dealing with it. It is impossible to know how far we may blame the individual for doing that which all of his competitors and his associates consider legitimate; at the same time, social changes can only be inaugurated by those who feel the unrighteousness of contemporary conditions, and the expression of their scruples may be the one opportunity for pushing forward moral tests into that dubious area wherein wealth is accumulated.

In the course of time a new clubhouse was built by an old friend of Hull-House much interested in working girls, and this has been occupied for twelve years by the very successful coöperating Jane Club. The incident of the early refusal is associated in my mind with a long talk upon the subject of questionable money I held with the warden of Toynbee Hall, whom I visited at Bristol where he was then canon in the Cathedral. By way of illustration he showed me a beautiful little church which had been built by the last slave-trading merchant in Bristol, who had been much disapproved of by his fellow townsmen and had hoped by this transmutation of ill-gotten money into exquisite Gothic architecture to reconcile himself both to God and man. His impulse to build may have been born from his own scruples or from the quickened consciences of his neighbors who saw that the world-old iniquity of enslaving men must at length come to an end. The Abolitionists may have regarded this beautiful building as the fruit of a contrite heart, or they may have scorned it as an attempt to magnify the goodness of a slave trader and thus perplex the doubting citizens of Bristol in regard to the entire moral issue.

Canon Barnett did not pronounce judgment on the Bristol merchant. He was, however, quite clear upon the point that a higher moral standard for industrial life must be embodied in legislation as rapidly as possible, that it may bear equally upon all, and that an individual endeavoring to secure this legislation must forbear harsh judgment. This was doubtless a sound position, but during all the period of hot discussion concerning tainted money I never felt clear enough on the general principle involved, to accept the many invitations to write and speak upon the subject, although I received much instruction in the many letters of disapproval sent to me by radicals of various schools because I was a member of the university extension staff of the then new University of Chicago, the righteousness of whose foundation they challenged.

A little incident of this time illustrated to me the confusion in the minds of at least many older men between religious teaching and advancing morality. One morning I received a letter from the head of a Settlement in New York expressing his perplexity over the fact that his board of trustees had asked money from a man notorious for his unscrupulous business methods. My correspondent had placed his resignation in the hands of his board, that they might accept it at any time when they felt his utterances on the subject of tainted money were offensive, for he wished to be free to openly discuss a subject of such grave moral import. The very morning when my mind was full of the questions raised by this letter, I received a call from the daughter of the same businessman whom my friend considered so unscrupulous. She was passing through Chi-

cago and came to ask me to give her some arguments
which she might later use with her father to confute the
charge that Settlements were irreligious. She said, "You
see, he has been asked to give money to our Settlement and would like to do it, if his conscience was
only clear; he disapproves of Settlements because they
give no religious instruction; he has always been a very
devout man."

I remember later discussing the incident with Washington Gladden who was able to parallel it from his
own experience. Now that this discussion upon tainted
money has subsided, it is easy to view it with a certain
detachment impossible at the moment, and it is even
difficult to understand why the feeling should have been
so intense, although it doubtless registered genuine moral
concern.

There was room for discouragement in the many unsuccessful experiments in coöperation which were carried on in Chicago during the early nineties; a carpenter
shop on Van Buren Street near Halsted, a labor exchange started by the unemployed, not so paradoxical
an arrangement as it seems, and a very ambitious plan
for a country colony which was finally carried out at
Ruskin, Tennessee. In spite of failures, coöperative
schemes went on, some of the same men appearing in
one after another with irrepressible optimism. I remember during a coöperative congress, which met at Hull-
House in the World's Fair summer that Mr. Henry D.
Lloyd, who collected records of coöperative experiments
with the enthusiasm with which other men collect coins
or pictures, put before the congress some of the remarkable successes in Ireland and North England,
which he later embodied in his book on "Copartner-
ship." One of the old-time coöperators denounced the
modern method as "too much like cut-throat business"
and declared himself in favor of "principles which may
have failed over and over again, but are nevertheless
as sound as the law of gravitation." Mr. Lloyd and I
agreed that the fiery old man presented as fine a spectacle of devotion to a lost cause as either of us had
ever seen, although we both possessed memories well
stored with such romantic attachments.

And yet this dream that men shall cease to waste strength in competition and shall come to pool their powers of production is coming to pass all over the face of the earth. Five years later in the same Hull-House hall in which the coöperative congress was held, an Italian senator told a large audience of his fellow countrymen of the successful system of coöperative banks in north Italy and of their coöperative methods of selling produce to the value of millions of francs annually; still later Sir Horace Plunkett related the remarkable successes in coöperation in Ireland.

I have seldom been more infected by enthusiasm than I once was in Dulwich at a meeting of English coöperators where I was fairly overwhelmed by the fervor underlying the businesslike proceedings of the congress, and certainly when I served as a juror in the Paris Exposition of 1900, nothing in the entire display in the department of Social Economy was so imposing as the building housing the exhibit, which had been erected by coöperative trades-unions without the assistance of a single contractor.

And so one's faith is kept alive as one occasionally meets a realized ideal of better human relations. At least traces of successful coöperation are found even in individualistic America. I recall my enthusiasm on the day when I set forth to lecture at New Harmony, Indiana, for I had early been thrilled by the tale of Robert Owen, as every young person must be who is interested in social reform; I was delighted to find so much of his spirit still clinging to the little town which had long ago held one of his ardent experiments, although the poor old coöperators, who for many years claimed friendship at Hull-House because they heard that we "had once tried a coöperative coal association," might well have convinced me of the persistency of the coöperative ideal.

Many experiences in those early years, although vivid, seemed to contain no illumination; nevertheless they doubtless permanently affected our judgments concerning what is called crime and vice. I recall a series of striking episodes on the day when I took the wife and child as well as the old godfather, of an Italian convict to visit him in the State Penitentiary. When we approached the prison, the sight of its heavy stone walls and armed sentries threw the godfather into a paroxysm of rage; he cast his hat upon the ground and stamped upon it, tore his hair, and loudly fulminated in weird Italian oaths, until one of the guards, seeing his strange actions, came to inquire if "the gentleman was having a fit." When we finally saw the convict, his wife, to my extreme distress, talked of nothing but his striped clothing, until the poor man wept with chagrin. Upon our return journey to Chicago, the little son aged eight presented me with two oranges so affectionately and gaily that I was filled with reflections upon the advantage of each generation making a fresh start, when the train boy, finding the stolen fruit in my lap, violently threatened to arrest the child. But stranger than any episode was the fact itself that neither the convict, his wife, nor his godfather for a moment considered him a criminal. He had merely gotten excited over cards and had stabbed his adversary with a knife. "Why should a man who took his luck badly be kept forever from the sun?" was their reiterated inquiry.

I recall our perplexity over the first girls who had "gone astray"—the poor, little, forlorn objects, fifteen and sixteen years old, with their moral natures apparently untouched and unawakened; one of them whom the police had found in a professional house and asked us to shelter for a few days until she could be used as a witness, was clutching a battered doll which she had kept with her during her six months of an "evil life." Two of these prematurely aged children came to us one day directly from the maternity ward of the Cook County hospital, each with a baby in her arms, asking for protection, because they did not want to go home for fear of "being licked." For them were no jewels nor idle living such as the storybooks portrayed. The first of the older women whom I knew came to Hull-House to ask that her young sister, who was about to arrive from Germany, might live near us; she wished to find her respectable work and wanted her to have the "decent pleasures" that Hull-House afforded. After the arrangement had been completed and I had in a measure recovered from my astonishment at the businesslike way in which she spoke of her own life, I ventured to ask her history. In a very few words she told me that she had come from Germany as a music teacher to an American family. At the end of two years, in order to avoid a scandal involving the head of the house, she had come to Chicago where her child was born, but when the remittances ceased after its death, finding herself without home and resources, she had gradually become involved in her present mode of life. By dint of utilizing her family solicitude, we finally induced her to move into decent lodgings before her sister arrived, and for a difficult year she supported herself by her exquisite embroidery. At the end of that time, she gave up the struggle, the more easily as her young sister, well established in the dressmaking department of a large shop, had begun to suspect her past life.

But discouraging as these and other similar efforts often were, nevertheless the difficulties were infinitely less in those days when we dealt with "fallen girls" than in the years following when the "white slave traffic" became gradually established and when agonized parents, as well as the victims themselves, were totally unable to account for the situation. In the light of recent disclosures, it seems as if we were unaccountably dull not to have seen what was happening, especially to the Jewish girls among whom "the home trade of the white slave traffic" was first carried on and who were thus made to break through countless generations of chastity. We early encountered the difficulties of that old problem of restoring the woman, or even the child, into the society she had once outraged. I well remember our perplexity when we attempted to help two girls straight from a Virginia tobacco factory, who had been decoyed into a disreputable house when innocently seeking a lodging on the late evening of their arrival. Although they had been rescued promptly, the stigma remained, and we found it impossible to permit them to join any of the social clubs connected with Hull-House not so much because there was danger of contamination, as because the parents of the club members would have resented their presence most hotly. One of our trustees succeeded in persuading a repentant girl, four

teen years old, whom we tried to give a fresh start in
another part of the city, to attend a Sunday School class
of a large Chicago church. The trustee hoped that the
contact with nice girls, as well as the moral training,
would help the poor child on her hard road. But unfortunately tales of her shortcomings reached the superintendent who felt obliged, in order to protect the other
girls, to forbid her the school. She came back to tell
us about it, defiant as well as discouraged, and had it
not been for the experience with our own clubs, we
could easily have joined her indignation over a church
which "acted as if its Sunday School was a show window for candy kids."

In spite of poignant experiences or, perhaps, because
of them, the memory of the first years, at Hull-House
is more or less blurred with fatigue, for we could of
course become accustomed only gradually to the unending activity and to the confusion of a house constantly
filling and refilling with groups of people. The little
children who came to the kindergarten in the morning
were followed by the afternoon clubs of older children,
and those in turn made way for the educational and
social organization of adults, occupying every room in
the house every evening. All one's habits of living had
to be readjusted, and any student's tendency to sit with
a book by the fire was of necessity definitely abandoned.

To thus renounce "the luxury of personal preference"
was, however, a mere trifle compared to our perplexity
over the problems of an industrial neighborhood situated
in an unorganized city. Life pressed hard in many directions and yet it has always seemed to me rather interesting that when we were so distressed over its stern
aspects and so impressed with the lack of municipal
regulations, the first building erected for Hull-House
should have been designed for an art gallery, for although it contained a reading room on the first floor
and a studio above, the largest space on the second
floor was carefully designed and lighted for art exhibits,
which had to do only with the cultivation of that which
appealed to the powers of enjoyment as over against
a wage-earning capacity. It was also significant that a

Chicago business man, fond of pictures himself, responded to this first appeal of the new and certainly puzzling undertaking called a Settlement.

The situation was somewhat complicated by the fact that at the time the building was erected in 1891, our free lease of the land upon which Hull-House stood expired in 1895. The donor of the building, however, overcame the difficulty by simply calling his gift a donation of a thousand dollars a year. This restriction of course necessitated the simplest sort of a structure, although I remember on the exciting day when the new building was promised to us that I looked up my European notebook which contained the record of my experience in Ulm, hoping that I might find a description of what I then thought "a Cathedral of Humanity" ought to be. The description was "low and widespreading as to include all men in fellowship and mutual responsibility even as the older pinnacles and spires indicated communion with God." The description did not prove of value as an architectural motive, I am afraid, although the architects, who have remained our friends through all the years, performed marvels with a combination of complicated demands and little money. At the moment when I read this girlish outbreak it gave me much comfort, for in those days in addition to our other perplexities Hull-House was often called irreligious.

These first buildings were very precious to us and it afforded us the greatest pride and pleasure as one building after another was added to the Hull-House group. They clothed in brick and mortar and made visible to the world that which we were trying to do; they stated to Chicago that education and recreation ought to be extended to the immigrants. The boys came in great numbers to our provisional gymnasium fitted up in a former saloon, and it seemed to us quite as natural that a Chicago man, fond of athletics, should erect a building for them, as that the boys should clamor for more room.

I do not wish to give a false impression, for we were often bitterly pressed for money and worried by the prospect of unpaid bills, and we gave up one golden scheme after another because we could not afford it; we cooked the meals and kept the books and washed the windows without a thought of hardship if we thereby saved money for the consummation of some ardently desired undertaking.

But in spite of our financial stringency, I always believed that money would be given when we had once clearly reduced the Settlement idea to the actual deed. This chapter, therefore, would be incomplete if it did not record a certain theory of nonresistance or rather universal good will which I had worked out in connection with the Settlement idea and which was later so often and so rudely disturbed. At that time I had come to believe that if the activities of Hull-House were ever misunderstood, it would be either because there was not time to fully explain or because our motives had become mixed, for I was convinced that disinterested action was like truth or beauty in its lucidity and power of appeal.

But more gratifying than any understanding or response from without could possibly be was the consciousness that a growing group of residents was gathering at Hull-House, held together in that soundest of all social bonds, the companionship of mutual interests. These residents came primarily because they were genuinely interested in the social situation and believed that the Settlement was valuable as a method of approach to it. A house in which the men residents lived was opened across the street, and at the end of the first five years the Hull-House residential force numbered fifteen, a majority of whom still remain identified with the Settlement.

Even in those early years we caught glimpses of the fact that certain social sentiments, which are "the difficult and cumulating product of human growth" and which like all higher aims live only by communion and fellowship, are cultivated most easily in the fostering soil of a community life.

Occasionally I obscurely felt as if a demand were being made upon us for a ritual which should express and carry forward the hope of the social movement. I was constantly bewildered by the number of requests I received to officiate at funeral services and by the curious confessions made to me by total strangers. For a time

I accepted the former and on one awful occasion furnished "the poetic part" of a wedding ceremony really performed by a justice of the peace, but I soon learned to steadfastly refuse such offices, although I saw that for many people without church affiliations the vague humanitarianism the Settlement represented was the nearest approach they could find to an expression of their religious sentiments.

These hints of what the Settlement might mean to at least a few spirits among its contemporaries became clear to me for the first time one summer's day in rural England, when I discussed with John Trevor his attempts to found a labor church and his desire to turn the toil and danger attached to the life of the working-man into the means of a universal fellowship. That very year a papyrus leaf brought to the British Museum from Egypt, containing among other sayings of Jesus, "Raise the stone, and there thou shalt find me; cleave the wood and I am there," was a powerful reminder to all England of the basic relations between daily labor and Christian teaching.

In those early years at Hull-House we were, however, in no danger of losing ourselves in mazes of speculation or mysticism, and there was shrewd penetration in a compliment I received from one of our Scotch neighbors. He came down Polk Street as I was standing near the foundations of our new gymnasium, and in response to his friendly remark that "Hull-House was spreading out," I replied that "Perhaps we were spreading out too fast." "Oh, no," he rejoined, "you can afford to spread out wide, you are so well planted in the mud," giving the compliment, however, a practical turn, as he glanced at the deep mire on the then unpaved street. It was this same condition of Polk Street which had caused the crown prince of Belgium when he was brought upon a visit to Hull-House to shake his head and meditatively remark, "There is not such a street— no, not one—in all the territory of Belgium."

At the end of five years the residents of Hull-House published some first found facts and our reflections thereon in a book called *Hull-House Maps and Papers*. The maps were taken from information collected by one of the residents for the United States Bureau of Labor in the investigation into "the slums of great cities" and the papers treated of various neighborhood matters with candor and genuine concern if not with skill. The first edition became exhausted in two years, and apparently the Boston publisher did not consider the book worthy of a second.

🌅 *Chapter* 8

PROBLEMS OF POVERTY

THAT neglected and forlorn old age is daily brought to the attention of a Settlement which undertakes to bear its share of the neighborhood burden imposed by poverty was pathetically clear to us during our first months of residence at Hull-House. One day a boy of ten led a tottering old lady into the House, saying that she had slept for six weeks in their kitchen on a bed made up next to the stove; that she had come when her son died, although none of them had ever seen her before; but because her son had "once worked in the same shop with Pa she thought of him when she had nowhere to go." The little fellow concluded by saying that our house was so much bigger than theirs that he thought we would have more room for beds. The old woman herself said absolutely nothing, but looking on with that gripping fear of the poorhouse in her eyes, she was a living embodiment of that dread which is so heartbreaking that the occupants of the County Infirmary themselves seem scarcely less wretched then those who are making their last stand against it.

This look was almost more than I could bear for only a few days before some frightened women had bidden me to come quickly to the house of an old German woman, whom two men from the county agent's office were attempting to remove to the County Infirmary. The poor old creature had thrown herself bodily upon a small and battered chest of drawers and clung there, clutching it so firmly that it would have been impossible to remove her without also taking the piece of furniture. She did not weep nor moan nor indeed make any human sound, but between her broken gasps for breath she squealed shrilly like a frightened animal caught in a trap. The little group of women and children gathered at her door stood aghast at this realization of the black dread which always clouds the lives of the very poor when work is slack, but which constantly grows more imminent and threatening as old age approaches. The neighborhood women and I hastened to make all sorts of promises as to the support of the old woman and the county officials, only too glad to be rid of their unhappy duty, left her to our ministrations. This dread of the poorhouse, the result of centuries of deterrent Poor Law administration, seemed to me not without some justification one summer when I found myself perpetually distressed by the unnecessary idleness and forlornness of the old women in the Cook County Infirmary, many of whom I had known in the years when activity was still a necessity, and when they felt bustlingly important. To take away from an old woman whose life has been spent in household cares all the foolish little belongings to which her affections cling and to which her very fingers have become accustomed is to take away her last incentive to activity, almost to life itsel. To give an old woman only a chair and a bed, to leave her no cupboard in which her treasures may be stowed, not only that she may take them out when she desires occupation, but that her mind may dwell upon them in moments of revery, is to reduce living almost beyond the limit of human endurance.

The poor creature who clung so desperately to her chest of drawers was really clinging to the last remnant of normal living—a symbol of all she was asked to renounce. For several years after this summer I invited five or six old women to take a two weeks' vacation from the poorhouse which they eagerly and even gaily accepted. Almost all the old men in the County Infirmary wander away each summer taking their chances for finding food or shelter and return much refreshed by the little "tramp," but the old women cannot do this unless they have some help from the outside, and yet the expenditure of a very little money secures for them the coveted vacation. I found that a few pennies paid their carfare into town, a dollar a week procured lodging with an old acquaintance; assured of two good meals a day in the Hull-House coffeehouse they could count upon numerous cups of tea among old friends to whom they would airily state that they had 'come out for a little change" and hadn't yet made up their minds about "going in again for the winter." They thus enjoyed a two weeks' vacation to the top of their bent and returned with wondrous tales of their adventures, with which they regaled the other paupers during the long winter.

The reminiscenses of these old women, their shrewd comments upon life, their sense of having reached a point where they may at last speak freely with nothing to lose because of their frankness, makes them often the most delightful of companions. I recall one of my guests, the mother of many scattered children, whose one bright spot through all the dreary years had been the wedding feast of her son Mike—a feast which had become transformed through long meditation into the nectar and ambrosia of the very gods. As a farewell fling before she went "in" again, we dined together upon chicken pie, but it did not taste like "the chicken pie at Mike's wedding" and she was disappointed after all.

Even death itself sometimes fails to bring the dignity and serenity which one would fain associate with old age. I recall the dying hour of one old Scotchwoman whose long struggle to "keep respectable" had so embittered her that her last words were gibes and taunts for those who were trying to minister to her. "So you came in yourself this morning, did you? You only sent things yesterday. I guess you knew when the doctor was coming. Don't try to warm my feet with anything but that old jacket that I've got there; it belonged to my boy who was drowned at sea nigh thirty years ago, but it's warmer yet with human feelings than any of your damned charity hot-water bottles." Suddenly the harsh gasping voice was stilled in death and I awaited the doctor's coming shaken and horrified.

The lack of municipal regulation already referred to was, in the early days of Hull-House, paralleled by the inadequacy of the charitable efforts of the city and an unfounded optimism that there was no real poverty among us. Twenty years ago there was no Charity Organization Society in Chicago and the Visiting Nurse Association had not yet begun its beneficent work, while the relief societies, although conscientiously administered, were inadequate in extent and antiquated in method.

As social reformers gave themselves over to discussion of general principles, so the poor invariably accused poverty itself of their destruction. I recall a certain Mrs. Moran, who was returning one rainy day from the office of the county agent with her arms full of paper bags containing beans and flour which alone lay between her children and starvation. Although she had no money she boarded a street car in order to save her booty from complete destruction by the rain, and as the burst bags dropped "flour on the ladies' dresses" and "beans all over the place," she was sharply reprimanded by the conductor, who was further exasperated when he discovered she had no fare. He put her off, as she had hoped he would, almost in front of Hull-House. She related to us her state of mind as she stepped off the car and saw the last of her wares disappearing; she admitted she forgot the proprieties and "cursed a little," but, curiously enough, she pronounced her malediction, not against the rain nor the conductor, nor yet against the worthless husband who had been sent up to the city prison, but, true to the Chicago spirit of the moment, went to the root of the matter and roundly "cursed poverty."

This spirit of generalization and lack of organization among the charitable forces of the city was painfully revealed in that terrible winter after the World's Fair, when the general financial depression throughout the country was much intensified in Chicago by the numbers of unemployed stranded at the close of the exposition.

When the first cold weather came the police stations and the very corridors of the city hall were crowded by men who could afford no other lodging. They made huge demonstrations on the lake front, reminding one of the London gatherings in Trafalgar Square.

It was the winter in which Mr. Stead wrote his indictment of Chicago. I can vividly recall his visits to Hull-House, some of them between eleven and twelve o'clock at night, when he would come in wet and hungry from an investigation of the levee district, and, while he was drinking hot chocolate before an open fire, would relate in one of his curious monologues, his experience as an out-of-doors laborer standing in line without an overcoat for two hours in the sleet, that he might have a chance to sweep the streets; or his adventures with a crook, who mistook him for one of his own kind and offered him a place as an agent for a gambling house, which he promptly accepted. Mr. Stead was much impressed with the mixed goodness in Chicago, the lack of rectitude in many high places, the simple kindness of the most wretched to each other. Before he published "If Christ Came to Chicago" he made his attempt to rally the diverse moral forces of the city in a huge mass meeting, which resulted in a temporary organization, later developing into the Civic Federation. I was a member of the committee of five appointed to carry out the suggestions made in this remarkable meeting, and our first concern was to appoint a committee to deal with the unemployed. But when has a committee ever dealt satisfactorily with the unemployed? Relief stations were opened in various parts of the city, temporary lodging houses were established, Hull-House undertaking to lodge the homeless women who could be received nowhere else; employment stations were opened giving sewing to the women, and street sweeping for the men was organized. It was in connection with the latter that the perplexing question of the danger of permanently lowering wages at such a crisis, in the praiseworthy effort to bring speedy relief, was brought home to me. I insisted that it was better to have the men work half a day for seventy-five cents than a whole day for a dollar, better that they should earn three dollars in two days than in three days. I resigned from the street-cleaning committee in despair of making the rest of the committee understand that, as our real object was not street cleaning but the help of the unemployed, we must treat the situation in such wise that the men would not be worse off when they returned to their normal occupations. The discussion opened up situations new to me and carried me far afield in perhaps the most serious economic reading I have ever done.

A beginning also was then made toward a Bureau of Organized Charities, the main office being put in charge of a young man recently come from Boston, who lived at Hull-House. But to employ scientific methods for the first time at such a moment involved difficulties, and the most painful episode of the winter came for me from an attempt on my part to conform to carefully received instructions. A shipping clerk whom I had known for a long time had lost his place, as so many people had that year, and came to the relief station established at Hull-House four or five times to secure help for his family. I told him one day of the opportunity for work on the drainage canal and intimated that if any employment were obtainable, he ought to exhaust that possibility before asking for help. The man replied that he had always worked indoors and that he could not endure outside work in winter. I am grateful to remember that I was too uncertain to be severe, although I held to my instructions. He did not come again for relief, but worked for two days digging on the canal, where he contracted pneumonia and died a week later. I have never lost trace of the two little children he left behind him, although I cannot see them without a bitter consciousness that it was at their expense I learned that life cannot be administered by definite rules and regulations; that wisdom to deal with a man's difficulties comes only through some knowledge of his life and habits as a whole; and that to treat an isolated episode is almost sure to invite blundering.

It was also during this winter that I became permanently impressed with the kindness of the poor to each other; the woman who lives upstairs will willingly share her breakfast with the family below because she knows they "are hard up"; the man who boarded with them last winter will give a month's rent because he knows the father of the family is out of work; the baker across the street who is fast being pushed to the wall by his downtown competitors, will send across three loaves of stale bread because he has seen the children looking longingly into his window and suspects they are hungry. There are also the families who, during times of business depression, are obliged to seek help from the county or some benevolent society, but who are themselves most anxious not to be confounded with the pauper class, with whom indeed they do not in the least belong. Charles Booth, in his brilliant chapter on the unemployed, expresses regret that the problems of the working class are so often confounded with the problems of the inefficient and the idle, that although working people live in the same street with those in need of charity, to thus confound two problems is to render the solution of both impossible.

In a Tenement House, Sick Mother and Children

I remember one family in which the father had been out of work for this same winter, most of the furniture had been pawned, and as the worn-out shoes could not be replaced the children could not go to school. The mother was ill and barely able to come for the supplies and medicines. Two years later she invited me to supper one Sunday evening in the little home which had been completely restored, and she gave as a reason for the invitation that she couldn't bear to have me remember them as they had been during that one winter, which she insisted, had been unique in her twelve years of married life. She said that it was as she had met me, not as I am ordinarily, but as I should appear misshapen with rheumatism or with a face distorted by neuralgic pain; that it was not fair to judge poor people that way. She perhaps unconsciously illustrated the difference between the relief-station relation to the poor and the Settlement relation to its neighbors, the latter wishing to know them through all the varying conditions of life, to stand by when they are in distress, but by no means to drop intercourse with them when normal prosperity has returned, enabling the relation to become more social and free from economic disturbance.

Possibly something of the same effort has to be made within the Settlement itself to keep its own sense of proportion in regard to the relation of the crowded city quarter to the rest of the country. It was in the spring following this terrible winter, during a journey to meet lecture engagements in California, that I found myself amazed at the large stretches of open country and prosperous towns through which we passed day by day, whose existence I had quite forgotten.

In the latter part of the summer of 1895, I served as a member on a commission appointed by the mayor of Chicago to investigate conditions in the county poorhouse, public attention having become centered on it through one of those distressing stories, which exaggerates the wrong in a public institution while at the same time it reveals conditions which need to be rectified. However necessary publicity is for securing reformed administration, however useful such exposures may be for political purposes, the whole is attended by such a waste of the most precious human emotions, by such a tearing of living tissue, that it can scarcely be endured. Everytime I entered Hull-House during the days of the investigation, I would find waiting for me from twenty to thirty people whose friends and relatives were in the suspected institution, all in such acute distress of mind that to see them was to look upon the victims of deliberate torture. In most cases my visitor would state that it seemed impossible to put their invalids in any other place, but if these stories were true, something must be done. Many of the patients were taken out only to be returned after a few days or weeks to meet the sullen hostility of their attendants and with their own attitude changed from confidence to timidity and alarm.

This piteous dependence of the poor upon the good will of public officials was made clear to us in an early experience with a peasant woman straight from the fields of Germany, whom we met during our first six months at Hull-House. Her four years in America had been spent in patiently carrying water up and down two flights of stairs, and in washing the heavy flannel suits of iron foundry workers. For this her pay had averaged thirty-five cents a day. Three of her daughters had fallen victims to the vice of the city. The mother was bewildered and distressed, but understood nothing. We were able to induce the betrayer of one daughter to marry her; the second, after a tedious lawsuit, supported his child; with the third we were able to do nothing. This woman is now living with her family in a little house seventeen miles from the city. She has made two payments on her land and is a lesson to all beholders as she pastures her cow up and down the railroad tracks and makes money from her ten acres. She did not need charity for she had an immense capacity for hard work, but she sadly needed the service of the State's attorney office, enforcing the laws designed for the protection of such girls as her daughters.

We early found ourselves spending many hours in efforts to secure support for deserted women, insurance for bewildered widows, damages for injured operators, furniture from the clutches of the installment store. The Settlement is valuable as an information and interpretation bureau. It constantly acts between the various institutions of the city and the people for whose benefit these institutions were erected. The hospitals, the county agencies, and State asylums are often but vague rumors to the people who need them most. Another function of the Settlement to its neighborhood resembles that of the big brother whose mere presence on the playground protects the little one from bullies.

We early learned to know the children of hard-driven mothers who went out to work all day, sometimes leaving the little things in the casual care of a neighbor, but often locking them into their tenement rooms. The first three crippled children we encountered in the neighborhood had all been injured while their mothers were at work: one had fallen out of a third-story window, another had been burned, and the third had a curved spine due to the fact that for three years he had been tied all day long to the leg of the kitchen table, only released at noon by his older brother who hastily ran in from a neighboring factory to share his lunch with him. When the hot weather came the restless children could not brook the confinement of the stuffy rooms, and, as it was not considered safe to leave the doors open because of sneak thieves, many of the children were locked out. During our first summer an increasing number of these poor little mites would wander into the cool hallway of Hull-House. We kept them there and fed them at noon, in return for which we were sometimes offered a hot penny which had been held in a tight little fist "ever since mother left this morning, to buy something to eat with." Out of kindergarten hours our little guests noisily enjoyed the hospitality of our bedrooms under the so-called care of any resident who volunteered to keep an eye on them, but later they were moved into a neighboring apartment under more systematic supervision.

Hull-House was thus committed to a day nursery which we sustained for sixteen years first in a little cottage on a side street and then in a building designed for its use called the Children's House. It is now carried on by the United Charities of Chicago in a finely equipped building on our block, where the immigrant mothers are cared for as well as the children, and where they are taught the things

which will make life in America more possible. Our early
day nursery brought us into natural relations with the poorest women of the neighborhood, many of whom were bearing the burden of dissolute and incompetent husbands in
addition to the support of their children. Some of them
presented an impressive manifestation of that miracle of
affection which outlives abuse, neglect, and crime,—the
affection which cannot be plucked from the heart where
it has lived, although it may serve only to torture and
torment. "Has your husband come back?" you inquire of
Mrs. S., whom you have known for eight years as an overworked woman bringing her three delicate children every
morning to the nursery; she is bent under the double burden of earning the money which supports them and giving
them the tender care which alone keeps them alive. The
oldest two children have at last gone to work, and Mrs.
S. has allowed herself the luxury of staying at home two
days a week. And now the worthless husband is back
again—the "gentlemanly gambler" type who, through all
vicissitudes, manages to present a white shirtfront and a
gold watch to the world, but who is dissolute, idle and
extravagant. You dread to think how much his presence
will increase the drain upon the family exchequer, and you
know that he stayed away until he was certain that the
children were old enough to earn money for his luxuries.
Mrs. S. does not pretend to take his return lightly, but she
replies in all seriousness and simplicity, "You know my
feeling for him has never changed. You may think me
foolish, but I was always proud of his good looks and
educated appearance. I was lonely and homesick during
those eight years when the children were little and needed
so much doctoring, but I could never bring myself to feel
hard toward him, and I used to pray the good Lord to
keep him from harm and bring him back to us; so, of
course, I'm thankful now." She passes on with a dignity
which gives one a new sense of the security of affection.

I recall a similar case of a woman who had supported
her three children for five years, during which time her
dissolute husband constantly demanded money for drink
and kept her perpetually worried and intimidated. One Saturday, before the "blessed Easter," he came back from a
long debauch, ragged and filthy, but in a state of lachry-

mose repentance. The poor wife received him as a returned prodigal, believed that his remorse would prove lasting, and felt sure that if she and the children went to church with him on Easter Sunday and he could be induced to take the pledge before the priest, all their troubles would be ended. After hours of vigorous effort and the expenditure of all her savings, he finally sat on the front doorstep the morning of Easter Sunday, bathed, shaved and arrayed in a fine new suit of clothes. She left him sitting there in the reluctant spring sunshine while she finished washing and dressing the children. When she finally opened the front door with the three shining children that they might all set forth together, the returned prodigal had disappeared, and was not seen again until midnight, when he came back in a glorious state of intoxication from the proceeds of his pawned clothes and clad once more in the dingiest attire. She took him in without comment, only to begin again the wretched cycle. There were of course instances of the criminal husband as well as of the merely vicious. I recall one woman who, during seven years, never missed a visiting day at the penitentiary when she might see her husband, and whose little children in the nursery proudly reported the messages from father with no notion that he was in disgrace, so absolutely did they reflect the gallant spirit of their mother.

While one was filled with admiration for these heroic women, something was also to be said for some of the husbands, for the sorry men who, for one reason or another, had failed in the struggle of life. Sometimes this failure was purely economic and the men were competent to give the children, whom they were not able to support, the care and guidance and even education which were of the highest value. Only a few months ago I met upon the street one of the early nursery mothers who for five years had been living in another part of the city, and in response to my query as to the welfare of her five children, she bitterly replied, "All of them except Mary have been arrested at one time or another, thank you." In reply to my remark that I thought her husband had always had such admirable control over them, she burst out, "That has been the whole trouble. I got tired taking care of him and didn't believe that his laziness was all due to his health, as he said, so I left him and said that I would support the children, but not him. From that minute the trouble with the four boys began. I never knew what they were doing, and after every sort of a scrape I finally put Jack and the twins into institutions where I pay for them. Joe has gone to work at last, but with a disgraceful record behind him. I tell you I ain't so sure that because a woman can make big money that she can be both father and mother to her children."

As I walked on, I could but wonder in which particular we are most stupid—to judge a man's worth so solely by his wage-earning capacity that a good wife feels justified in leaving him, or in holding fast to that wretched delusion that a woman can both support and nurture her children.

One of the most piteous revelations of the futility of the latter attempt came to me through the mother of "Goosie," as the children for years called a little boy who, because he was brought to the nursery wrapped up in his mother's shawl, always had his hair filled with the down and small feathers from the feather brush factory where she worked. One March morning, Goosie's mother was hanging out the washing on a shed roof before she left for the factory. Five-year-old Goosie was trotting at her heels handing her clothespins, when he was suddenly blown off the roof by the high wind into the alley below. His neck was broken by the fall, and as he lay piteous and limp on a pile of frozen refuse, his mother cheerily called him to "climb up again," so confident do overworked mothers become that their children cannot get hurt. After the funeral, as the poor mother sat in the nursery postponing the moment when she must go back to her empty rooms, I asked her, in a futile effort to be of comfort, if there was anything more we could do for her. The overworked, sorrow-stricken woman looked up and replied, "If you could give me my wages for tomorrow, I would not go to work in the factory at all. I would like to stay at home all day and hold the baby. Goosie was always asking me to take him and I never had any time." This statement revealed the condition of many nursery mothers who are obliged to forego the joys and solaces which belong to even the most poverty-stricken. The long hours of factory labor necessary for earning the support of a child leave no time for the tender care and caressing which may enrich the life of the most piteous baby.

With all of the efforts made by modern society to nurture and educate the young, how stupid it is to permit the mothers of young children to spend themselves in the coarser work of the world! It is curiously inconsistent that with the emphasis which this generation has placed upon the mother and upon the prolongation of infancy, we constantly allow the waste of this most precious material. I cannot recall without indignation a recent experience. I was detained late one evening in an office building by a prolonged committee meeting of the Board of Education. As I came out at eleven o'clock, I met in the corridor of the fourteenth floor a woman whom I knew, on her knees scrubbing the marble tiling. As she straightened up to greet me, she seemed so wet from her feet up to her chin, that I hastily inquired the cause. Her reply was that she left home at five o'clock every night and had no opportunity for six hours to nurse her baby. Her mother's milk mingled with the very water with which she scrubbed the floors until she should return at midnight, heated and exhausted, to feed her screaming child with what remained within her breasts.

These are only a few of the problems connected with the lives of the poorest people with whom the residents in a Settlement are constantly brought in contact.

I cannot close this chapter without a reference to that gallant company of men and women among whom my acquaintance is so large, who are fairly indifferent to starvation itself because of their preoccupation with higher ends. Among them are visionaries and enthusiasts, unsuccessful artists, writers, and reformers. For many years at Hull-House, we knew a well-bred German woman who was completely absorbed in the experiment of expressing musical phrases and melodies by means of colors. Because she was small and deformed, she stowed herself into her trunk every night, where she slept on a canvas stretched hammock-wise from the four corners and her food was of the meagerest; nevertheless if a visitor left an off⸗ upon her table, it was largely spent for apparatus o⸍ cately colored silk floss, with which to pursue the f⸍ ing experiment. Another sadly crippled old wor widow of a sea captain, although living almost exclusively upon malted milk tablets as affording a cheap form of prepared food, was always eager to talk of the beautiful illuminated manuscripts she had sought out in her travels and to show specimens of her own work as an illuminator. Still another of these impressive old women was an inveterate inventor. Although she had seen prosperous days in England, when we knew her, she subsisted largely upon the samples given away at the demonstration counters of the department stores, and on bits of food which she cooked on a coal shovel in the furnace of the apartment house whose basement back room she occupied. Although her inventions were not practicable, various experts to whom they were submitted always pronounced them suggestive and ingenious. I once saw her receive this complimentary verdict —"this ribbon to stick in her coat"—with such dignity and gravity that the words of condolence for her financial disappointment died upon my lips.

These indomitable souls are but three out of many whom I might instance to prove that those who are handicapped in the race for life's goods sometimes play a magnificent trick upon the jade, life herself, by ceasing to know whether or not they possess any of her tawdry goods and chattels.

✿✿ Chapter 9

A DECADE OF
ECONOMIC DISCUSSION

THE Hull-House residents were often bewildered by
the desire for constant discussion which characterized
Chicago twenty years ago, for although the residents in
the early Settlements were in many cases young persons
who had sought relief from the consciousness of social
maladjustment in the "anodyne of work" afforded by
philanthropic and civic activities, their former experiences had not thrown them into company with radicals.
The decade between 1890-1900 was, in Chicago, a
period of propaganda as over against constructive social
effort; the moment for marching and carrying banners,
for stating general principles and making a demonstration, rather than the time for uncovering the situation
and for providing the legal measures and the civic organization through which new social hopes might make
themselves felt.

When Hull-House was established in 1889, the events
of the Haymarket riot were already two years old, but
during that time Chicago had apparently gone through
the first period of repressive measures, and in the winter of 1889-1890, by the advice and with the active par-

ticipation of its leading citizens, the city had reached the conclusion that the only cure for the acts of anarchy was free speech and an open discussion of the ills of which the opponents of government complained. Great open meetings were held every Sunday evening in the recital hall of the then new auditorium, presided over by such representative citizens as Lyman Gage, and every possible shade of opinion was freely expressed. A man who spoke constantly at these meetings used to be pointed out to the visiting stranger as one who had been involved with the group of convicted anarchists, and who doubtless would have been arrested and tried, but for the accident of his having been in Milwaukee when the explosion occurred. One cannot imagine such meetings being held in Chicago today, nor that such a man should be encouraged to raise his voice in a public assemblage presided over by a leading banker. It is hard to tell just what change has come over our philosophy or over the minds of those citizens who were then convinced that if these conferences had been established earlier, the Haymarket riot and all its sensational results might have been avoided.

At any rate, there seemed a further need for smaller clubs, where men who differed widely in their social theories might meet for discussion, where representatives of the various economic schools might modify each other, and at least learn tolerance and the futility of endeavoring to convince all the world of the truth of one position. Fanaticism is engendered only when men, finding no contradiction to their theories, at last believe that the very universe lends itself as an exemplification of one point of view. "The Working People's Social Science Club" was organized at Hull-House in the spring of 1890 by an English workingman, and for seven years it held a weekly meeting. At eight o'clock every Wednesday night the secretary called to order from forty to one hundred people; a chairman for the evening was elected, a speaker was introduced who was allowed to talk until nine o'clock; his subject was then thrown open to discussion and a lively debate ensued until ten o'clock, at which hour the meeting was declared adjourned. The enthusiasm of this club seldom lagged. Its zest for discussion was unceasing, and any attempt to turn it into a study or reading club always met with the strong disapprobation of the members.

In these weekly discussions in the Hull-House drawing room everything was thrown back upon general principles and all discussion save that which "went to the root of things," was impatiently discarded as an unworthy, halfway measure. I recall one evening in this club when an exasperated member had thrown out the statement that "Mr. B. believes that socialism will cure the toothache." Mr. B. promptly rose to his feet and said that it certainly would, that when every child's teeth were systematically cared for from the beginning, toothaches would disappear from the face of the earth, belonging, as it did, to the extinct competitive order, as the black plague had disappeared from the earth with the ill-regulated feudal regime of the Middle Ages. "But," he added, "why do we spend time discussing trifles like the toothache when great social changes are to be considered which will of themselves reform these minor ills?" Even the man who had been humorous fell into the solemn tone of the gathering. It was, perhaps, here that the socialist surpassed everyone else in the fervor of economic discussion. He was usually a German or a Russian, with a turn for logical presentation, who saw in the concentration of capital and the growth of monopolies an inevitable transition to the socialistic state. He pointed out that the concentration of capital in fewer hands but increased the mass of those whose interests were opposed to a maintenance of its power, and vastly simplified its final absorption by the community; that monopoly "when it is finished doth bring forth socialism." Opposite to him, springing up in every discussion was the individualist, or, as the socialist called him, the anarchist, who insisted that we shall never secure just human relations until we have equality of opportunity; that the sole function of the state is to maintain the freedom of each, guarded by the like freedom of all, in order that each man may be able to work out the problems of his own existence.

That first winter was within three years of the Henry George campaign in New York, when his adherents all over the country were carrying on a successful and effective propaganda. When Henry George himself came to Hull-House one Sunday afternoon, the gymnasium which was already crowded with men to hear Father Huntington's address on "Why should a free thinker believe in Christ," fairly rocked on its foundations under the enthusiastic and prolonged applause which greeted this great leader and constantly interrupted his stirring address, filled, as all of his speeches were, with high moral enthusiasm and humanitarian fervor. Of the remarkable congresses held in connection with the World's Fair, perhaps those inaugurated by the advocates of single tax exceeded all others in vital enthusiasm. It was possibly significant that all discussions in the department of social science had to be organized by partisans in separate groups. The very committee itself on social science composed of Chicago citizens, of whom I was one, changed from week to week, as partisan members had their feelings hurt because their cause did not receive "due recognition." And yet in the same building adherents of the most diverse religious creeds, eastern and western, met in amity and good fellowship. Did it perhaps indicate that their presentation of the eternal problems of life were cast in an older and less sensitive mold than this presentation in terms of social experience, or was it rather that the new social science was not yet a science at all but merely a name under cover of which we might discuss the perplexing problems of the industrial situation? Certainly the difficulties of our committee were not minimized by the fact that the then new science of sociology had not yet defined its own field. The University of Chicago, opened only the year before the World's Fair, was the first great institution of learning to institute a department of sociology.

In the meantime the Hull-House Social Science Club grew in numbers and fervor as various distinguished people who were visiting the World's Fair came to address it. I recall a brilliant Frenchwoman who was filled with amazement because one of the shabbiest men reflected a reading of Schopenhauer. She considered the statement of another member most remarkable—that when he saw a carriage driving through the streets occupied by a capitalist who was no longer even an entrepreneur, he felt quite as sure that his days were numbered and that his very lack of function to society would speedily bring him to extinction, as he did when he saw a drunkard reeling along the same street.

The club at any rate convinced the residents that no one so poignantly realizes the failures in the social structure as the man at the bottom, who has been most directly in contact with those failures and has suffered most. I recall the shrewd comments of a certain sailor who had known the disinherited in every country; of a Russian who had served his term in Siberia; of an old Irishman who called himself an atheist but who in moments of excitement always blamed the good Lord for "setting supinely" when the world was so horribly out of joint.

It was doubtless owing largely to this club that Hull-House contracted its early reputation for radicalism. Visitors refused to distinguish between the sentiments expressed by its members in the heat of discussion and the opinions held by the residents themselves. At that moment in Chicago the radical of every shade of opinion was vigorous and dogmatic; of the sort that could not resign himself to the slow march of human improvement; of the type who knew exactly "in what part of the world Utopia standeth."

During this decade Chicago seemed divided into two classes; those who held that "business is business" and who were therefore annoyed at the very notion of social control, and the radicals, who claimed that nothing could be done to really moralize the industrial situation until society should be reorganized.

A Settlement is above all a place for enthusiasms, a spot to which those who have a passion for the equalization of human joys and opportunities are early attracted. It is this type of mind which is in itself so often obnoxious to the man of conquering business faculty, to whom the practical world of affairs seems so supremely rational that he would never vote to change the type of it even if he could. The man of social enthusiasm is to him an annoyance and an affront. He does not like to hear him talk and considers him *per se* "unsafe." Such a businessman would admit, as an abstract proposition, that society is susceptible of modification and would even agree that all human institutions imply progressive development, but at the same time he deeply distrusts those who seek to reform existing conditions. There is a certain common-sense foundation for this distrust, for too often the reformer is the rebel who defies things as they are, because of the restraints which they impose upon his individual desires rather than because of the general defects of the system. When such a rebel poses for a reformer, his shortcomings are heralded to the world, and his downfall is cherished as an awful warning to those who refuse to worship "the god of things as they are."

And yet as I recall the members of this early club, even those who talked the most and the least rationally, seem to me to have been particularly kindly and "safe." The most pronounced anarchist among them has long since become a convert to a religious sect, holding Buddhistic tenets which imply little food and a distrust of all action; he has become a wraith of his former self but he still retains his kindly smile.

In the discussion of these themes, Hull-House was of course quite as much under the suspicion of one side as the other. I remember one night when I addressed a club of secularists, which met at the corner of South Halsted and Madison streets, a rough-looking man called out: "You are all right now, but, mark my words, when you are subsidized by the millionaires, you will be afraid to talk like this." The defense of free speech was a sensitive point with me, and I quickly replied that while I did not intend to be subsidized by millionaires, neither did I propose to be bullied by workingmen, and that I should state my honest opinion without consulting either of them. To my surprise, the audience of radicals broke into applause, and the discussion turned upon the need of resisting tyranny wherever found, if democratic institutions were to endure. This desire to bear independent witness to social righteousness often resulted in a sense of compromise difficult to endure, and at many times it seemed to me that we were destined to alienate everybody. I should have been most grateful at that time to accept the tenets of socialism, and I conscientiously made my effort, both by reading and by many discussions with the comrades. I found that I could easily give an affirmative answer to the heated question "Don't you see that just as the hand mill created a society with a feudal lord, so the steam mill creates a society with an industrial capitalist?" But it was a little harder to give an affirmative reply to the proposition that the social relation thus established proceeds to create principles, ideas, and categories as merely historical and transitory products.

Of course I use the term "socialism" technically and do not wish to confuse it with the growing sensitiveness which recognizes that no personal comfort nor individual development can compensate a man for the misery of his neighbors, nor with the increasing conviction that social arrangements can be transformed through man's conscious and deliberate effort. Such a definition would not have been accepted for a moment by the Russians, who then dominated the socialist party in Chicago and among whom a crude interpretation of the class conflict was the test of the faith.

During those first years on Halsted Street nothing was more painfully clear than the fact that pliable human nature is relentlessly pressed upon by its physical environment. I saw nowhere a more devoted effort to understand and relieve that heavy pressure than the socialists were making, and I should have been glad to have had the comradeship of that gallant company had they not firmly insisted that fellowship depends upon identity of creed. They repudiated similarity of aim and social sympathy as tests which were much too loose and wavering as they did that vague socialism which for thousands has come to be a philosophy or rather religion embodying the hope of the world and the protection of all who suffer.

I also longed for the comfort of a definite social creed, which should afford at one and the same time an explanation of the social chaos and the logical steps toward its better ordering. I came to have an exaggerated sense of responsibility for the poverty in the midst of which I was living and which the socialists constantly forced me to defend. My plight was not unlike that which might have resulted in my old days of skepticism regarding foreordination, had I then been compelled to defend the confusion arising from the clashing of free wills as an alternative to an acceptance of the doctrine. Another difficulty in the way of accepting this economic determinism, so baldly dependent upon the theory of class consciousness, constantly arose when I lectured in country towns and there had opportunities to read human documents of prosperous people as well as those of my neighbors who were crowded into the city. The former were stoutly unconscious of any classes in America, and the class consciousness of the immigrants was fast being broken into by the necessity for making new and unprecedented connections in the industrial life all about them.

In the meantime, although many men of many minds met constantly at our conferences, it was amazing to find the incorrigible good nature which prevailed. Radicals are accustomed to hot discussion and sharp differences of opinion and take it all in the day's work. I recall that the secretary of the Hull-House Social Science Club at the anniversary of the seventh year of its existence read a report in which he stated that, so far as he could remember, but twice during that time had a speaker lost his temper, and in each case it had been a college professor who "wasn't accustomed to being talked back to."

He also added that but once had all the club members united in applauding the same speaker; only Samuel Jones, who afterward became "the golden rule" mayor of Toledo, had been able to overcome all their dogmatic differences, when he had set forth a plan of endowing a group of workingmen with a factory plant and a working capital for experimentation in hours and wages, quite as groups of scholars are endowed for research.

Chicago continued to devote much time to economic

discussion and remained in a state of youthful glamour throughout the nineties. I recall a young Methodist minister who, in order to free his denomination from any entanglement in his discussion of the economic and social situation, moved from his church building into a neighboring hall. The congregation and many other people followed him there, and he later took to the street corners because he found that the shabbiest men liked that the best. Professor Herron filled to overflowing a downtown hall every noon with a series of talks entitled "Between Cæsar and Jesus"—an attempt to apply the teachings of the Gospel to the situations of modern commerce. A half dozen publications edited with some ability and much moral enthusiasm have passed away, perhaps because they represented pamphleteering rather than journalism and came to a natural end when the situation changed. Certainly their editors suffered criticism and poverty on behalf of the causes which they represented.

Trades-unionists, unless they were also socialists, were not prominent in those economic discussions, although they were steadily making an effort to bring order into the unnecessary industrial confusion. They belonged to the second of the two classes into which Mill divides all those who are dissatisfied with human life as it is, and whose feelings are wholly identified with its radical amendment. He states that the thoughts of one class are in the region of ultimate aims, of "the highest ideals of human life," while the thoughts of the other are in the region of the "immediately useful, and practically attainable."

The meetings of our Social Science Club were carried on by men of the former class, many of them with a strong religious bias who constantly challenged the Church to assuage the human spirit thus torn and bruised "in the tumult of a time disconsolate." These men were so serious in their demand for religious fellowship, and several young clergymen were so ready to respond to the appeal, that various meetings were arranged at Hull-House, in which a group of people met together to consider the social question, not in a spirit of discussion, but in prayer and meditation. These clergymen were making heroic efforts to induce their churches to formally consider the labor situation, and during the years which have elapsed since then, many denominations of the Christian Church have organized labor committees; but at that time there was nothing of the sort beyond the society in the established Church of England "to consider the conditions of labor."

During that decade even the most devoted of that pioneer church society failed to formulate the fervid desire for juster social conditions into anything more convincing than a literary statement, and the Christian Socialists, at least when the American branch held its annual meeting at Hull-House, afforded but a striking portrayal of that "between-age mood" in which so many of our religious contemporaries are forced to live. I remember that I received the same impression when I attended a meeting called by the canon of an English cathedral to discuss the relation of the Church to labor. The men quickly indicted the cathedral for its uselessness, and the canon asked them what in their minds should be its future. The men promptly replied that any new social order would wish, of course, to preserve beautiful historic buildings, that although they would dismiss the bishop and all the clergy, they would want to retain one or two scholars as custodians and interpreters. "And what next?" the imperturbable ecclesiastic asked. "We would democratize it," replied the men. But when it came to a more detailed description of such an undertaking, the discussion broke into a dozen bits, although illuminated by much shrewd wisdom and affording a clue, perhaps as to the destruction of the bishop's palace by the citizens of this same town, who had attacked it as a symbol of swollen prosperity during the bread riots of the earlier part of the century.

On the other hand the workingmen who continue to demand help from the Church thereby acknowledge their kinship, as does the son who continues to ask bread from the father who gives him a stone. I recall an incident connected with a prolonged strike in Chicago on the part of the typographical unions for an

eight-hour day. The strike had been conducted in a
most orderly manner and the union men, convinced of
the justice of their cause, had felt aggrieved because
one of the religious publishing houses in Chicago had
constantly opposed them. Some of the younger clergymen of the denominations who were friendly to the
strikers' cause came to a luncheon at Hull-House,
where the situation was discussed by the representatives
of all sides. The clergymen, becoming much interested
in the idealism with which an officer of the State Federation of Labor presented the cause, drew from him the
story of his search for fraternal relation: he said that at
fourteen years of age he had joined a church, hoping to
find it there; he had later become a member of many
fraternal organizations and mutual benefit societies, and,
although much impressed by their rituals, he was disappointed in the actual fraternity. He had finally found,
so it seemed to him, in the cause of organized labor,
what these other organizations had failed to give him—
an opportunity for sacrificial effort.

Chicago thus took a decade to discuss the problems
inherent in the present industrial organization and to
consider what might be done, not, so much against deliberate aggression as against brutal confusion and neglect; quite as the youth of promise passed through a
mist of rose-colored hope before he settles in the land
of achievement where he becomes all too dull and literal
minded. And yet as I hastily review the decade in Chicago which followed this one given over to discussion,
the actual attainment of these early hopes, so far as
they have been realized at all, seem to have come from
men of affairs rather than from those given to speculation. Was the whole decade of discussion an illustration
of that striking fact which has been likened to the
changing of swords in Hamlet; that the abstract minds
at length yield to the inevitable or at least grow less
ardent in their propaganda, while the concrete minds,
dealing constantly with daily affairs, in the end demonstrate the reality of abstract notions?

I remember when Frederic Harrison visited Hull-
House that I was much disappointed to find that the

Positivists had not made their ardor for humanity a more potent factor in the English social movement, as I was surprised during a visit from John Morley to find that he, representing perhaps the type of man whom political life seemed to have pulled away from the ideals of his youth, had yet been such a champion of democracy in the full tide of reaction. My observations were much too superficial to be of value and certainly both men were well groomed in philosophy ånd theory of social reform and had long before carefully formulated their principles, as the new English Labor Party, which is destined to break up the reactionary period, is now being created by another set of theorists. There were certainly moments during the heated discussions of this decade when nothing seemed so important as right theory: this was borne in upon me one brilliant evening at Hull-House when Benjamin Kidd, author of the much-read *Social Evolution,* was pitted against Victor Berger of Milwaukee, even then considered a rising man in the Socialist Party.

At any rate the residents at Hull-House discovered that while their first impact with city poverty allied them to groups given over to discussion of social theories, their sober efforts to' heal neighborhood ills allied them to general public movements which were without challenging creeds. But while we discovered that we most easily secured the smallest of much-needed improvements by attaching our efforts to those of organized bodies, nevertheless these very organizations would have been impossible, had not the public conscience been aroused and the community sensibility quickened by these same ardent theorists.

As I review these very first impressions of the workers in unskilled industries, living in a depressed quarter of the city, I realize how easy it was for us to see exceptional cases of hardship as typical of the average lot, and yet, in spite of alleviating philanthropy and labor legislation, the indictment of Tolstoy applied to Moscow thirty years ago still fits every American city: "Wherever we may live, if we draw a circle around us of a hundred thousand, or a thousand, or even of ten miles circumference, and look at the lives of those men and women who are inside our circle, we shall find half-starved children, old people, pregnant women, sick and weak persons, working beyond their strength, who have neither food nor rest enough to support them, and who, for this reason, die before their time; we shall see others, full-grown, who are injured and needlessly killed by dangerous and hurtful tasks."

As the American city is awakening to self-consciousness, it slowly perceives the civic significance of these industrial conditions, and perhaps Chicago has been foremost in the effort to connect the unregulated overgrowth of the huge centers of population, with the astonishingly rapid development of industrial enterprises; quite as Chicago was foremost to carry on the preliminary discussion through which a basis was laid for like-mindedness and the coördination of diverse wills. I remember an astute English visitor, who had been a guest in a score of American cities, observed that it was hard to understand the local pride he constantly encountered; for in spite of the boasting on the part of leading citizens in the western, eastern, and southern towns, all American cities seemed to him essentially alike and all equally the results of an industry totally unregulated by well-considered legislation.

I am inclined to think that perhaps all this general discussion was inevitable in connection with the early Settlements, as they in turn were the inevitable result of theories of social reform, which in their full enthusiasm reached America by way of England, only in the last decade of the century. There must have been tough fiber somewhere; for, although the residents of Hull-House were often baffled by the radicalism within the Social Science Club and harassed by the criticism from outside, we still continued to believe that such discussion should be carried on, for if the Settlement seeks its expression through social activity, it must learn the difference between mere social unrest and spiritual impulse.

The group of Hull-House residents, which by the end of the decade comprised twenty-five, differed widely in social beliefs, from the girl direct from the country who looked upon all social unrest as mere anarchy, to the resident, who had become a socialist when a student in Zurich, and who had long before translated from the German Engel's *Conditions of the Working Class in England,* although at this time she had been read out of the Socialist Party because the Russian and German Impossibilists suspected her fluent English, as she always lightly explained. Although thus diversified in social beliefs, the residents became solidly united through our mutual experience in an industrial quarter, and we became not only convinced of the need for social control and protective legislation but also of the value of this preliminary argument.

This decade of discussion between 1890 and 1900 already seems remote from the spirit of Chicago of today. So far as I have been able to reproduce this earlier period, it must reflect the essential provisionality of

Hull-House on Halsted Street,
Apartment House in Foreground

everything; "the perpetual moving on to something future which shall supersede the present," that paramount
impression of life itself, which affords us at one and the
same time, ground for despair and for endless and
varied anticipation.

Chapter 10

Pioneer Labor
Legislation in Illinois

Our very first Christmas at Hull-House, when we as
yet knew nothing of child labor, a number of little girls
refused the candy which was offered them as part of
the Christmas good cheer, saying simply that they
"worked in a candy factory and could not bear the
sight of it." We discovered that for six weeks they had
worked from seven in the morning until nine at night,
and they were exhausted as well as satiated. The sharp
consciousness of stern economic conditions was thus
thrust upon us in the midst of the season of good will.

During the same winter three boys from a Hull-
House club were injured at one machine in a neighboring factory for lack of a guard which would have cost but
a few dollars. When the injury of one of these boys
resulted in his death, we felt quite sure that the owners
of the factory would share our horror and remorse, and
that they would do everything possible to prevent the
recurrence of such a tragedy. To our surprise they did
nothing whatever, and I made my first acquaintance
then with those pathetic documents signed by the par-

ents of working children, that they will make no claim for damages resulting from "carelessness."

The visits we made in the neighborhood constantly discovered women sewing upon sweatshop work, and often they were assisted by incredibly small children. I remember a little girl of four who pulled out basting threads hour after hour, sitting on a stool at the feet of her Bohemian mother, a little bunch of human misery. But even for that there was no legal redress, for the only child-labor law in Illinois with any provision for enforcement had been secured by the coal miners' unions, and was confined to children employed in mines.

We learned to know many families in which the working children contributed to the support of their parents, not only because they spoke English better than the older immigrants and were willing to take lower wages, but because their parents gradually found it easy to live upon their earnings. A South Italian peasant who has picked olives and packed oranges from his toddling babyhood cannot see at once the difference between the outdoor healthy work which he had performed in the varying seasons, and the long hours of monotonous factory life which his child encounters when he goes to work in Chicago. An Italian father came to us in great grief over the death of his eldest child, a little girl of twelve, who had brought the largest wages into the family fund. In the midst of his genuine sorrow he said: "She was the oldest kid I had. Now I shall have to go back to work again until the next one is able to take care of me." The man was only thirty-three and had hoped to retire from work at least during the winters. No foreman cared to have him in a factory, untrained and unintelligent as he was. It was much easier for his bright, English-speaking little girl to get a chance to paste labels on a box than for him to secure an opportunity to carry pig iron. The effect on the child was what no one concerned thought about, in the abnormal effort she made thus prematurely to bear the weight of life. Another little girl of thirteen, a Russian-Jewish child employed in a laundry at a heavy task beyond her strength, committed suicide, because she had borrowed three dollars from a companion which she could not repay unless she confided the story to her parents and gave up an entire week's wages—but what could the family live upon that week in case she did! Her child mind, of course, had no sense of proportion, and carbolic acid appeared inevitable.

While we found many pathetic cases of child labor and hard-driven victims of the sweating system who could not possibly earn enough in the short busy season to support themselves during the rest of the year, it became evident that we must add carefully collected information to our general impression of neighborhood conditions if we would make it of any genuine value.

There was at that time no statistical information on Chicago industrial conditions, and Mrs. Florence Kelley, an early resident of Hull-House, suggested to the Illinois State Bureau of Labor that they investigate the sweating system in Chicago with its attendant child labor. The head of the Bureau adopted this suggestion and engaged Mrs. Kelley to make the investigation. When the report was presented to the Illinois Legislature, a special committee was appointed to look into the Chicago conditions. I well recall that on the Sunday the members of this commission came to dine at Hull-House, our hopes ran high, and we believed that at last some of the worst ills under which our neighbors were suffering would be brought to an end.

As a result of its investigations, this committee recommended to the Legislature the provisions which afterward became those of the first factory law of Illinois, regulating the sanitary conditions of the sweatshop and fixing fourteen as the age at which a child might be employed. Before the passage of the law could be secured, it was necessary to appeal to all elements of the community, and a little group of us addressed the open meetings of trades-unions and of benefit societies, church organizations, and social clubs literally every evening for three months. Of course the most energetic help as well as intelligent understanding came from the trades-unions. The central labor body of Chicago, then called the Trades and Labor Assembly, had previously appointed a committee of investigation to inquire into the sweating system. This committee consisted of five delegates

from the unions and five outside their membership. Two
of the latter were residents of Hull-House, and continued
with the unions in their well-conducted campaign until
the passage of Illinois's first Factory Legislation was
secured, a statute which has gradually been built upon
by many public-spirited citizens until Illinois stands
well among the States, at least in the matter of pro-
tecting her children. The Hull-House residents that winter had their first experience in lobbying. I remember
that I very much disliked the word and still more the
prospect of the lobbying itself, and we insisted that
well-known Chicago women should accompany this first
little group of Settlement folk who with trades-unionists
moved upon the state capitol in behalf of factory legislation. The national or, to use its formal name, The
General Federation of Woman's Clubs had been organized in Chicago only the year before this legislation
was secured. The Federation was then timid in regard
to all legislation because it was anxious not to frighten
its new membership, although its second president, Mrs.
Henrotin, was most untiring in her efforts to secure this
law.

It was, perhaps, a premature effort, though certainly
founded upon a genuine need, to urge that a clause
limiting the hours of all women working in factories or
workshops to eight a day, or forty-eight a week, should
be inserted in the first factory legislation of the State.
Although we had lived at Hull-House but three years
when we urged this legislation, we had known a large
number of young girls who were constantly exhausted
by night work; for whatever may be said in defense of
night work for men, few women are able to endure it.
A man who works by night sleeps regularly by day, but
a woman finds it impossible to put aside the household
duties which crowd upon her, and a conscientious girl
finds it hard to sleep with her mother washing and
scrubbing within a few feet of her bed. One of the
most painful impressions of those first years is that of
pale, listless girls, who worked regularly in a factory of
the vicinity which was then running full night time.
These girls also encountered a special danger in the
early morning hours as they returned from work, de-

bilitated and exhausted, and only too easily convinced that a drink and a little dancing at the end of the balls in the saloon dance halls, was what they needed to brace them. One of the girls whom we then knew, whose name, Chloe, seemed to fit her delicate charm, craving a drink to dispel her lassitude before her tired feet should take the long walk home, had thus been decoyed into a saloon, where the soft drink was followed by an alcoholic one containing "knockout drops," and she awoke in a disreputable rooming house—too frightened and disgraced to return to her mother.

Thus confronted by that old conundrum of the interdependence of matter and spirit, the conviction was forced upon us that long and exhausting hours of work are almost sure to be followed by lurid and exciting pleasures; that the power to overcome temptation reaches its limit almost automatically with that of physical resistance. The eight-hour clause in this first factory law met with much less opposition in the Legislature than was anticipated, and was enforced for a year before it was pronounced unconstitutional by the Supreme Court of Illinois. During the halcyon months when it was a law, a large and enthusiastic Eight-Hour Club of working women met at Hull-House, to read the literature on the subject and in every way to prepare themselves to make public sentiment in favor of the measure which meant so much to them. The adverse decision in the test case, the progress of which they had most intelligently followed, was a matter of great disappointment. The entire experience left on my mind a distrust of all legislation which was not preceded by full discussion and understanding. A premature measure may be carried through a legislature by perfectly legitimate means and still fail to possess vitality and a sense of maturity. On the other hand, the administration of an advanced law acts somewhat as a referendum. The people have an opportunity for two years to see the effects of its operation. If they choose to reopen the matter at the next General Assembly, it can be discussed with experience and conviction; the very operation of the law has performed the function of the "referendum" in a limited use of the term.

Founded upon some such compunction, the sense that the passage of the child labor law would in many cases work hardship, was never absent from my mind during the earliest years of its operation. I addressed as many mothers' meetings and clubs among working women as I could, in order to make clear the object of the law and the ultimate benefit to themselves as well as to their children. I am happy to remember that I never met with lack of understanding among the hard-working widows, in whose behalf many prosperous people were so eloquent. These widowed mothers would say, "Why, of course, that is what I am working for—to give the children a chance. I want them to have more education than I had"; or another, "That is why we came to America, and I don't want to spoil his start, even although his father is dead"; or "It's different in America. A boy gets left if he isn't educated." There was always a willingness, even among the poorest women, to keep on with the hard night scrubbing or the long days of washing for the children's sake.

The bitterest opposition to the law came from the large glass companies, who were so accustomed to use the labor of children that they were convinced the manufacturing of glass could not be carried on without it.

Fifteen years ago the State of Illinois, as well as Chicago, exhibited many characteristics of the pioneer country in which untrammeled energy and an "early start" were still the most highly prized generators of success. Although this first labor legislation was but bringing Illinois into line with the nations in the modern industrial world, which "have long been obliged for their own sakes to come to the aid of the workers by which they live—that the child, the young person and the woman may be protected from their own weakness and necessity—" nevertheless from the first it ran counter to the instinct and tradition, almost to the very religion of the manufacturers of the state, who were for the most part self-made men.

This first attempt in Illinois for adequate factory legislation also was associated in the minds of businessmen with radicalism, because the law was secured during the term of Governor Altgeld and was first enforced during his administration. While nothing in its genesis or spirit could be further from "anarchy" than factory legislation, and while the first law in Illinois was still far behind Massachusetts and New York, the fact that Governor Altgeld pardoned from the state's prison the anarchists who had been sentenced there after the Haymarket riot, gave the opponents of this most reasonable legislation a quickly utilized opportunity to couple it with that detested word; the State document which accompanied Governor Altgeld's pardon gave these ungenerous critics a further opportunity, because a magnanimous action was marred by personal rancor, betraying for the moment the infirmity of a noble mind. For all of these reasons this first modification of the undisturbed control of the aggressive captains of industry could not be enforced without resistance marked by dramatic episodes and revolts. The inception of the law had already become associated with Hull-House, and when its ministration was also centered there, we inevitably received all the odium which these first efforts entailed. Mrs. Kelley was appointed the first factory inspector with a deputy and a force of twelve inspectors to enforce the law. Both Mrs. Kelley and her assistant, Mrs. Stevens, lived at Hull-House; the office was on Polk Street directly opposite, and one of the most vigorous deputies was the president of the Jane Club. In addition, one of the early men residents, since dean of a state law school, acted as prosecutor in the cases brought against the violators of the law.

Chicago had for years been notoriously lax in the administration of law, and the enforcement of an unpopular measure was resented equally by the president of a large manufacturing concern and by the former victim of a sweatshop who had started a place of his own. Whatever the sentiments toward the new law on the part of the employers, there was no doubt of its enthusiastic reception by the trades-unions, as the securing of the law had already come from them, and through the years which have elapsed since, the experience of the Hull-House residents would coincide with that of an English statesman who said that "a common rule for the standard of life and the condition of labor may be secured by legislation, but it must be maintained by trades unionism."

This special value of the trades-unions first became clear to the residents of Hull-House in connection with the sweating system. We early found that the women in the sewing trades were sorely in need of help. The trade was thoroughly disorganized, Russian and Polish tailors competing against English-speaking tailors, unskilled Bohemian and Italian women competing against both. These women seem to have been best helped through the use of the label when unions of specialized workers in the trade are strong enough to insist that the manufacturers shall "give out work" only to those holding union cards. It was certainly impressive when the garment makers themselves in this way finally succeeded in organizing six hundred of the Italian women in our immediate vicinity, who had finished garments at home for the most wretched and precarious wages. To be sure, the most ignorant women only knew that "you couldn't get clothes to sew" from the places where they paid the best, unless "you had a card," but through the veins of most of them there pulsed the quickened blood of a new fellowship, a sense of comfort and aid which had been laid out to them by their fellow workers.

During the fourth year of our residence at Hull-House we found ourselves in a large mass meeting ardently advocating the passage of a Federal measure called the Sulzer Bill. Even in our short struggle with the evils of the sweating system it did not seem strange that the center of the effort had shifted to Washington, for by that time we had realized that the sanitary regulation of sweatshops by city officials, and a careful enforcement of factory legislation by state factory inspectors will not avail, unless each city and State shall be able to pass and enforce a code of comparatively uniform legislation. Although the Sulzer Act failed to utilize the Interstate Commerce legislation for its purpose, many of the national representatives realized for the first time that only by federal legislation could their constituents in remote country places be protected from contagious diseases raging in New York or Chicago,

for many country doctors testify as to the outbreak of
scarlet fever in rural neighborhoods after the children
have begun to wear the winter overcoats and cloaks
which have been sent from infected city sweatshops.

Through our efforts to modify the sweating system,
the Hull-House residents gradually became committed
to the fortunes of the Consumers' League, an organization which for years has been approaching the question
of the underpaid sewing woman from the point of
view of the ultimate responsibility lodged in the con-
sumer. It becomes more reasonable to make the presentation of the sweatshop situation through this League,
as it is more effectual to work with them for the extension of legal provisions in the slow upbuilding of that
code of legislation which is alone sufficient to protect
the home from the dangers incident to the sweating system.

The Consumers' League seems to afford the best
method of approach for the protection of girls in department stores; I recall a group of girls from a neighboring
"emporium" who applied to Hull-House for dancing parties on alternate Sunday afternoons. In reply to our protest
they told us they not only worked late every evening,
in spite of the fact that each was supposed to have "two
nights a week off," and every Sunday morning, but that on
alternate Sunday afternoons they were required "to sort the
stock." Over and over again, meetings called by the Clerks
Union and others have been held at Hull-House protesting
against these incredibly long hours. Little modification has
come about, however, during our twenty years of residence, although one large store in the Bohemian
quarter closes all day on Sunday and many of the
others for three nights a week. In spite of the Sunday work, these girls prefer the outlying department
stores to those downtown; there is more social intercourse with the customers, more kindliness and social
equality between the saleswomen and the managers, and
above all the girls have the protection naturally afforded
by friends and neighbors and they are free from that
suspicion which so often haunts the girls downtown, that
their fellow workers may not be "nice girls."

In the first years of Hull-House we came across no

trades-unions among the women workers, and I think, perhaps, that only one union, composed solely of women, was to be found in Chicago then—that of the bookbinders. I easily recall the evening when the president of this pioneer organization accepted an invitation to take dinner at Hull-House. She came in rather a recalcitrant mood, expecting to be patronized, and so suspicious of our motives that it was only after she had been persuaded to become a guest of the house for several weeks in order to find out about us for herself, that she was convinced of our sincerity and of the ability of "outsiders" to be of any service to working women. She afterward became closely identified with Hull-House, and her hearty coöperation was assured until she moved to Boston and became a general organizer for the American Federation of Labor.

The women shirtmakers and the women cloakmakers were both organized at Hull-House as was also the Dorcas Federal Labor Union, which had been founded through the efforts of a working woman, then one of the residents. The latter union met once a month in our drawing room. It was composed of representatives from all the unions in the city which included women in their membership and also received other women in sympathy with unionism. It was accorded representation in the central labor body of the city, and later it joined its efforts with those of others to found the Woman's Union Label League. In what we considered a praiseworthy effort to unite it with other organizations, the president of a leading Woman's Club applied for membership. We were so sure of her election that she stood just outside of the drawing-room door, or, in trades-union language, "the wicket gate," while her name was voted upon. To our chagrin she did not receive enough votes to secure her admission, not because the working girls, as they were careful to state, did not admire her, but because she "seemed to belong to the other side." Fortunately, the big-minded woman so thoroughly understood the vote and her interest in working women was so genuine that it was less than a decade afterward when she was elected to the presidency of the National Woman's Trades Union League. The incident and the sequel registers, perhaps, the change in Chicago toward the labor movement, the recognition of the fact that it is a general social movement concerning all members of society and not merely a class struggle.

Some such public estimate of the labor movement was brought home to Chicago during several conspicuous strikes; at least labor legislation has twice been inaugurated because its need was thus made clear. After the Pullman strike various elements in the community were unexpectedly brought together that they might soberly consider and rectify the weakness in the legal structure which the strike had revealed. These citizens arranged for a large and representative convention to be held in Chicago on Industrial Conciliation and Abitration. I served as secretary of the committee from the new Civic Federation having the matter in charge, and our hopes ran high when, as a result of the agitation, the Illinois legislature passed a law creating a State Board of Conciliation and Arbitration. But even a state board cannot accomplish more than public sentiment authorizes and sustains, and we might easily have been discouraged in those early days could we have foreseen some of the industrial disturbances which have since disgraced Chicago. This law embodied the best provisions of the then existing laws for the arbitration of industrial disputes. At the time the word arbitration was still a word to conjure with, and many Chicago citizens were convinced, not only of the danger and futility involved in the open warfare of opposing social forces, but further believed that the search for justice and righteousness in industrial relations was made infinitely more difficult thereby.

The Pullman strike afforded much illumination to many Chicago people. Before it, there had been nothing in my experience to reveal that distinct cleavage of society, which a general strike at least momentarily affords. Certainly, during all those dark days of the Pullman strike, the growth of class bitterness was most obvious. The fact that the Settlement maintained avenues of intercourse with both sides seemed to give it opportunity for nothing but a realization of the bitterness and division along class lines. I had known Mr. Pullman and had seen his genuine pride and pleasure in the

model town he had built with so much care; and I had
an opportunity to talk to many of the Pullman employees during the strike when I was sent from a so-called
"Citizens' Arbitration Committee" to their first meetings held in a hall in the neighboring village of Ken-
sington, and when I was invited to the modest supper
tables laid in the model houses. The employees then
expected a speedy settlement and no one doubted but
that all the grievances connected with the "straw bosses" would be quickly remedied and that the benevolence which had built the model town would not fail
them. They were sure that the "straw bosses" had
misrepresented the state of affairs, for this very first
awakening to class consciousness bore many traces of
the servility on one side and the arrogance on the other
which had so long prevailed in the model town. The
entire strike demonstrated how often the outcome of
far-reaching industrial disturbances is dependent upon
the personal will of the employer or the temperament
of a strike leader. Those familiar with strikes know only
too well how much they are influenced by poignant
domestic situations, by the troubled consciences of the
minority directors, by the suffering women and children,
by the keen excitement of the struggle, by the religious
scruples sternly suppressed but occasionally asserting
themselves, now on one side and now on the other, and
by that undefined psychology of the crowd which we
understand so little. All of these factors also influence
the public and do much to determine popular sympathy
and judgment. In the early days of the Pullman strike,
as I was coming down in the elevator of the Auditorium hotel from one of the futile meetings of the Arbitration Committee, I met an acquaintance, who angrily
said "that the strikers ought all to be shot." As I had
heard nothing so bloodthirsty as this either from the
most enraged capitalist or from the most desperate of
the men, and was interested to find the cause of such
a senseless outbreak, I finally discovered that the first
ten thousand dollars which my acquaintance had ever
saved, requiring, he said, years of effort from the time
he was twelve years old until he was thirty, had been
lost as the result of a strike; he clinched his argument

that he knew what he was talking about, with the statement that "no one need expect him to have any sympathy with strikers or with their affairs."

A very intimate and personal experience revealed, at least to myself, my constant dread of the spreading ill will. At the height of the sympathetic strike my oldest sister, who was convalescing from a long illness in a hospital near Chicago, became suddenly very much worse. While I was able to reach her at once, every possible obstacle of a delayed and blocked transportation system interrupted the journey of her husband and children who were hurrying to her bedside from a distant state. As the end drew nearer and I was obliged to reply to my sister's constant inquiries that her family had not yet come, I was filled with a profound apprehension lest her last hours should be touched with resentment toward those responsible for the delay; lest her unutterable longing should at the very end be tinged with bitterness. She must have divined what was in my mind, for at last she said each time after the repetition of my sad news: "I don't blame any one, I am not judging them." My heart was comforted and heavy at the same time; but how many more such moments of sorrow and death were being made difficult and lonely throughout the land, and how much would these experiences add to the lasting bitterness, that touch of self-righteousness which makes the spirit of forgiveness well-nigh impossible.

When I returned to Chicago from the quiet country I saw the Federal troops encamped about the post office; almost everyone on Halsted Street wearing a white ribbon, the emblem of the strikers' side; the residents at Hull-House divided in opinion as to the righteousness of this or that measure; and no one able to secure any real information as to which side was burning the cars. After the Pullman strike I made an attempt to analyze in a paper which I called *The Modern King Lear* the inevitable revolt of human nature against the plans Mr. Pullman had made for his employees, the miscarriage of which appeared to him such black ingratitude. It seemed to me unendurable not to make some effort to gather together the social implications of

the failure of this benevolent employer and its relation
to the demand for a more democratic administration
of industry. Doubtless the paper represented a certain
"excess of participation," to use a gentle phrase of
Charles Lamb's in preference to a more emphatic one
used by Mr. Pullman himself. The last picture of the
Pullman strike which I distinctly recall was three years
later when one of the strike leaders came to see me.
Although out of work for most of the time since the
strike, he had been undisturbed for six months in the
repair shops of a street-car company, under an assumed
name, but he had at that moment been discovered and
dismissed. He was a superior type of English workingman, but as he stood there, broken and discouraged,
believing himself so black-listed that his skill could never be used again, filled with sorrow over the loss of his
wife who had recently died after an illness with distressing mental symptoms, realizing keenly the lack of the
respectable way of living he had always until now been
able to maintain, he seemed to me an epitome of the
wretched human waste such a strike implies. I fervently
hoped that the new arbitration law would prohibit in
Chicago forever more such brutal and ineffective methods of settling industrial disputes. And yet even as
early as 1896, we found the greatest difficulty in apply-
ing the arbitration law to the garment workers' strike,
although it was finally accomplished after various mass
meetings had urged it. The cruelty and waste of the
strike as an implement for securing the most reasonable
demands came to me at another time, during the long
strike of the clothing cutters. They had protested, not
only against various wrongs of their own, but against
the fact that the tailors employed by the custom merchants were obliged to furnish their own workshops and
thus bore a burden of rent which belonged to the employer. One of the leaders in this strike, whom I had
known for several years as a sober, industrious, and unusually intelligent man, I saw gradually break down during the many trying weeks and at last suffer a complete
moral collapse.

He was a man of sensitive organization under the
necessity, as is every leader during a strike, to address

the same body of men day after day with an appeal
sufficiently emotional to respond to their sense of injury; to receive callers at any hour of the day or night;
to sympathize with all the distress of the strikers who
see their families daily suffering; he must do it all with
the sickening sense of the increasing privation in his
own home, and in this case with the consciousness that
failure was approaching nearer each day. This man, accustomed to the monotony of his workbench and suddenly thrown into a new situation, showed every sign
of nervous fatigue before the final collapse came. He
disappeared after the strike and I did not see him for
ten years, but when he returned he immediately began
talking about the old grievances which he had repeated
so often that he could talk of nothing else. It was easy
to recognize the same nervous symptoms which the
broken-down lecturer exhibits who has depended upon
the exploitation of his own experiences to keep himself
going. One of his stories was indeed pathetic. His employer, during the busy season, had met him one Sunday afternoon in Lincoln Park whither he had taken
his three youngest children, one of whom had been ill.
The employer scolded him for thus wasting his time
and roughly asked why he had not taken home enough
work to keep himself busy through the day. The story
was quite credible because the residents of Hull-House
have had many opportunities to see the worker driven
ruthlessly during the season and left in idleness for long
weeks afterward. We have slowly come to realize that
periodical idleness as well as the payment of wages insufficient for maintenance of the manual worker in full
industrial and domestic efficiency, stand economically on
the same footing with the "sweated" industries, the overwork of women, and employment of children.

But of all the aspects of social misery nothing is so
heartbreaking as unemployment, and it was inevitable
that we should see much of it in a neighborhood where
low rents attracted the poorly paid worker and many
newly arrived immigrants who were first employed in
gangs upon railroad extensions and similar undertakings.
The sturdy peasants eager for work were either the victims of the padrone who fleeced them unmercifully,

both in securing a place to work and then in supplying them with food, or they became the mere sport of unscrupulous employment agencies. Hull-House made an investigation both of the padrone and of the agencies in our immediate vicinity, and the outcome confirming what we already suspected, we eagerly threw ourselves into a movement to procure free employment bureaus under State control until a law authorizing such bureaus and giving the officials intrusted with their management power to regulate private employment agencies, passed the Illinois Legislature in 1899. The history of these bureaus demonstrates the tendency we all have to consider a legal enactment in itself an achievement and to grow careless in regard to its administration and actual results; for an investigation into the situation ten years later discovered that immigrants were still shamefully imposed upon. A group of Bulgarians were found who had been sent to work in Arkansas where their services were not needed; they walked back to Chicago only to secure their next job in Oklahoma and to pay another railroad fare as well as another commission to the agency. Not only was there no method by which the men not needed in Arkansas could know that there was work in Oklahoma unless they came back to Chicago to find it out, but there was no certainty that they might not be obliged to walk back from Oklahoma because the Chicago agency had already sent out too many men.

This investigation of the employment bureau resources of Chicago was undertaken by the League for the Protection of Immigrants, with whom it is possible for Hull-House to coöperate whenever an investigation of the immigrant colonies in our immediate neighborhood seems necessary, as was recently done in regard to the Greek colonies of Chicago. The superintendent of this League, Miss Grace Abbott, is a resident of Hull-House and all of our later attempts to secure justice and opportunity for immigrants are much more effective through the League, and when we speak before a congressional committee in Washington concerning the needs of Chicago immigrants, we represent the League as well as our own neighbors.

It is in connection with the first factory employment of newly arrived immigrants and the innumerable difficulties attached to their first adjustment that some of the most profound industrial disturbances in Chicago have come about. Under any attempt at classification these strikes belong more to the general social movement than to the industrial conflict, for the strike is an implement used most rashly by unorganized labor who, after they are in difficulties, call upon the trades-unions for organization and direction. They are similar to those strikes which are inaugurated by the unions on behalf of unskilled labor. In neither case do the hastily organized unions usually hold after the excitement of the moment has subsided, and the most valuable result of such strikes is the expanding consciousness of the solidarity of the workers. This was certainly the result of the Chicago stockyard strike in 1905, inaugurated on behalf of the immigrant laborers and so conspicuously carried on without violence that, although twenty-two thousand workers were idle during the entire summer, there were fewer arrests in the stockyards district than the average summer months afford. However, the story of this strike should not be told from Hull-House, but from the University of Chicago Settlement, where Miss Mary McDowell performed such signal public service during that trying summer. It would be interesting to trace how much of the subsequent exposure of conditions and attempts at governmental control of this huge industry had their genesis in this first attempt of the unskilled workers to secure a higher standard of living. Certainly the industrial conflict when epitomized in a strike, centers public attention on conditions as nothing else can do. A strike is one of the most exciting episodes in modern life, and as it assumes the characteristics of a game, the entire population of a city becomes divided into two cheering sides. In such moments the fair-minded public, who ought to be depended upon as a referee, practically disappears. Anyone who tries to keep the attitude of nonpartisanship, which is perhaps an impossible one, is quickly under suspicion by both sides. At least that was the fate of a group of citizens appointed by the mayor of Chicago to arbitrate during the stormy teamsters' strike which occurred in 1905. We sat through a long Sunday afternoon in the mayor's office in the City Hall, talking first with the labor men and then with the group of capitalists. The undertaking was the more futile in that we were all practically the dupes of a new type of "industrial conspiracy" successfully inaugurated in Chicago by a close compact between the coal teamsters' union and the coal team owners' association, who had formed a kind of monopoly hitherto new to a monopoly-ridden public.

The stormy teamsters' strike, ostensibly undertaken in defense of the garment workers, but really arising from causes so obscure and dishonorable that they have never yet been made public, was the culmination of a type of trades-unions which had developed in Chicago during the preceding decade in which corruption had flourished almost as openly as it had previously done in the City Hall. This corruption sometimes took the form of grafting after the manner of Samuel Parks in New York; sometimes that of political deals in the "delivery of the labor vote"; and sometimes that of a combination between capital and labor hunting together. At various times during these years the better type of trades-unionists had made a firm stand against this corruption and a determined effort to eradicate it from the labor movement, not unlike the general reform effort of many American cities against political corruption. This reform movement in the Chicago Federation of Labor had its martyrs, and more than one man nearly lost his life through the "slugging" methods employed by the powerful corruptionists. And yet even in the midst of these things were found touching examples of fidelity to the earlier principles of brotherhood totally untouched by the corruption. At one time the scrub-women in the downtown office buildings had a union of their own affiliated with the elevator men and the janitors. Although the union was used merely as a weapon in the fight of the coal teamsters against the use of natural gas in downtown buildings, it did not prevent the women from getting their first glimpse into the fellowship and the sense of protection which is the great gift of trades-unionism to the unskilled, unbefriended worker. I remember in a meeting held at Hull-House one Sunday afternoon, that the president of a "local" of scrubwomen stood up to relate her experience. She told first of the long years in which the fear of losing her job and the fluctuating pay were harder to bear than the hard work itself, when she had regarded all the other women who scrubbed in the same building merely as rivals and was most afraid of the most miserable, because they offered to work for less and less as they were pressed harder and harder by debt. Then she told of the change that had come when the elevator men and even the lordly janitors had talked to her about an organization and had said that they must all stand together. She told how gradually she came to feel sure of her job and of her regular pay, and she was even starting to buy a house now that she could "calculate" how much she "could have for sure." Neither she nor any of the other members knew that the same combination which had organized the scrubwomen into a union later destroyed it during a strike inaugurated for their own purposes.

That a Settlement is drawn into the labor issues of its city can seem remote to its purpose only to those who fail to realize that so far as the present industrial system thwarts our ethical demands, not only for social righteousness but for social order, a Settlement is committed to an effort to understand and, as far as possible, to alleviate it. That in this effort it should be drawn into fellowship with the local efforts of trades-unions is most obvious. This identity of aim apparently commits the Settlement in the public mind to all the faiths and works of actual trades-unions. Fellowship has so long implied similarity of creed that the fact that the Settlement often differs widely from the policy pursued by trades-unionists and clearly expresses that difference does not in the least change public opinion in regard to its identification. This is especially true in periods of industrial disturbance, although it is exactly at such moments that the trades-unionists themselves are suspicious of all but their "own kind." It is during the much longer periods between strikes that the Settlement's fellowship with trades-unions is most satisfactory

in the agitation for labor legislation and similar undertakings. The first officers of the Chicago Woman's
Trades Union League were residents of Settlements, although they can claim little share in the later record
the League made in securing the passage of the Illinois
Ten-Hour Law for Women and in its many other fine
undertakings.

Nevertheless the reaction of strikes upon Chicago Settlements affords an interesting study in social psychology. For whether Hull-House is in any wise identified
with the strike or not, makes no difference. When
"Labor" is in disgrace we are always regarded as belonging to it and share the opprobrium. In the public
excitement following the Pullman strike Hull-House lost
many friends; later the teamsters' strike caused another
such defection, although my office in both cases had
been solely that of a duly appointed arbitrator.

There is, however, a certain comfort in the assumption I have often encountered that wherever one's judgment might place the justice of a given situation, it is
understood that one's sympathy is not alienated by
wrongdoing, and that through this sympathy one is still
subject to vicarious suffering. I recall an incident during
a turbulent Chicago strike which brought me much
comfort. On the morning of the day of a luncheon to
which I had accepted an invitation, the waitress, whom
I did not know, said to my prospective hostess that
she was sure I could not come. Upon being asked for
her reason she replied that she had seen in the morning
paper that the strikers had killed a "scab" and she was
sure that I would feel quite too badly about such a
thing to be able to keep a social engagement. In spite
of the confused issues, she evidently realized my despair
over the violence in a strike quite as definitely as if she
had been told about it. Perhaps that sort of suffering
and the attempt to interpret opposing forces to each
other will long remain a function of the Settlement,
unsatisfactory and difficult as the role often becomes.

There has gradually developed between the various
Settlements of Chicago a warm fellowship founded upon
a like-mindedness resulting from similar experiences,
quite as identity of interest and endeavor develop an

enduring relation between the residents of the same Settlement. This sense of comradeship is never stronger than during the hardships and perplexities of a strike of unskilled workers revolting against the conditions which drag them even below the level of their European life. At such times the residents in various Settlements are driven to a standard of life argument running somewhere in this wise—that as the very existence of the State depends upon the character of its citizens, therefore if certain industrial conditions are forcing the workers below the standard of decency, it becomes possible to deduce the right of State regulation. Even as late as the stockyard strike this line of argument was denounced as "socialism" although it has since been confirmed as wise statesmanship by a decision of the Supreme Court of the United States which was apparently secured through the masterly argument of the Brandeis brief in the Oregon ten-hour case.

In such wise the residents of an industrial neighborhood gradually comprehend the close connection of their own difficulties with national and even international movements. The residents in the Chicago Settlements became pioneer members in the American branch of the International League for Labor Legislation, because their neighborhood experiences had made them only too conscious of the dire need for protective legislation. In such a league, with its ardent members in every industrial nation of Europe, with its encouraging reports of the abolition of all night work for women in six European nations, with its careful observations on the results of employer's liability legislation and protection of machinery, one becomes identified with a movement of world-wide significance and manifold manifestation.

Chapter 11

IMMIGRANTS AND
THEIR CHILDREN

FROM our very first months at Hull-House we found it much easier to deal with the first generation of crowded city life than with the second or third, because it is more natural and cast in a simpler mold. The Italian and Bohemian peasants who live in Chicago still put on their bright holiday clothes on a Sunday and go to visit their cousins. They tramp along with at least a suggestion of having once walked over plowed fields and breathed country air. The second generation of city poor too often have no holiday clothes and consider their relations a "bad lot." I have heard a drunken man in a maudlin stage babble of his good country mother and imagine he was driving the cows home, and I knew that his little son who laughed loud at him would be drunk earlier in life and would have no pastoral interlude to his ravings. Hospitality still survives among foreigners, although it is buried under false pride among the poorest Americans. One thing seemed clear in regard to entertaining immigrants; to preserve and keep whatever of value their past life contained and to bring them in contact with a better type of Americans. For

several years, every Saturday evening the entire families
of our Italian neighbors were our guests. These evenings
were very popular during our first winters at Hull-House.
Many educated Italians helped us, and the house became
known as a place where Italians were welcome and where
national holidays were observed. They come to us with
their petty lawsuits, sad relics of the *vendetta,* with their
incorrigible boys, with their hospital cases, with their as-
pirations for American clothes, and with their needs for
an interpreter.

An editor of an Italian paper made a genuine connection between us and the Italian colony, not only with the
Neapolitans and the Sicilians of the immediate neighborhood, but with the educated *connazionali* throughout the
city, until he went south to start an agricultural colony in
Alabama, in the establishment of which Hull-House heartily coöperated.

Possibly the South Italians more than any other immigrants represent the pathetic stupidity of agricultural
people crowded into city tenements, and we were much
gratified when thirty peasant families were induced to move
upon the land which they knew so well how to cultivate.
The starting of this colony, however, was a very expensive affair in spite of the fact that the colonists purchased
the land at two dollars an acre; they needed much more
than raw land, and although it was possible to collect the
small sums necessary to sustain them during the hard time
of the first two years, we were fully convinced that undertakings of this sort could be conducted properly only by
colonization societies such as England has established, or,
better still, by enlarging the functions of the Federal Department of Immigration.

An evening similar in purpose to the one devoted to the
Italians was organized for the Germans, in our first year.
Owing to the superior education of our Teutonic guests and
the clever leading of a cultivated German woman, these
evenings reflected something of that cozy social intercourse which is found in its perfection in the fatherland.
Our guests sang a great deal in the tender minor of the
German folksong or in the rousing spirit of the Rhine,
and they slowly but persistently pursued a course in German history and literature, recovering something of that

poetry and romance which they had long since resigned with other good things. We found strong family affection between them and their English-speaking children, but their pleasures were not in common, and they seldom went out together. Perhaps the greatest value of the Settlement to them was in placing large and pleasant rooms with musical facilities at their disposal, and in reviving their almost forgotten enthusiams. I have seen sons and daughters stand in complete surprise as their mother's knitting needles softly beat time to the song she was singing, or her worn face turned rosy under the hand-clapping as she made an old-fashioned curtsy at the end of a German poem. It was easy to fancy a growing touch of respect in her children's manner to her, and a rising enthusiasm for German literature and reminiscence on the part of all the family, an effort to bring together the old life and the new, a respect for the older cultivation, and not quite so much assurance that the new was the best.

This tendency upon the part of the older immigrants to lose the amenities of European life without sharing those of America has often been deplored by keen observers from the home countries. When Professor Masurek of Prague gave a course of lectures in the University of Chicago, he was much distressed over the materialism into which the Bohemians of Chicago had fallen. The early immigrants had been so stirred by the opportunity to own real estate, an appeal perhaps to the Slavic land hunger, and their energies had become so completely absorbed in money-making that all other interests had apparently dropped away. And yet I recall a very touching incident in connection with a lecture Professor Masurek gave at Hull-House, in which he had appealed to his countrymen to arouse themselves from this tendency to fall below their home civilization and to forget the great enthusiasm which had united them into the Pan-Slavic Movement. A Bohemian widow who supported herself and her two children by scrubbing, hastily sent her youngest child to purchase, with the twenty-five cents which was to have supplied them with food the next day, a bunch of red roses which she presented to the lecturer in appreciation of his testimony to the reality of the things of the spirit.

An overmastering desire to reveal the humbler immi-

grant parents to their own children lay at the base of what
has come to be called the Hull-House Labor Museum. This
was first suggested to my mind one early spring day when
I saw an old Italian woman, her distaff against her homesick face, patiently spinning a thread by the simple stick
spindle so reminiscent of all southern Europe. I was walking down Polk Street, perturbed in spirit, because it seemed
so difficult to come into genuine relations with the Italian
women and because they themselves so often lost their
hold upon their Americanized children. It seemed to me
that Hull-House ought to be able to devise some educational enterprise which should build a bridge between European and American experiences in such wise as to give
them both more meaning and a sense of relation. I medi-
tated that perhaps the power to see life as a whole is more
needed in the immigrant quarter of a large city than anywhere else, and that the lack of this power is the most
fruitful source of misunderstanding between European immigrants and their children, as it is between them and
their American neighbors; and why should that chasm between fathers and sons, yawning at the feet of each generation, be made so unnecessarily cruel and impassable to
these bewildered immigrants? Suddenly I looked up and
saw the old woman with her distaff, sitting in the sun on
the steps of a tenement house. She might have served as
a model for one of Michelangelo's Fates, but her face
brightened as I passed and, holding up her spindle for
me to see, she called out that when she had spun a little
more yarn, she would knit a pair of stockings for her
goddaughter. The occupation of the old woman gave me
the clue that was needed. Could we not interest the young
people working in the neighborhood factories in these older forms of industry, so that, through their own parents
and grandparents, they would find a dramatic representation of the inherited resources of their daily occupation. If
these young people could actually see that the complicated
machinery of the factory had been evolved from simple
tools, they might at least make a beginning toward that
education which Dr. Dewey defines as "a continuing reconstruction of experience." They might also lay a foundation for reverence of the past which Goethe declares to be
the basis of all sound progress.

My exciting walk on Polk Street was followed by many talks with Dr. Dewey and with one of the teachers in his school who was a resident at Hull-House. Within a month a room was fitted up to which we might invite those of our neighbors who were possessed of old crafts and who were eager to use them.

We found in the immediate neighborhood at least four varieties of these most primitive methods of spinning and three distinct variations of the same spindle in connection with wheels. It was possible to put these seven into historic sequence and order and to connect the whole with the present method of factory spinning. The same thing was done for weaving, and on every Saturday evening a little exhibit was made of these various forms of labor in the textile industry. Within one room a Syrian woman, a Greek, an Italian, a Russian, and an Irishwoman enabled even the most casual observer to see that there is no break in orderly evolution if we look at history from the industrial standpoint; that industry develops similarly and peacefully year by year among the workers of each nation, heedless of differences in language, religion, and political experiences.

And then we grew ambitious and arranged lectures upon industrial history. I remember that after an interesting lecture upon the industrial revolution in England and a portrayal of the appalling conditions throughout the weaving districts of the north, which resulted from the hasty gathering of the weavers into the new towns, a Russian tailor in the audience was moved to make a speech. He suggested that whereas time had done much to alleviate the first difficulties in the transition of weaving from hand work to steam power, that in the application of steam to sewing we are still in our first stages, illustrated by the isolated woman who tries to support herself by hand needlework at home until driven out by starvation, as many of the hand weavers had been.

The historical analogy seemed to bring a certain comfort to the tailor, as did a chart upon the wall showing the infinitesimal amount of time that steam had been applied to manufacturing processes compared to the centuries of hand labor. Human progress is slow and perhaps never more cruel than in the advance of industry, but is not the

worker comforted by knowing that other historial periods
have existed similar to the one in which he finds himself,
and that the readjustment may be shortened and allevi-
ated by judicious action; and is he not entitled to the
solace which an artistic portrayal of the situation might
give him? I remember the evening of the tailor's speech
that I felt reproached because no poet or artist has endeared the sweaters' victim to us as George Eliot has made
us love the belated weaver, Silas Marner. The textile museum is connected directly with the basket weaving, sewing, millinery, embroidery, and dressmaking constantly
being taught at Hull-House, and so far as possible with the
other educational departments; we have also been able to
make a collection of products, of early implements, and of
photographs which are full of suggestion. Yet far beyond
its direct educational value, we prize it because it so often
puts the immigrants into the position of teachers, and we
imagine that it affords them a pleasant change from the
tutelage in which all Americans, including their own children, are so apt to hold them. I recall a number of Russian women working in a sewing room near Hull-House,
who heard one Christmas week that the House was going
to give a party to which they might come. They arrived

Italian Spinner in the Hull-House Labor Museum

one afternoon, when, unfortunately, there was no party
on hand and, although the residents did their best to entertain them with impromptu music and refreshments, it was
quite evident that they were greatly disappointed. Finally
it was suggested that they be shown the Labor Museum—
where gradually the thirty sodden, tired women were transformed. They knew how to use the spindles and were delighted to find the Russian spinning frame. Many of them
had never seen the spinning wheel, which has not penetrated to certain parts of Russia, and they regarded it as a
new and wonderful invention. They turned up their
dresses to show their homespun petticoats; they tried the
looms; they explained the difficulty of the old patterns; in
short, from having been stupidly entertained, they themselves did the entertaining. Because of a direct appeal to
former experiences, the immigrant visitors were able for
the moment to instruct their American hostesses in an old
and honored craft, as was indeed becoming to their age
and experience.

In some such ways as these have the Labor Museum and
the shops pointed out the possibilities which Hull-House
has scarcely begun to develop, of demonstrating that culture is an understanding of the long-established occupations and thoughts of men, of the arts with which they
have solaced their toil. A yearning to recover for the
household arts something of their early sanctity and
meaning arose strongly within me one evening when I was
attending a Passover Feast to which I had been invited
by a Jewish family in the neighborhood, where the
traditional and religious significance of the woman's daily
activity was still retained. The kosher food the Jewish
mother spread before her family had been prepared
according to traditional knowledge and with constant care
in the use of utensils; upon her had fallen the responsibility
to make all ready according to Mosaic instructions that the
great crisis in a religious history might be fittingly set forth
by her husband and son. Aside from the grave religious
significance in the ceremony, my mind was filled with
shifting pictures of woman's labor with which travel makes
one familiar; the Indian women grinding grain outside
of their huts as they sing praises to the sun and rain; a
file of white-clad Moorish women whom I had once seen

waiting their turn at a well in Tangiers; south Italian women kneeling in a row along the stream and beating their wet clothes against the smooth white stones; the milking, the gardening, the marketing in thousands of hamlets, which are such direct expressions of the solicitude and affection at the basis of all family life.

There has been some testimony that the Labor Museum has revealed the charm of woman's primitive activities. I recall a certain Italian girl who came every Saturday evening to a cooking class in the same building in which her mother spun in the Labor Museum exhibit; and yet Angelina always left her mother at the front door while she herself went around to a side door because she did not wish to be too closely identified in the eyes of the rest of the cooking class with an Italian woman who wore a kerchief over her head, uncouth boots, and short petticoats. One evening, however, Angelina saw her mother surrounded by a group of visitors from the School of Education who much admired the spinning, and she concluded from their conversation that her mother was "the best stick-spindle spinner in America." When she inquired from me as to the truth of this deduction, I took occasion to describe the Italian village in which her mother had lived, something of her free life, and how, because of the opportunity she and the other women of the village had to drop their spindles over the edge of a precipice, they had developed a skill in spinning beyond that of the neighboring towns. I dilated somewhat on the freedom and beauty of that life—how hard it must be to exchange it all for a two-room tenement, and to give up a beautiful homespun kerchief for an ugly department store hat. I intimated it was most unfair to judge her by these things alone, and that while she must depend on her daughter to learn the new ways, she also had a right to expect her daughter to know something of the old ways.

That which I could not convey to the child, but upon which my own mind persistently dwelt, was that her mother's whole life had been spent in a secluded spot under the rule of traditional and narrowly localized observances, until her very religion clung to local sanctities—to the shrine before which she had always prayed, to the pavement and walls of the low vaulted church—and then suddenly she was torn from it all and literally put out to sea, straight away from the solid habits of her religious and domestic life, and she now walked timidly but with poignant sensibility upon a new and strange shore.

It was easy to see that the thought of her mother with any other background than that of the tenement was new to Angelina, and at least two things resulted; she allowed her mother to pull out of the big box under the bed the beautiful homespun garments which had been previously hidden away as uncouth; and she openly came into the Labor Museum by the same door as did her mother, proud at least of the mastery of the craft which had been so much admired.

A club of necktie workers formerly meeting at Hull-House persistently resented any attempt on the part of their director to improve their minds. The president once said that she "wouldn't be caught dead at a lecture," that she came to the club "to get some fun out of it," and indeed it was most natural that she should crave recreation after a hard day's work. One evening I saw the entire club listening to quite a stiff lecture in the Labor Museum and to my rather wicked remark to the president that I was surprised to see her enjoying a lecture, she replied that she did not call this a lecture, she called this "getting next to the stuff you work with all the time." It was perhaps the sincerest tribute we have ever received as to the success of the undertaking.

The Labor Museum continually demanded more space as it was enriched by a fine textile exhibit lent by the Field Museum, and later by carefully selected specimens of basketry from the Philippines. The shops have finally included a group of three or four women, Irish, Italian, Danish, who have become a permanent working force in the textile department which has developed into a self-supporting industry through the sale of its homespun products.

These women and a few men, who come to the museum to utilize their European skill in pottery, metal, and wood, demonstrate that immigrant colonies might yield to our American life something very valuable, if their resources were intelligently studied and developed. I recall an Italian, who had decorated the doorposts of his tenement with a beautiful pattern he had previously used in carving the reredos of a Neapolitan church, who was "fired" by his landlord on the ground of destroying property. His feelings were hurt, not so much that he had been put out of his house, as that his work had been so disregarded; and he said that when people traveled in Italy they liked to look at wood carvings but that in America "they only made money out of you."

Sometimes the suppression of the instinct of workmanship is followed by more disastrous results. A Bohemian whose little girl attended classes at Hull-House, in one of her periodic drunken spells had literally almost choked her to death, and later had committed suicide when in delirium tremens. His poor wife, who stayed a week at Hull-House after the disaster until a new tenement could be arranged for her, one day showed me a gold ring which her husband had made for their betrothal. It exhibited the most exquisite workmanship, and she said that although in the old country he had been a goldsmith, in America he had for twenty years shoveled coal in a furnace room of a large manufacturing plant; that whenever she saw one of his "restless fits," which preceded his drunken periods, "coming on," if she could provide him with a bit of metal and persuade him to stay at home and work at it, he was all right and the time passed without disaster, but that "nothing else would do it." This story threw a flood of light upon the dead man's struggle and on the stupid maladjustment which had broken him down. Why had we never been told? Why had our interest in the remarkable musical ability of his child blinded us to the hidden artistic ability of the father? We had forgotten that a long-established occupation may form the very foundations of the moral life, that the art with which a man has solaced his toil may be the salvation of his uncertain temperament.

There are many examples of touching fidelity to immigrant parents on the part of their grown children; a young man who day after day attends ceremonies which no longer express his religious convictions and who makes his vain effort to interest his Russian Jewish father in social problems; a daughter who might earn much more money as a stenographer could she work from Monday morning till Saturday night, but who quietly and docilely makes neckties for low wages because she can thus abstain from work Saturdays to please her father; these young people, like poor Maggie Tulliver, through many painful experiences have reached the conclusion that pity, memory, and faithfulness are natural ties with paramount claims.

This faithfulness, however, is sometimes ruthlessly imposed upon by immigrant parents who, eager for money and accustomed to the patriarchal authority of peasant households, hold their children in a stern bondage which requires a surrender of all their wages and concedes no time or money for pleasures.

There are many convincing illustrations that this parental harshness often results in juvenile delinquency. A Polish boy of seventeen came to Hull-House one day to ask a contribution of fifty cents "towards a flower piece for the funeral of an old Hull-House club boy." A few questions made it clear that the object was fictitious, whereupon the boy broke down and half-defiantly stated that he wanted to buy two twenty-five cent tickets, one for his girl and one for himself, to a dance of the Benevolent Social Twos; that he hadn't a penny of his own although he had worked in a brass foundry for three years and had been advanced twice, because he always had to give his pay envelope unopened to his father; "just look at the clothes he buys me" was his concluding remark.

Perhaps the girls are held even more rigidly. In a recent investigation of two hundred working girls it was found that only five per cent had the use of their own money and that sixty-two per cent turned in all they earned, literally every penny, to their mothers. It was through this little investigation that we first knew Marcella, a pretty young German girl who helped her widowed mother year after year to care for a large family of younger children. She was content for the most part although her mother's old-country notions of dress gave her but an infinitesimal amount of her own wages to spend on her clothes, and she was quite sophisticated as to proper dressing because she sold silk in a neighborhood department store. Her mother approved of the young man who was showing her various attentions and agreed that Marcella should accept his invitation to a ball, but would allow her not a penny toward a new gown to replace one impossibly plain and shabby. Marcella spent a sleepless night and wept bitterly, although she well knew that the doctor's bill for the children's scarlet fever was not yet paid. The next day as she was cutting off three yards of shining pink silk, the thought came to her that it would make her a fine new waist to wear to the ball. She wistfully saw it wrapped in paper and carelessly stuffed into the muff of the purchaser, when suddenly the parcel fell upon the floor. No one was looking and quick as a flash the girl picked it up and pushed it into her blouse. The theft was discovered by the relentless department store detective who, for "the sake of the example," insisted upon taking the case into court. The poor mother wept bitter tears over this downfall of her "frommes Mädchen" and no one had the heart to tell her of her own blindness.

I know a Polish boy whose earnings were all given to his father who gruffly refused all requests for pocket money. One Christmas his little sisters, having been told by their mother that they were too poor to have any Christmas presents, appealed to the big brother as to one who was earning money of his own. Flattered by the implication, but at the same time quite impecunious, the night before Christmas he nonchalantly walked through a neighboring department store and stole a manicure set for one little sister and a string of beads for the other. He was caught at the door by the house detective as one of those children whom each local department store arrests in the weeks before Christmas at the daily rate of eight to twenty. The youngest of these offenders are seldom taken into court but are either sent home with a warning or turned over to the officers of the Juvenile Protective Association. Most of these premature law breakers are in search of Americanized clothing and others are only looking for playthings. They are all distracted by the profusion and variety of the display, and their moral sense is confused by the general air of openhandedness.

These disastrous efforts are not unlike those of many younger children who are constantly arrested for petty thieving because they are too eager to take home food or fuel which will relieve the distress and need they so constantly hear discussed. The coal on the wagons, the vegetables displayed in front of the grocery shops, the very

wooden blocks in the loosened street paving are a challenge to their powers to help out at home. A Bohemian
boy who was out on parole from the old detention home of
the Juvenile Court itself brought back five stolen chickens
to the matron for Sunday dinner, saying that he knew the
Committee were "having a hard time to fill up so many
kids and perhaps these fowl would help out." The honest
immigrant parents, totally ignorant of American laws and
municipal regulations, often send a child to pick up coal on
the railroad tracks or to stand at three o'clock in the
morning before the side door of a restaurant which gives
away broken food, or to collect grain for the chickens at
the base of elevators and standing cars. The latter custom
accounts for the large number of boys arrested for breaking the seals on grain freight cars. It is easy for a child thus
trained to accept the proposition of a junk dealer to bring
him bars of iron stored in freight yards. Four boys quite
recently had thus carried away and sold to one man two
tons of iron.

Four fifths of the children brought into the Juvenile
Court in Chicago are the children of foreigners. The Germans are the greatest offenders, Polish next. Do their children suffer from the excess of virtue in those parents so
eager to own a house and lot? One often sees a grasping
parent in the court, utterly broken down when the Americanized youth who has been brought to grief clings as
piteously to his peasant father as if he were still a frightened little boy in the steerage.

Many of these children have come to grief through their
premature fling into city life, having thrown off parental
control as they have impatiently discarded foreign ways.
Boys of ten and twelve will refuse to sleep at home, pre-
ferring the freedom of an old brewery vault or an empty
warehouse to the obedience required by their parents, and
for days these boys will live on the milk and bread which
they steal from the back porches after the early morning
delivery. Such children complain that there is "no fun" at
home. One little chap who was given a vacant lot to cultivate by the City Garden Association insisted upon rais-
ing only popcorn and tried to present the entire crop to
Hull-House "to be used for the parties," with the stipulation that he would have "to be invited every single time."

Then there are little groups of dissipated young men who pride themselves upon their ability to live without working and who despise all the honest and sober ways of their immigrant parents. They are at once a menace and a center of demoralization. Certainly the bewildered parents, unable to speak English and ignorant of the city, whose children have disappeared for days or weeks, have often come to Hull-House, evincing that agony which fairly separates the marrow from the bone, as if they had discovered a new type of suffering, devoid of the healing in familiar sorrows. It is as if they did not know how to search for the children without the assistance of the children themselves. Perhaps the most pathetic aspect of such cases is their revelation of the premature dependence of the older and wiser upon the young and foolish, which is in itself often responsible for the situation because it has given the children an undue sense of their own importance and a false security that they can take care of themselves.

On the other hand, an Italian girl who has had lessons in cooking at the public school will help her mother to connect the entire family with American food and household habits. That the mother has never baked bread in Italy—only mixed it in her own house and then taken it out to the village oven—makes all the more valuable her daughter's understanding of the complicated cooking stove. The same thing is true of the girl who learns to sew in the public school, and more than anything else, perhaps, of the girl who receives the first simple instruction in the care of little children—that skillful care which every tenement-house baby requires if he is to be pulled through his second summer. As a result of this teaching I recall a young girl who carefully explained to her Italian mother that the reason the babies in Italy were so healthy and the babies in Chicago were so sickly, was not, as her mother had firmly insisted, because her babies in Italy had goat's milk and her babies in America had cow's milk, but because the milk in Italy was clean and the milk in Chicago was dirty. She said that when you milked your own goat before the door, you knew that the milk was clean, but when you bought milk from the grocery store after it had been carried for many miles in the country, you couldn't tell whether it was fit for the baby to drink until the men from the City

Hall who had watched it all the way said that it was all right.

Thus through civic instruction in the public schools, the Italian woman slowly became urbanized in the sense in which the word was used by her own Latin ancestors, and thus the habits of her entire family were modified. The public schools in the immigrant colonies deserve all the praise as Americanizing agencies which can be bestowed upon them, and there is little doubt that the fast-changing curriculum in the direction of the vacation-school experiments will react more directly upon such households.

It is difficult to write of the relation of the older and most foreign-looking immigrants to the children of other people—the Italians whose fruitcarts are upset simply because they are "dagoes" or the Russian peddlers who are stoned and sometimes badly injured because it has become a code of honor in a gang of boys to thus express their derision. The members of a Protective Association of Jewish Peddlers organized at Hull-House related daily experiences in which old age had been treated with such irreverence, cherished dignity with such disrespect, that a listener caught the passion of Lear in the old texts, as a platitude enunciated by a man who discovers in it his own experience thrills us as no unfamiliar phrases can possibly do. The Greeks are filled with amazed rage when their very name is flung at them as an opprobrious epithet. Doubtless these difficulties would be much minimized in America, if we faced our own race problem with courage and intelligence, and these very Mediterranean immigrants might give us valuable help. Certainly they are less conscious than the Anglo-Saxon of color distinctions, perhaps because of their traditional familiarity with Carthage and Egypt. They listened with respect and enthusiasm to a scholarly address delivered by Professor Du Bois at Hull-House on a Lincoln's birthday, with apparently no consciousness of that race difference which color seems to accentuate so absurdly, and upon my return from various conferences held in the interest of "the advancement of colored people," I have had many illuminating conversations with my cosmopolitan neighbors.

The celebration of national events has always been a source of new understanding and companionship with the

members of the contiguous foreign colonies not only between them and their American neighbors but between
them and their own children. One of our earliest Italian
events was a rousing commemoration of Garibaldi's birthday, and his imposing bust, presented to Hull-House that
evening, was long the chief ornament of our front hall.
It called forth great enthusiasm from the *connazionali*
whom Ruskin calls, not the "common people" of Italy,
but the "companion people" because of their power for
swift sympathy.

A huge Hellenic meeting held at Hull-House, in which
the achievements of the classic period were set forth both
in Greek and English by scholars of well-known repute,
brought us into a new sense of fellowship with all our
Greek neighbors. As the mayor of Chicago was seated
upon the right hand of the dignified senior priest of the
Greek Church and they were greeted alternately in the
national hymns of America and Greece, one felt a curious
sense of the possibility of transplanting to new and crude
Chicago some of the traditions of Athens itself, so deeply
cherished in the hearts of this group of citizens.

The Greeks indeed gravely consider their traditions as
their most precious possession and more than once in
meetings of protest held by the Greek colony against the
aggressions of the Bulgarians in Macedonia, I have heard
it urged that the Bulgarians are trying to establish a protectorate, not only for their immediate advantage, but that
they may claim a glorious history for the "barbarous country." It is said that on the basis of this protectorate, they
are already teaching in their schools that Alexander the
Great was a Bulgarian and that it will be but a short time
before they claim Aristotle himself, an indignity the Greeks
will never suffer!

To me personally the celebration of the hundredth anniversary of Mazzini's birth was a matter of great interest.
Throughout the world that day Italians who believed in a
United Italy came together. They recalled the hopes of
this man who, with all his devotion to his country was
still more devoted to humanity and who dedicated to
the workingmen of Italy an appeal so philosophical,
so filled with a yearning for righteousness, that it tran-
scended all national boundaries and became a bugle call

for "The Duties of Man." A copy of this document was given to every school child in the public schools of Italy on this one hundredth anniversary, and as the Chicago branch of the Society of Young Italy marched into our largest hall and presented to Hull-House an heroic bust of Mazzini, I found myself devoutly hoping that the Italian youth, who have committed their future to America, might indeed become "the Apostle of the fraternity of nations" and that our American citizenship might be built without disturbing these foundations which were laid of old time.

TOLSTOYISM

THE administration of charity in Chicago during the winter following the World's Fair had been of necessity most difficult, for, although large sums had been given to the temporary relief organization which endeavored to care for the thousands of destitute strangers stranded in the city, we all worked under a sense of desperate need and a paralyzing consciousness that our best efforts were most inadequate to the situation.

During the many relief visits I paid that winter in tenement houses and miserable lodgings, I was constantly shadowed by a certain sense of shame that I should be comfortable in the midst of such distress. This resulted at times in a curious reaction against all the educational and philanthropic activities in which I had been engaged. In the face of the desperate hunger and need, these could not but seem futile and superficial. The hard winter in Chicago had turned the thoughts of many of us to these stern matters. A young friend of mine who came daily to Hull-House consulted me in regard to going into the paper warehouse belonging to her father that she might there sort rags with the Polish girls; another young girl took a place in a sweatshop for

a month, doing her work so simply and thoroughly that
the proprietor had no notion that she had not been
driven there by need; still two others worked in a shoe
factory;—and all this happened before such adventures
were undertaken in order to procure literary material.
It was in the following winter that the pioneer effort in
this direction, Walter Wyckoff's account of his vain attempt to find work in Chicago, compelled even the
sternest businessman to drop his assertion that "any
man can find work if he wants it."

The dealing directly with the simplest human wants
may have been responsible for an impression which I
carried about with me almost constantly for a period
of two years and which culminated finally in a visit to
Tolstoy—that the Settlement, or Hull-House at least,
was a mere pretense and travesty of the simple impulse
"to live with the poor," so long as the residents did not
share the common lot of hard labor and scant fare.

Actual experience had left me in much the same state
of mind I had been in after reading Tolstoy's *What to
Do,* which is a description of his futile efforts to relieve
the unspeakable distress and want in the Moscow winter
of 1881, and his inevitable conviction that only he who
literally shares his own shelter and food with the needy
can claim to have served them.

Doubtless it is much easier to see "what to do" in
rural Russia, where all the conditions tend to make the
contrast as broad as possible between peasant labor and
noble idleness, than it is to see "what to do" in the in-
terdependencies of the modern industrial city. But for
that very reason perhaps, Tolstoy's clear statement is
valuable for that type of conscientious person in every
land who finds it hard, not only to walk in the path of
righteousness, but to discover where the path lies.

I had read the books of Tolstoy steadily all the
years since *My Religion* had come into my hands immediately after I left college. The reading of that book
had made clear that men's poor little efforts to do right
are put forth for the most part in the chill of self-dis-
trust; I became convinced that if the new social order
ever came, it would come by gathering to itself all the
pathetic human endeavor which had indicated the for-

ward direction. But I was most eager to know whether Tolstoy's undertaking to do his daily share of the physical labor of the world, that labor which is "so disproportionate to the unnourished strength" of those by whom it is ordinarily performed, had brought him peace!

I had time to review carefully many things in my mind during the long days of convalescence following an illness of typhoid fever which I suffered in the autumn of 1895. The illness was so prolonged that my health was most unsatisfactory during the following winter, and the next May I went abroad with my friend, Miss Smith, to effect if possible a more complete recovery.

The prospect of seeing Tolstoy filled me with the hope of finding a clue to the tangled affairs of city poverty. I was but one of thousands of our contemporaries who were turning toward this Russian, not as to a seer —his message is much too confused and contradictory for that—but as to a man who has had the ability to lift his life to the level of his conscience, to translate his theories into action.

Our first few weeks in England were most stimulating. A dozen years ago London still showed traces of "that exciting moment in the life of the nation when its youth is casting about for new enthusiasms," but it evinced still more of that British capacity to perform the hard work of careful research and self-examination which must precede any successful experiments in social reform. Of the varied groups and individuals whose suggestions remained with me for years, I recall perhaps as foremost those members of the new London County Council whose far-reaching plans for the betterment of London could not but enkindle enthusiasm. It was a most striking expression of that effort which would place beside the refinement and pleasure of the rich, a new refinement and a new pleasure born of the commonwealth and the common joy of all the citizens, that at this moment they prized the municipal pleasure boats upon the Thames no less than the extensive schemes for the municipal housing of the poorest people. Ben Tillet, who was then an alderman, "the docker sitting beside the duke," took me in a rowboat down the Thames on a journey made exciting by the hundreds of dockers who cheered him as we passed one wharf after another on our way to his home at Greenwich; John Burns showed us his wonderful civic accomplishments at Battersea, the plant turning street sweepings into cement pavements, the technical school teaching boys brick laying and plumbing, and the public bath in which the children of the Board School were receiving a swimming lesson—these measures anticipating our achievements in Chicago by at least a decade and a half. The new Education Bill which was destined to drag on for twelve years before it developed into the children's charter, was then a storm center in the House of Commons. Miss Smith and I were much pleased to be taken to tea on the Parliament terrace by its author, Sir John Gorst, although we were quite bewildered by the arguments we heard there for church schools *versus* secular.

We heard Keir Hardie before a large audience of workingmen standing in the open square of Canning Town outline the great things to be accomplished by the then new Labor Party, and we joined the vast body of men in the booming hymn

> When wilt Thou save the people,
> O God of Mercy, when!

finding it hard to realize that we were attending a political meeting. It seemed that moment as if the hopes of democracy were more likely to come to pass on English soil than upon our own. Robert Blatchford's stirring pamphlets were in everyone's hands, and a reception given by Karl Marx's daughter, Mrs. Aveling, to Liebknecht before he returned to Germany to serve a prison term for his *lèse majesté* speech in the Reichstag, gave us a glimpse of the old-fashioned orthodox Socialist who had not yet begun to yield to the biting ridicule of Bernard Shaw, although he flamed in their midst that evening.

Octavia Hill kindly demonstrated to us the principles upon which her well-founded business of rent collecting was established, and with pardonable pride showed us the Red Cross Square with its cottages marvelously picturesque and comfortable, on two sides, and on the third a public hall and common drawing room for the use of all the tenants; the interior of the latter had been decorated by pupils of Walter Crane with mural frescoes portraying the heroism in the life of the modern workingman.

While all this was warmly human, we also had opportunities to see something of a group of men and women who were approaching the social problem from the study of economics; among others Mr. and Mrs. Sidney Webb who were at work on their Industrial Democracy; Mr. John Hobson who was lecturing on the evolution of modern capitalism.

We followed factory inspectors on a round of duties performed with a thoroughness and a trained intelligence which were a revelation of the possibilities of public service. When it came to visiting Settlements, we were at least reassured that they were not falling into identical lines of effort. Canon Ingram, who has since become Bishop of London, was then warden of Oxford House and in the midst of an experiment which pleased me greatly, the more because it was carried on by a churchman. Oxford House had hired all the concert halls—vaudeville shows we later called them in Chicago—which were found in Bethnal Green, for every Saturday night. The residents had censored the programs, which they were careful to keep popular, and any workingman who attended a show in Bethnal Green on a Saturday night, and thousands of them did, heard a program the better for this effort.

One evening in University Hall Mrs. Humphry Ward, who had just returned from Italy, described the effect of the Italian salt tax in a talk which was evidently one in a series of lectures upon the economic wrongs which pressed heaviest upon the poor; at Browning House, at the moment, they were giving prizes to those of their costermonger neighbors who could present the best cared-for-donkeys, and the warden, Herbert Stead, exhibited almost the enthusiasm of his well-known brother, for that crop of kindliness which can be garnered most easily from the acreage where human beings grow the thickest; at the Bermondsey Settlement they were rejoicing that their University Extension students had successfully passed the examinations for the University of London. The entire impression received in England of research, of scholarship, of organized public spirit, was in marked contrast to the impressions of my next visit in 1900, when the South African War had absorbed the enthusiasm of the nation and the wrongs at "the heart of the empire" were disregarded and neglected.

London, of course, presented sharp differences to Russia where social conditions were written in black and white with little shading, like a demonstration of the Chinese proverb, "Where one man lives in luxury, another is dying of hunger."

The fair of Nijni-Novgorod seemed to take us to the very edge of civilization so remote and eastern that the merchants brought their curious goods upon the backs of camels or on strange craft riding at anchor on the broad Volga. But even here our letter of introduction to Korolenko, the novelist, brought us to a realization of that strange mingling of a remote past and a self-conscious present which Russia presents on every hand. This same contrast was also shown by the pilgrims trudging on pious errands to monasteries, to tombs, and to the Holy Land itself, with their bleeding feet bound in rags and thrust into bast sandals, and, on the other hand, by the revolutionists even then advocating a Republic which should obtain not only in political but also in industrial affairs.

We had letters of introduction to Mr. and Mrs. Aylmer Maude of Moscow, since well known as the translators of *Resurrection* and other of Tolstoy's later works, who at that moment were on the eve of leaving Russia in order to form an agricultural colony in South England where they might support themselves by the labor of their hands. We gladly accepted Mr. Maude's offer to take us to Yasnaya Polyana and to introduce us to Count Tolstoy, and never did a disciple journey toward his master with more enthusiasm than did our guide. When, however, Mr. Maude actually presented Miss Smith and myself to Count Tolstoy, knowing well his master's attitude toward philanthropy, he endeavored to make Hull-House appear much more noble and unique than I should have ventured to do.

Tolstoy, standing by clad in his peasant garb, listened gravely but, glancing distrustfully at the sleeves of my traveling gown which unfortunately at that season were monstrous in size, he took hold of an edge and pulling out one sleeve to an interminable breadth, said quite simply that "there was enough stuff on one arm to make a frock for a little girl," and asked me directly if I did not find "such a dress" a "barrier to the people." I was too disconcerted to make a very clear explanation, although I tried to say that monstrous as my sleeves were they did not compare in size with those of the working girls in Chicago and that nothing would more effectively separate me from "the people" than a cotton blouse following the simple lines of the human form; even if I had wished to imitate him and "dress as a peasant," it would have been hard to choose which peasant among the thirty-six nationalities we had recently counted in our ward. Fortunately the countess came to my rescue with a recital of her former attempts to clothe hypothetical little girls in yards of material cut from a train and other superfluous parts of her best gown until she had been driven to a firm stand which she advised me to take at once. But neither Countess Tolstoy nor any other friend was on hand to help me out of my predicament later, when I was asked who "fed" me, and how did I obtain "shelter"? Upon my reply that a farm a hundred miles from Chicago supplied me with the necessities of life, I fairly anticipated the next scathing question: "So you are an absentee landlord? Do you think you will help the people more by adding yourself to the crowded city than you would by tilling your own soil?" This new sense of discomfort over a failure to till my own soil was increased when Tolstoy's second daughter appeared at the five-o'clock tea table set under the trees, coming straight from the harvest field where she had been working with a group of peasants since five o'clock in the morning, not pretending to work but really taking the place of a peasant woman who had hurt her foot. She was plainly much exhausted, but neither expected nor received sym-

pathy from the members of a family who were quite
accustomed to see each other carry out their convictions in spite of discomfort and fatigue. The martyrdom
of discomfort, however, was obviously much easier to
bear than that to which, even to the eyes of the casual
visitor, Count Tolstoy daily subjected himself, for his
study in the basement of the conventional dwelling,
with its short shelf of battered books and its scythe and
spade leaning against the wall, had many times lent
itself to that ridicule which is the most difficult form
of martyrdom.

That summer evening as we sat in the garden with
a group of visitors from Germany, from England and
America, who had traveled to the remote Russian village that they might learn of this man, one could not
forbear the constant inquiry to one's self, as to why he
was so regarded as sage and saint that this party of
people should be repeated each day of the year. It
seemed to me then that we were all attracted by this
sermon of the deed, because Tolstoy had made the one
supreme personal effort, one might almost say the one
frantic personal effort, to put himself into right relations
with the humblest people, with the men who tilled his soil,
blacked his boots, and cleaned his stables. Doubtless
the heaviest burden of our contemporaries is a consciousness of a divergence between our democratic theory on
the one hand, that working people have a right to the
intellectual resources of society, and the actual fact on
the other hand, that thousands of them are so over-
burdened with toil that there is no leisure nor energy
left for the cultivation of the mind. We constantly suffer
from the strain and indecision of believing this theory
and acting as if we did not believe it, and this man
who years before had tried "to get off the backs of the
peasants," who had at least simplified his life and worked
with his hands, had come to be a prototype to many of
his generation.

Doubtless all of the visitors sitting in the Tolstoy
garden that evening had excused themselves from laboring with their hands upon the theory that they were doing something more valuable for society in other ways.
No one among our contemporaries has dissented from

this point of view so violently as Tolstoy himself, and yet no man might so easily have excused himself from hard and rough work on the basis of his genius and of his intellectual contributions to the world. So far, however, from considering his time too valuable to be spent in labor in the field or in making shoes, our great host was too eager to know life to be willing to give up this companionship of mutual labor. One instinctively found reasons why it was easier for a Russian than for the rest of us to reach this conclusion; the Russian peasants have a proverb which says: "Labor is the house that love lives in," by which they mean that no two people nor group of people can come into affectionate relations with each other unless they carry on together a mutual task, and when the Russian peasant talks of labor he means labor on the soil, or, to use the phrase of the great peasant, Bondereff, "bread labor." Those monastic orders founded upon agricultural labor, those philosophical experiments like Brook Farm and many another have attempted to reduce to action this same truth. Tolstoy himself has written many times his own convictions and attempts in this direction, perhaps never more tellingly than in the description of Levin's morning spent in the harvest field, when he lost his sense of grievance and isolation and felt a strange new brotherhood for the peasants, in proportion as the rhythmic motion of his scythe became one with theirs.

At the long dinner table laid in the garden were the various traveling guests, the grown-up daughters, and the younger children with their governess. The countess presided over the usual European dinner served by men, but the count and the daughter, who had worked all day in the fields, ate only porridge and black bread and drank only kvas, the fare of the hay-making peasants. Of course we are all accustomed to the fact that those who perform the heaviest labor eat the coarsest and simplest fare at the end of the day, but it is not often that we sit at the same table with them while we ourselves eat the more elaborate food prepared by someone else's labor. Tolstoy ate his simple supper without remark or comment upon the food his family and guests

preferred to eat, assuming that they, as well as he, had
settled the matter with their own consciences.

The Tolstoy household that evening was much interested in the fate of a young Russian spy who had
recently come to Tolstoy in the guise of a country school-
master, in order to obtain a copy of "Life," which had
been interdicted by the censor of the press. After spending the night in talk with Tolstoy, the spy had gone
away with a copy of the forbidden manuscript but, unfortunately for himself, having become converted to Tolstoy's views he had later made a full confession to the
authorities and had been exiled to Siberia. Tolstoy, holding
that it was most unjust to exile the disciple while he, the
author of the book, remained at large, had pointed out
this inconsistency in an open letter to one of the Moscow
newspapers. The discussion of this incident, of course,
opened up the entire subject of nonresidence, and curiously enough I was disappointed in Tolstoy's position in the
matter. It seemed to me that he made too great a distinction between the use of physical force and that moral
energy which can override another's differences and
scruples with equal ruthlessness.

With that inner sense of mortification with which one
finds one's self at difference with the great authority, I
recalled the conviction of the early Hull-House residents; that whatever of good the Settlement had to
offer should be put into positive terms, that we might
live with opposition to no man, with recognition of the
good in every man, even the most wretched. We had
often departed from this principle, but had it not in
every case been a confession of weakness, and had we
not always found antagonism a foolish and unwarrant-
able expenditure of energy?

The conversation at dinner and afterward, although
conducted with animation and sincerity, for the moment
stirred vague misgivings within me. Was Tolstoy more
logical than life warrants? Could the wrongs of life be
reduced to the terms of unrequited labor and all be
made right if each person performed the amount necessary to satisfy his own wants? Was it not always easy
to put up a strong case if one took the naturalistic view

of life? But what about the historic view, the inevitable shadings and modifications which life itself brings to its own interpretation? Miss Smith and I took a night train back to Moscow in that tumult of feeling which is always produced by contact with a conscience making one more of those determined efforts to probe to the very foundations of the mysterious world in which we find ourselves. A horde of perplexing questions, concerning those problems of existence of which in happier moments we catch but fleeting glimpses and at which we even then stand aghast, pursued us relentlessly on the long journey through the great wheat plains of South Russia, through the crowded Ghetto of Warsaw, and finally into the smiling fields of Germany where the peasant men and women were harvesting the grain. I remember that through the sight of those toiling peasants, I made a curious connection between the bread labor advocated by Tolstoy and the comfort the harvest fields are said to have once brought to Luther when, much perturbed by many theological difficulties, he suddenly forgot them all in a gush of gratitude for mere bread, exclaiming, "How it stands, that golden yellow corn, on its fine tapered stem; the meek earth, at God's kind bidding, has produced it once again!" At least the toiling poor had this comfort of bread labor, and perhaps it did not matter that they gained it unknowingly and painfully, if only they walked in the path of labor. In the exercise of that curious power possessed by the theorist to inhibit all experiences which do not enhance his doctrine, I did not permit myself to recall that which I knew so well—that exigent and unremitting labor grants the poor no leisure even in the supreme moments of human suffering and that "all griefs are lighter with bread."

I may have wished to secure this solace for myself at the cost of the least possible expenditure of time and energy, for during the next month in Germany, when I read everything of Tolstoy's that had been translated into English, German, or French, there grew up in my mind a conviction that what I ought to do upon my return to Hull-House was to spend at least two hours every morning in the little bakery which we

had recently added to the equipment of our coffeehouse. Two hours' work would be but a wretched compromise, but it was hard to see how I could take more
time out of each day. I had been taught to bake bread
in my childhood not only as a household accomplish-
ment, but because my father, true to his miller's tradition, had insisted that each one of his daughters on
her twelfth birthday must present him with a satisfactory
wheat loaf of her own baking, and he was most exigent
as to the quality of this test loaf. What could be more
in keeping with my training and tradition than baking
bread? I did not quite see how my activity would fit in
with that of the German union baker who presided over
the Hull-House bakery, but all such matters were sec-
ondary and certainly could be arranged. It may be that
I had thus to pacify my aroused conscience before I
could settle down to hear Wagner's "Ring" at Beyreuth;
it may be that I had fallen a victim to the phrase,
"bread labor"; but at any rate I held fast to the belief
that I should do this, through the entire journey home-
ward, on land and sea, until I actually arrived in Chicago when suddenly the whole scheme seemed to me as
utterly preposterous as it doubtless was. The half dozen
people invariably waiting to see me after breakfast, the
piles of letters to be opened and answered, the demand
of actual and pressing human wants—were these all to
be pushed aside and asked to wait while I saved my
soul by two hours' work at baking bread?

Although my resolution was abandoned, this may be
the best place to record the efforts of more doughty
souls to carry out Tolstoy's conclusions. It was perhaps
inevitable that Tolstoy colonies should be founded, although Tolstoy himself has always insisted that each
man should live his life as nearly as possible in the
place in which he was born. The visit Miss Smith and
I made a year or two later to a colony in one of the
southern States portrayed for us most vividly both the
weakness and the strange august dignity of the Tolstoy
position. The colonists at Commonwealth held but a
short creed. They claimed in fact that the difficulty is
not to state truth but to make moral conviction opera-
tive upon actual life, and they announced it their inten-

tion "to obey the teachings of Jesus in all matters of labor and the use of property." They would thus transfer the vindication of creed from the church to the open field, from dogma to experience.

The day Miss Smith and I visited the Commonwealth colony of threescore souls, they were erecting a house for the family of a one-legged man, consisting of a wife and nine children who had come the week before in a forlorn prairie schooner from Arkansas. As this was the largest family the little colony contained, the new house was to be the largest yet erected. Upon our surprise at this literal giving "to him that asketh," we inquired if the policy of extending food and shelter to all who applied, without test of creed or ability, might not result in the migration of all the neighboring poorhouse population into the colony. We were told that this actually had happened during the winter until the colony fare of corn meal and cow peas had proved so unattractive that the paupers had gone back, for even the poorest of the southern poorhouses occasionally supplied bacon with the pone if only to prevent scurvy from which the colonists themselves had suffered. The difficulty of the poorhouse people had thus settled itself by the sheer poverty of the situation, a poverty so biting that the only ones willing to face it were those sustained by a conviction of its righteousness. The fields and gardens were being worked by an editor, a professor, a clergyman, as well as by artisans and laborers, the fruit thereof to be eaten by themselves and their families or by any other families who might arrive from Arkansas. The colonists were very conventional in matters of family relationship and had broken with society only in regard to the conventions pertaining to labor and property. We had a curious experience at the end of the day, when we were driven into the nearest town. We had taken with us as a guest the wife of the president of the colony, wishing to give her a dinner at the hotel, because she had girlishly exclaimed during a conversation that at times during the winter she had become so eager to hear good music that it had seemed to her as if she were actually hungry for it, almost as hungry as she was for a beefsteak. Yet as we drove away we had the curious sensation that while the experiment was obviously coming to an end, in the midst of its privations it yet embodied the peace of mind which comes to him who insists upon the logic of life whether it is reasonable or not—the fanatic's joy in seeing his own formula translated into action. At any rate, as we reached the commonplace southern town of workaday men and women, for one moment its substantial buildings, its solid brick churches, its ordered streets, divided into those of the rich and those of the poor, seemed much more unreal to us than the little struggling colony we had left behind. We repeated to each other that in all the practical judgments and decisions of life, we must part company with logical demonstration; that if we stop for it in each case, we can never go on at all; and yet, in spite of this, when conscience does become the dictator of the daily life of a group of men, it forces our admiration as no other modern spectacle has power to do. It seemed but a mere incident that this group should have lost sight of the facts of life in their earnest endeavor to put to the test the things of the spirit.

I knew little about the colony started by Mr. Maude at Purleigh containing several of Tolstoy's followers who were not permitted to live in Russia, and we did not see Mr. Maude again until he came to Chicago on his way from Manitoba, whither he had transported the second group of Dukhobors, a religious sect who had interested all of Tolstoy's followers because of their literal acceptance of nonresistance and other Christian doctrines which are so strenuously advocated by Tolstoy. It was for their benefit that Tolstoy had finished and published "Resurrection," breaking through his long-kept resolution against novel writing. After the Dukhobors were settled in Canada, of the five hundred dollars left from the "Resurrection" funds, one-half was given to Hull-House. It seemed possible to spend this fund only for the relief of the most primitive wants of food and shelter on the part of the most needy families.

☙ ☙ *Chapter* 13

PUBLIC ACTIVITIES AND
INVESTIGATIONS

ONE of the striking features of our neighborhood twenty years ago, and one to which we never became reconciled, was the presence of huge wooden garbage boxes fastened to the street pavement in which the undisturbed refuse accumulated day by day. The system of garbage collecting was inadequate throughout the city but it became the greatest menace in a ward such as ours, where the normal amount of waste was much increased by the decayed fruit and vegetables discarded by the Italian and Greek fruit peddlers, and by the residuum left over from the piles of filthy rags which were fished out of the city dumps and brought to the homes of the rag pickers for further sorting and washing.

The children of our neighborhood twenty years ago played their games in and around these huge garbage boxes. They were the first objects that the toddling child learned to climb; their bulk afforded a barricade and their contents provided missiles in all the battles of the older boys; and finally they became the seats upon which absorbed lovers held enchanted converse. We are obliged to remember that all children eat everything which they find and that odors have a curious and intimate power of

Rear Tenement in Hull-House Neighborhood

entwining themselves into our tenderest memories, before even the residents of Hull-House can understand their own early enthusiasm for the removal of these boxes and the establishment of a better system of refuse collection.

It is easy for even the most conscientious citizen of Chicago to forget the foul smells of the stockyards and the garbage dumps, when he is living so far from them that he is only occasionally made conscious of their existence, but the residents of a Settlement are perforce constantly surrounded by them. During our first three years on Halsted Street, we had established a small incinerator at Hull-House and we had many times reported the untoward conditions of the ward to the city hall. We had also arranged many talks for the immigrants, pointing out that although a woman may sweep her own doorway in her native village and allow the refuse to innocently decay in the open air and sunshine, in a crowded city quarter, if the garbage is not properly collected and destroyed, a tenement-house mother may see her children sicken and die, and that the immigrants must therefore not only keep their own houses clean, but must also help the authorities to keep the city clean.

Possibly our efforts slightly modified the worst conditions, but they still remained intolerable, and the fourth summer the situation became for me absolutely desperate when I realized in a moment of panic that my delicate little nephew for whom I was guardian could not be with me at Hull-House at all unless the sickening odors were reduced. I may well be ashamed that other delicate children who were torn from their families, not into boarding school but into eternity, had not long before driven me into effective action. Under the direction of the first man who came as a resident to Hull-House we began a systematic investigation of the city system of garbage collection, both as to its efficiency in other wards and its possible connection with the death rate in the various wards of the city.

The Hull-House Woman's Club had been organized the year before by the resident kindergartner who had first inaugurated a mothers' meeting. The members came together, however, in quite a new way that summer when we discussed with them the high death rate so persistent in our ward. After several club meetings devoted to the subject, despite the fact that the death rate rose highest in the congested foreign colonies and not in the streets in which most of the Irish American club women lived, twelve of their number undertook in connection with the residents, to carefully investigate the condition of the alleys. During August and September the substantiated reports of violations of the law sent in from Hull-House to the health department were one thousand and thirty-seven.

For the club woman who had finished a long day's work of washing or ironing followed by the cooking of a hot supper, it would have been much easier to sit on her doorstep during a summer evening than to go up and down ill-kept alleys and get into trouble with her neighbors over the condition of their garbage boxes. It required both civic enterprise and moral conviction to be willing to do this three evenings a week during the hottest and most uncomfortable months of the year. Nevertheless, a certain number of women persisted, as did the residents, and three city inspectors in succession were transferred from the ward because of unsatisfactory services. Still the death rate remained high and the condition seemed little improved throughout the next winter. In sheer desperation, the following spring when the city contracts were awarded for the removal of garbage, with the backing of two well-known business men, I put in a bid for the garbage removal of the nineteenth ward. My paper was thrown out on a technicality but the incident induced the mayor to appoint me the garbage inspector of the ward.

The salary was a thousand dollars a year, and the loss of that political "plum" made a great stir among the politicians. The position was no sinecure whether regarded from the point of view of getting up at six in the morning to see that the men were early at work; or of following the loaded wagons, uneasily dropping their contents at intervals, to their dreary destination at the dump; or of insisting that the contractor must increase the number of his wagons from nine to thirteen and from thirteen to seventeen, although he assured me that he lost money on every one and that the former inspector had let him off with seven; or of taking careless landlords into court because they would not provide the proper garbage receptacles; or of arresting the tenant who tried to make the garbage wagons carry away the contents of his stable.

With the two or three residents who nobly stood by, we set up six of those doleful incinerators which are supposed to burn garbage with the fuel collected in the alley itself. The one factory in town which could utilize old tin cans was a window weight factory, and we deluged that with ten times as many tin cans as it could use—much less would pay for. We made desperate attempts to have the dead animals removed by the contractor who was paid most liberally by the city for that purpose but who, we slowly discovered, always made the police ambulances do the work, delivering the carcasses upon freight cars for shipment to a soap factory in Indiana where they were sold for a good price although the contractor himself was the largest stockholder in the concern. Perhaps our greatest achievement was the discovery of a pavement eighteen inches under the surface in a narrow street, although after it was found we triumphantly discovered a record of its existence in the city archives. The Italians living on the street were much interested but displayed little astonishment, perhaps because they were accustomed to see buried cities exhumed. This pavement became the *casus belli* between myself and the street commissioner when I insisted that its restoration belonged to him, after I had removed the first eight inches of garbage. The matter was finally settled by the mayor himself, who permitted me to drive him to the entrance of the street in what the children called my "garbage phaëton" and who took my side of the controversy.

A graduate of the University of Wisconsin, who had done some excellent volunteer inspection in both Chicago and Pittsburgh, became my deputy and performed the work in a most thoroughgoing manner for three years. During the last two she was under the regime of civil service, for in 1895, to the great joy of many citizens, the Illinois legislature made that possible.

Many of the foreign-born women of the ward were much shocked by this abrupt departure into the ways of men, and it took a great deal of explanation to convey the idea even remotely that if it were a womanly task to go about in tenement houses in order to nurse the sick, it might be quite as womanly to go through the same district in order to prevent the breeding of so-called "filth diseases." While some of the women enthusiastically approved the slowly changing conditions and saw that their housewifely duties logically extended to the adjacent alleys and streets, they yet were quite certain that "it was not a lady's job." A revelation of this attitude was made one day in a conversation which the inspector heard vigorously carried on in a laundry. One of the employees was leaving and was expressing her mind concerning the place in no measured terms, summing up her contempt for it as follows: "I would rather be the girl who goes about in the alleys than to stay here any longer!"

And yet the spectacle of eight hours' work for eight hours' pay, the even-handed justice to all citizens irrespective of "pull," the dividing of responsibility between landlord and tenant, and the readiness to enforce obedience to law from both, was, perhaps, one of the most valuable demonstrations which could have been made. Such daily living on the part of the office holder is of infinitely more value than many talks on civics for, after all, we credit most easily that which we see. The careful inspection, combined with other causes, brought about a great improvement in the cleanliness and comfort of the neighborhood and one happy day, when the death rate of our ward was found to have dropped from third to seventh in the list of city wards and was so reported to our Woman's Club, the applause which followed recorded the genuine sense of participation in the result, and a public spirit which had "made good." But the cleanliness of the ward was becoming much too popular to suit our all-powerful alderman and, although we felt fatuously secure under the regime of civil service, he found a way to circumvent us by eliminating the position altogether. He introduced an ordinance into the city council which combined the collection of refuse with the cleaning and repairing of the streets, the whole to be placed under a ward superintendent. The office of course was to be filled under civil service regulations but only men were eligible to the examination. Although this latter regulation was afterward modified in favor of one woman, it was retained long enough to put the nineteenth ward inspector out of office.

Of course our experience in inspecting only made us more conscious of the wretched housing conditions over which we had been distressed from the first. It was during the World's Fair summer that one of the Hull-House residents in a public address upon housing reform used as an example of indifferent landlordism a large block in the neighborhood occupied by small tenements and stables unconnected with a street sewer, as was much similar property in the vicinity. In the lecture the resident spared neither a description of the property nor the name of the owner. The young man who owned the property was justly indignant at this public method of attack and promptly came to investigate the condition of the property. Together we made a careful tour of the houses and stables and in the face of the conditions that we found there, I could not but agree with him that supplying South Italian peasants with sanitary appliances seemed a difficult undertaking. Nevertheless he was unwilling that the block should remain in its deplorable state, and he finally cut through the dilemma with the rash proposition that he would give a free lease of the entire tract to Hull-House, accompanying the offer, however, with the warning remark, that if we should choose to use the income from the rents in sanitary improvements we should be throwing our money away.

Even when we decided that the houses were so bad that we could not undertake the task of improving them, he was game and stuck to his proposition that we should have a free lease. We finally submitted a plan that the houses should be torn down and the entire tract turned into a playground, although cautious advisers intimated that it would be very inconsistent to ask for subscriptions for the support of Hull-House when we were known to have thrown away an income of two thousand dollars a year. We, however, felt that a spectacle of inconsistency was better than one of bad landlordism and so the worst of the houses were demolished, the best three were sold and moved across the street under careful provision that they might never be used for junk-shops or saloons, and a public playground was finally established. Hull-House became responsible for its management for ten years, at the end of which time it was turned over to the City Playground Commission, although from the first the city detailed a policeman who was responsible for its general order and who became a valued adjunct of the House.

During fifteen years this public-spirited owner of the property paid all the taxes, and when the block was finally sold he made possible the playground equipment of a nearby schoolyard. On the other hand, the dispossessed tenants, a group of whom had to be evicted by legal process before their houses could be torn down, have never ceased to mourn their former estates. Only the other day I met upon the street an old Italian harness maker, who said that he had never succeeded so well anywhere else nor found a place that "seemed so much like Italy."

Festivities of various sorts were held on this early playground, always a May day celebration with its Maypole dance and its May queen. I remember that one year the honor of being queen was offered to the little girl who should pick up the largest number of scraps of paper which littered all the streets and alleys. The children that spring had been organized into a league, and each member had been provided with a stiff piece of wire upon the sharpened point of which stray bits of paper were impaled and later soberly counted off into a large box in the Hull-House alley. The little Italian girl who thus won the scepter took it very gravely as the just reward of hard labor, and we were all so absorbed in the desire for clean and tidy streets that we were wholly oblivious to the incongruity of thus selecting "the queen of love and beauty."

It was at the end of the second year that we received a visit from the warden of Toynbee Hall and his wife, as they were returning to England from a journey around the world. They had lived in East London for many years, and had been identified with the public movements for its betterment. They were much shocked that, in a new country with conditions still plastic and hopeful, so little attention had been paid to experiments and methods of amelioration which had already been tried; and they looked in vain through our library for blue books and governmental reports which recorded painstaking study into the conditions of English cities.

They were the first of a long line of English visitors to express the conviction that many things in Chicago were untoward not through paucity of public spirit but through a lack of political machinery adapted to modern city life. This was not all of the situation but perhaps no casual visitor could be expected to see that these matters of detail seemed unimportant to a city in the first flush of youth, impatient of correction and convinced that all would be well with its future. The most obvious faults were those connected with the congested housing of the immigrant population, nine tenths of them from the country, who carried on all sorts of traditional activities in the crowded tenements. That a group of Greeks should be permitted to slaughter sheep in a basement, that Italian women should be allowed to sort over rags collected from the city dumps, not only within the city limits but in a court swarming with little children, that immigrant bakers should continue unmolested to bake bread for their neighbors in

An Alley Near Hull-House

unspeakably filthy spaces under the pavement, appeared incredible to visitors accustomed to careful city regulations. I recall two visits made to the Italian quarter by John Burns—the second, thirteen years after the first. During the latter visit it seemed to him unbelievable that a certain house owned by a rich Italian should have been permitted to survive. He remembered with the greatest minuteness the positions of the houses on the court, with the exact space between the front and rear tenements, and he asked at once whether we had been able to cut a window into a dark hall as he had recommended thirteen years before. Although we were obliged to confess that the landlord would not permit the window to be cut, we were able to report that a City Homes Association had existed for ten years; that following a careful study of tenement conditions in Chicago, the text of which had been written by a Hull-House resident, the association had obtained the enactment of a model tenement-house code, and that their secretary had carefully watched the administration of the law for years so that its operation might not be minimized by the granting of too many exceptions in the city council. Our progress still seemed slow to Mr. Burns because in Chicago the actual houses were quite unchanged, embodying features long since declared illegal in London. Only this year could we have reported to him, had he again come to challenge us, that the provisions of the law had at last been extended to existing houses and that a conscientious corps of inspectors under an efficient chief were fast remedying the most glaring evils, while a band of nurses and doctors were following hard upon the "trail of the white hearse."

The mere consistent enforcement of existing laws and efforts to their advance often placed Hull-House, at least temporarily, into strained relations with its neighbors. I recall a continuous warfare against local landlords who would move wrecks of old houses as a nucleus for new ones in order to evade the provisions of the building code, and a certain Italian neighbor who was filled with bitterness because his new rear tenement was discovered to be illegal. It seemed impossible to make him understand that the health of the tenants was in any wise as important as his undisturbed rents.

Nevertheless many evils constantly arise in Chicago from congested housing which wiser cities forestall and prevent; the inevitable boarders crowded into a dark tenement already too small for the use of the immigrant family occupying it; the surprisingly large number of delinquent girls who have become criminally involved with their own fathers and uncles; the school children who cannot find a quiet spot in which to read or study and who perforce go into the streets each evening; the tuberculosis superinduced and fostered by the inadequate rooms and breathing spaces. One of the Hull-House residents, under the direction of a Chicago physician who stands high as an authority on tuberculosis and who devotes a large proportion of his time to our vicinity, made an investigation into housing conditions as related to tuberculosis with a result as startling as that of the "lung block" in New York.

It is these subtle evils of wretched and inadequate housing which are often most disastrous. In the summer of 1902 during an epidemic of typhoid fever in which our ward, although containing but one thirty-sixth of the population of the city, registered one sixth of the total number of deaths, two of the Hull-House residents made an investigation of the methods of plumbing in the houses adjacent to conspicuous groups of fever cases. They discovered among the people who had been exposed to the infection a widow who had lived in the ward for a number of years, in a comfortable little house of her own. Although the Italian immigrants were closing in all around her, she was not willing to sell her property and to move away until she had finished the education of her children. In the meantime she held herself quite aloof from her Italian neighbors and could never be drawn into any of the public efforts to secure a better code of tenement-house sanitation. Her two daughters were sent to an eastern college. One June when one of them had graduated and the other still had two years before she took her degree, they came to the spotless little house and to their self-sacrificing mother for the summer holiday. They both fell ill with typhoid fever and one daughter died because the mother's utmost efforts could not keep the infection out of her own house. The entire disaster affords, perhaps, a fair illustration of the futility of the individual conscience which would isolate a family from the rest of the community and its interests.

The careful information collected concerning the juxaposition of the typhoid cases to the various systems of plumbing and nonplumbing was made the basis of a bacteriological study by another resident, Dr. Alice Hamilton, as to the possibility of the infection having been carried by flies. Her researches were so convincing that they have been incorporated into the body of scientific data supporting that theory, but there were also practical results from the investigation. It was discovered that the wretched sanitary appliances through which alone the infection could have become so widely spread would not have been permitted to remain, unless the city inspector had either been criminally careless or open to the arguments of favored landlords.

The agitation finally resulted in a long and stirring trial before the civil service board of half of the employees in the Sanitary Bureau, with the final discharge of eleven out of the entire force of twenty-four. The inspector in our neighborhood was a kindly old man, greatly distressed over the affair, and quite unable to understand why he should not have used his discretion as to the time when a landlord should be forced to put in modern appliances. If he was "very poor," or "just about to sell his place," or "sure that the house would be torn down to make room for a factory," why should one "inconvenience" him? The old man died soon after the trial, feeling persecuted to the very last and not in the least understanding what it was all about. We were amazed at the commercial ramifications which graft in the city hall involved and at the indignation which interference with it produced. Hull-House lost some large subscriptions as the result of this investigation, a loss which, if not easy to bear, was at least comprehensible. We also uncovered unexpected graft in connection with the plumbers' unions, and but for the fearless testimony of one of their members, could never have brought the trial to a successful issue.

Inevitable misunderstanding also developed in connection with the attempt on the part of Hull-House residents to prohibit the sale of cocaine to minors, which brought us into sharp conflict with many druggists. I recall an Italian

druggist living on the edge of the neighborhood who finally came with a committee of his fellow countrymen to see
what Hull-House wanted of him, thoroughly convinced
that no such effort could be disinterested. One dreary trial
after another had been lost through the inadequacy of the
existing legislation, and after many attempts to secure
better legal regulation of its sale, a new law with the coöperation of many agencies was finally secured in 1907.
Through all this the Italian druggist, who had greatly
profited by the sale of cocaine to boys, only felt outraged
and abused. And yet the thought of this campaign brings
before my mind with irresistible force, a young Italian boy
who died—a victim of the drug at the age of seventeen.
He had been in our kindergarten as a handsome merry
child, in our clubs as a vivacious boy, and then gradually
there was an eclipse of all that was animated and joyous
and promising, and when I at last saw him in his coffin, it
was impossible to connect that haggard shriveled body
with what I had known before.

A midwife investigation, undertaken in connection with
the Chicago Medical Society, while showing the great need
of further state regulation in the interest of the most ignorant mothers and helpless children, brought us into conflict with one of the most venerable of all customs. Was
all this a part of the unending struggle between the old
and new, or were these oppositions so unexpected and so
unlooked for merely a reminder of that old bit of wisdom
that "there is no guarding against interpretations"? Perhaps more subtle still, they were due to that very super-
refinement of disinterestedness which will not justify itself,
that it may feel superior to public opinion. Some of our
investigations of course had no such untoward results, such
as "An Intensive Study of Truancy" undertaken by a resident of Hull-House in connection with the compulsory education department of the Board of Education and the
Visiting Nurse Association. The resident, Mrs. Britton
who, having had charge of our children's clubs for many
years, knew thousands of children in the neighborhood,
made a detailed study of three hundred families tracing
back the habitual truancy of the children to economic
and social causes. This investigation preceded a most interesting conference on truancy held under a committee

of which I was a member from the Chicago Board of Education. It left lasting results upon the administration of the truancy law as well as the coöperation of volunteer bodies.

We continually conduct small but careful investigations at Hull-House, which may guide us in our immediate doings such as two recently undertaken by Mrs. Britton, one upon the reading of school children before new books were bought for the children's club libraries, and another on the proportion of tuberculosis among school children, before we opened a little experimental outdoor school on one of our balconies. Some of the Hull-House investigations are purely negative in result; we once made an attempt to test the fatigue of factory girls in order to determine how far overwork superinduced the tuberculosis to which such a surprising number of them were victims. The one scientific instrument it seemed possible to use was an ergograph, a complicated and expensive instrument kindly lent to us from the physiological laboratory of the University of Chicago. I remember the imposing procession we made from Hull-House to the factory full of working women, in which the proprietor allowed us to make the tests; first there was the precious instrument on a hand truck guarded by an anxious student and the young physician who was going to take the tests every afternoon; then there was Dr. Hamilton, the resident in charge of the investigation, walking with a scientist who was interested to see that the instrument was properly installed; I followed in the rear to talk once more to the proprietor of the factory to be quite sure that he would permit the experiment to go on. The result of all this preparation, however, was to have the instrument record less fatigue at the end of the day than at the beginning, not because the girls had not worked hard and were not "dog tired" as they confessed, but because the instrument was not fitted to find it out.

For many years we have administered a branch station of the federal post office at Hull-House, which we applied for in the first instance because our neighbors lost such a large percentage of the money they sent to Europe through the commissions to middle men. The experience in the post office constantly gave us data for urging the establishment of postal savings as we saw one perplexed immigrant after another turning away in bewilderment when he was told that the United States post office did not receive savings.

We find increasingly, however, that the best results are to be obtained in investigations as in other undertakings, by combining our researches with those of other public bodies or with the State itself. When all the Chicago Settlements found themselves distressed over the condition of the newsboys who, because they are merchants and not employees, do not come under the provisions of the Illinois child labor law, they united in the investigation of a thousand young newsboys, who were all interviewed on the streets during the same twenty-four hours. Their school and domestic status was easily determined later, for many of the boys lived in the immediate neighborhoods of the ten Settlements which had undertaken the investigation. The report embodying the results of the investigation recommended a city ordinance containing features from the Boston and Buffalo regulations, and although an ordinance was drawn up and a strenuous effort was made to bring it to the attention of the aldermen, none of them would introduce it into the city council without newspaper backing. We were able to agitate for it again at the annual meeting of the National Child Labor Committee which was held in Chicago in 1908, and which was of course reported in papers throughout the entire country. This meeting also demonstrated that local measures can sometimes be urged most effectively when joined to the efforts of a national body. Undoubtedly the best discussions ever held upon the operation and status of the Illinois law were those which took place then. The needs of the Illinois children were regarded in connection with the children of the nation, and advanced health measures for Illinois were compared with those of other states.

The investigations of Hull-House thus tend to be merged with those of larger organizations, from the investigation of the social value of saloons made for the Committee of Fifty in 1896, to the one on infant mortality in relation to nationality, made for the American Academy of Science in 1909. This is also true of Hull-House activities in regard to public movements, some of which are inaugurated by the residents of other Settlements, as the Chicago School of Civics and Philanthropy, founded by the splendid efforts of Dr. Graham Taylor, for many years head of Chicago Commons. All of our recent investigations into housing have been under the department of investigation of this school with which several of the Hull-House residents are identified, quite as our active measures to secure better housing conditions have been carried on with the City Homes Association and through the coöperation of one of our residents who several years ago was appointed a sanitary inspector on the city staff.

Perhaps Dr. Taylor himself offers the best possible example of the value of Settlement experience to public undertakings, in his manifold public activities of which one might instance his work at the moment upon a commission recently appointed by the governor of Illinois to report upon the best method of Industrial Insurance or Employer's Liability Acts, and his influence in securing another to study into the subject of Industrial Diseases. The actual factory investigation under the latter is in charge of Dr. Hamilton, of Hull-House, whose long residence in an industrial neighborhood as well as her scientific attainment give her peculiar qualifications for the undertaking.

And so a Settlement is led along from the concrete to the abstract, as may easily be illustrated. Many years ago a tailors' union meeting at Hull-House asked our coöperation in tagging the various parts of a man's coat in such wise as to show the money paid to the people who had made it; one tag for the cutting and another for the buttonholes, another for the finishing and so on, the resulting total to be compared with the selling price of the coat itself. It quickly became evident that we had no way of computing how much of this larger balance was spent for salesmen, commercial travelers, rent and management, and the poor tagged coat was finally left hanging limply in a closet as if discouraged with the attempt. But the desire of the manual worker to know the relation of his own labor to the whole is not only legitimate but must form the basis of any intelligent action for his improvement. It was therefore with the hope of reform in the sewing trades that the Hull-House residents testified before the Federal Industrial

Commission in 1900, and much later with genuine enthusiasm joined with trades-unionists and other public-spirited citizens in an industrial exhibit which made a graphic presentation of the conditions and rewards of labor. The large casino building in which it was held was filled every day and evening for two weeks, showing how popular such information is, if it can be presented graphically. As an illustration of this same moving from the smaller to the larger, I might instance the efforts of Miss McDowell of the University of Chicago Settlement and others in urging upon Congress the necessity for a special investigation into the condition of women and children in industry because we had discovered the insuperable difficulties of smaller investigations, notably one undertaken for the Illinois Bureau of Labor by Mrs. Van der Vaart of Neighborhood House and by Miss Breckinridge of the University of Chicago. This investigation made clear that it was as impossible to detach the girls working in the stockyards from their sisters in industry as it was to urge special legislation on their behalf.

In the earlier years of the American Settlements, the residents were sometimes impatient with the accepted methods of charitable administration and hoped, through residence in an industrial neighborhood, to discover more coöperative and advanced methods of dealing with the problems of poverty which are so dependent upon industrial maladjustment. But during twenty years, the Settlements have seen the charitable people, through their very knowledge of the poor, constantly approach nearer to those methods formerly designated as radical. The residents, so far from holding aloof from organized charity, find testimony, certainly in the National Conferences, that out of the most persistent and intelligent efforts to alleviate poverty will in all probability arise the most significant suggestions for eradicating poverty. In the hearing before a congressional committee for the establishment of a Children's Bureau, residents in American Settlements joined their fellow philanthropists in urging the need of this indispensable instrument for collecting and disseminating information which would make possible concerted intelligent action on behalf of children.

Mr. Howells has said that we are all so besotted with our

novel reading that we have lost the power of seeing certain aspects of life with any sense of reality because we are continually looking for the possible romance. The description might apply to the earlier years of the American settlement, but certainly the later years are filled with discoveries in actual life as romantic as they are unexpected. If I may illustrate one of these romantic discoveries from my own experience, I would cite the indications of an internationalism as sturdy and virile as it is unprecedented which I have seen in our cosmopolitan neighborhood: when a South Italian Catholic is forced by the very exigencies of the situation to make friends with an Austrian Jew representing another nationality and another religion, both of which cut into all his most cherished prejudices, he finds it harder to utilize them a second time and gradually loses them. He thus modifies his provincialism, for if an old enemy working by his side has turned into a friend, almost anything may happen. When, therefore, I became identified with the peace movement both in its International and National Conventions, I hoped that this internationalism engendered in the immigrant quarters of American cities might be recognized as an effective instrument in the cause of peace. I first set it forth with some misgiving before the Convention held in Boston in 1904 and it is always a pleasure to recall the hearty assent given to it by Professor William James.

I have always objected to the phrase "sociological laboratory" applied to us, because Settlements should be something much more human and spontaneous than such a phrase connotes, and yet it is inevitable that the residents should know their own neighborhoods more thoroughly than any other, and that their experiences there should affect their convictions.

Years ago I was much entertained by a story told at the Chicago Woman's Club by one of its ablest members in the discussion following a paper of mine on "The Outgrowths of Toynbee Hall." She said that when she was a little girl playing in her mother's garden, she one day discovered a small toad who seemed to her very forlorn and lonely, although as she did not in the least know how to comfort him, she reluctantly left him to his fate; later in the day, quite at the other end of the garden, she found a large toad, also apparently without family and friends. With a heart full of tender sympathy, she took a stick and by exercising infinite patience and some skill, she finally pushed the little toad through the entire length of the garden into the company of the big toad, when, to her inexpressible horror and surprise, the big toad opened his mouth and swallowed the little one. The moral of the tale was clear applied to people who lived "where they did not naturally belong," although I protested that was exactly what we wanted—to be swallowed and digested, to disappear into the bulk of the people.

Twenty years later I am willing to testify that something of the sort does take place after years of identification with an industrial community.

CIVIC COOPERATION

ONE of the first lessons we learned at Hull-House was that private beneficence is totally inadequate to deal with the vast numbers of the city's disinherited. We also quickly came to realize that there are certain types of wretchedness from which every private philanthropy shrinks and which are cared for only in those wards of the county hospital provided for the wrecks of vicious living or in the city's isolation hospital for smallpox patients.

I have heard a broken-hearted mother exclaim when her erring daughter came home at last too broken and diseased to be taken into the family she had disgraced, "There is no place for her but the top floor of the County Hospital; they will have to take her there," and this only after every possible expedient had been tried or suggested. This aspect of governmental responsibility was unforgettably borne in upon me during the smallpox epidemic following the World's Fair, when one of the residents, Mrs. Kelley, as State Factory Inspector, was much concerned in discovering and destroying clothing which was being finished in houses containing unreported cases of smallpox. The deputy most successful in locating such cases lived at Hull-House during the epidemic because he did not wish to expose his own family. Another resident, Miss Lathrop, as a member of the State Board of Charities, went back and forth to the crowded pest house which had been hastily constructed on a stretch of prairie west of the city. As Hull-House was already so exposed, it seemed best for the special smallpox inspectors from the Board of health to take their meals and change their clothing there before they went to their respective homes. All of these officials had accepted without question and as implicit in public office the obligation to carry on the dangerous and difficult undertakings for which private philanthropy is unfitted, as if the commonalty of compassion represented by the State was more comprehending than that of any individual group.

It was as early as our second winter on Halsted Street that one of the Hull-House residents received an appointment from the Cook County agent as a county visitor. She reported at the agency each morning, and all the cases within a radius of ten blocks from Hull-House were given to her for investigation. This gave her a legitimate opportunity for knowing the poorest people in the neighborhood and also for understanding the county method of outdoor relief. The commissioners were at first dubious of the value of such a visitor and predicted that a woman would be a perfect "coal chute" for giving away county supplies, but they gradually came to depend upon her suggestion and advice.

In 1893 this same resident, Miss Julia C. Lathrop, was appointed by the governor a member of the Illinois State Board of Charities. She served in this capacity for two consecutive terms and was later reappointed to a third term. Perhaps her most valuable contribution toward the enlargement and reorganization of the charitable institutions of the State came through her intimate knowledge of the beneficiaries, and her experience demonstrated that it is only through long residence among the poor that an official could have learned to view public institutions as she did, from the standpoint of the inmates rather than from that of the managers. Since that early day, residents of Hull-House have spent much time in working for the civil service methods of appointment for employees in the county and State institutions; for the establishment of State colonies for the care of epileptics; and for a dozen other enterprises which occupy that borderland between charitable effort and legislation. In this borderland we coöperate in many civic enterprises for I think we may claim that Hull-House has always held its activities lightly, ready to hand them over to whosoever would carry them on properly.

Miss Starr had early made a collection of framed photographs, largely of the paintings studied in her art class, which became the basis of a loan collection first used by the Hull-House students and later extended to the public schools. It may be fair to suggest that this effort was the nucleus of the Public School Art Society which was later formed in the city and of which Miss Starr was the first president.

In our first two summers we had maintained three baths in the basement of our own house for the use of the neighborhood, and they afforded some experience and argument for the erection of the first public bathhouse in Chicago, which was built on a neighboring street and opened under the city Board of Health. The lot upon which it was erected belonged to a friend of Hull-House who offered it to the city without rent, and this enabled the city to erect the first public bath from the small appropriation of ten thousand dollars. Great fear was expressed by the public authorities that the baths would not be used, and the old story of the bathtubs in model tenements which had been turned into coal bins was often quoted to us. We were supplied, however, with the incontrovertible argument that in our adjacent third square mile there were in 1892 but three bathtubs and that this fact was much complained of by many of the tenement-house dwellers. Our contention was justified by the immediate and overflowing use of the public baths, as we had before been sustained in the contention that an immigrant population would respond to opportunities for reading when the Public Library Board had established a branch reading room at Hull-House.

We also quickly discovered that nothing brought us

so absolutely into comradeship with our neighbors as mutual and sustained effort such as the paving of a street, the closing of a gambling house, or the restoration of a veteran police sergeant.

Several of these earlier attempts at civic coöperation were undertaken in connection with the Hull-House Men's Club, which had been organized in the spring of 1893, had been incorporated under a State charter of its own, and had occupied a club room in the gymnasium building. This club obtained an early success in one of the political struggles in the ward and thus fastened upon itself a specious reputation for political power. It was at last so torn by the dissensions of two political factions which attempted to capture it that, although it is still an existing organization, it has never regained the prestige of its first five years. Its early political success came in a campaign Hull-House had instigated against a powerful alderman who has held office for more than twenty years in the nineteenth ward, and who, although notoriously corrupt, is still firmly intrenched among his constituents.

Hull-House has had to do with three campaigns organized against him. In the first one he was apparently only amused at our "Sunday School" effort and did little to oppose the election to the aldermanic office of a member of the Hull-House Men's Club who thus became his colleague in the city council. When Hull-House, however, made an effort in the following spring against the re-election of the alderman himself, we encountered the most determined and skillful opposition. In these campaigns we doubtless depended too much upon the idealistic appeal for we did not yet comprehend the element of reality always brought into the political struggle in such a neighborhood where politics deal so directly with getting a job and earning a living.

We soon discovered that approximately one out of every five voters in the nineteenth ward at that time held a job dependent upon the good will of the alderman. There were no civil service rules to interfere, and the unskilled voter swept the street and dug the sewer, as secure in his position as the more sophisticated voter who tended a bridge or occupied an office chair in the city hall. The alderman was even more fortunate in finding places with the franchise-seeking corporations; it took us some time to understand why so large a proportion of our neighbors were street-car employees and why we had such a large club composed solely of telephone girls. Our powerful ᐧalderman had various methods of entrenching himself. Many people were indebted to him for his kindly services in the police station and the justice courts, for in those days Irish constituents easily broke the peace, and before the establishment of the Juvenile Court, boys were arrested for very trivial offenses; added to these were hundreds of constituents indebted to him for personal kindness, from the peddler who received a free license to the businessman who had a railroad pass to New York. Our third campaign against him, when we succeeded in making a serious impression upon his majority, evoked from his henchmen the same sort of hostility which a striker so inevitably feels against the man who would take his job, even sharpened by the sense that the movement for reform came from an alien source.

Another result of the campaign was an expectation on the part of our new political friends that Hull-House would perform like offices for them, and there resulted endless confusion and misunderstanding because in many cases we could not even attempt to do what the alderman constantly did with a right good will. When he protected a law breaker from the legal consequences of his act, his kindness appeared, not only to himself but to all beholders, like the deed of a powerful and kindly statesman. When Hull-House on the other hand insisted that a law must be enforced, it could but appear like the persecution of the offender. We were certainly not anxious for consistency nor for individual achievement, but in a desire to foster a higher political morality and not to lower our standards, we constantly clashed with the existing political code. We also unwittingly stumbled upon a powerful combination of which our alderman was the political head, with its banking, its ecclesiastical, and its journalistic representatives, and as we followed up the clue and naïvely told all we discovered, we of course laid the foundations for opposition which has manifested itself in many forms; the most striking expression of it was an attack upon Hull-House lasting through weeks and months by a Chicago daily newspaper which has since ceased publication.

During the third campaign I received many anonymous letters—those from the men often obscene, those from the women revealing that curious connection between prostitution and the lowest type of politics which every city tries in vain to hide. I had offers from the men in the city prison to vote properly if released; various communications from lodging-house keepers as to the prices of the vote they were ready to deliver; everywhere appeared that animosity which is evoked only when a man feels that his means of livelihood is threatened.

As I look back, I am reminded of the state of mind of Kipling's newspapermen who witnessed a volcanic eruption at sea, in which unbelievable deep-sea creatures were expelled to the surface, among them an enormous white serpent, blind and smelling of musk, whose death throes thrashed the sea into a fury. With professional instinct unimpaired, the journalists carefully observed the uncanny creature never designed for the eyes of men; but a few days later, when they found themselves in a comfortable second-class carriage, traveling from Southampton to London between trim hedgerows and smug English villages, they concluded that the experience was too sensational to be put before the British public, and it became improbable even to themselves.

Many subsequent years of living in kindly neighborhood fashion with the people of the nineteenth ward has produced upon my memory the soothing effect of the second-class railroad carriage and many of these political experiences have not only become remote but already seem improbable. On the other hand, these campaigns were not without their rewards; one of them was a quickened friendship both with the more substantial citizens in the ward and with a group of fine young voters whose devotion to Hull-House has never since failed; another was a sense of identification with public-spirited men throughout the city who contributed

money and time to what they considered a gallant
effort against political corruption. I remember a young
professor from the University of Chicago who with his
wife came to live at Hull-House, traveling the long distance every day throughout the autumn and winter that
he might qualify as a nineteenth-ward voter in the
spring campaign. He served as a watcher at the polls
and it was but a poor reward for his devotion that
he was literally set upon and beaten up, for in those
good old days such things frequently occurred. Many another case of devotion to our standard so recklessly
raised might be cited, but perhaps more valuable than
àny of these was the sense of identification we obtained
with the rest of Chicago.

So far as a Settlement can discern and bring to local
consciousness neighborhood needs which are common
needs, and can give vigorous help to the municipal
measures through which such needs shall be met, it
fulfills its most valuable function. To illustrate from our
first effort to improve the street paving in the vicinity,
we found that when we had secured the consent of the
majority of the property owners on a given street for
a new paving, the alderman checked the entire plan
through his kindly service to one man who had appealed
to him to keep the assessments down. The street long
remained a shocking mass of wet, dilapidated cedar
blocks, where children were sometimes mired as they
floated a surviving block in the water which speedily
filled the holes whence other blocks had been extracted for fuel. And yet when we were able to demonstrate
that the street paving had thus been reduced into cedar
pulp by the heavily loaded wagons of an adjacent factory, that the expense of its repaving should be borne
from a general fund and not by the poor property owners, we found that we could all unite in advocating
reform in the method of repaving assessments, and
the alderman himself was obliged to come into such a
popular movement. The Nineteenth Ward Improvement Association, which met at Hull-House during two
winters, was the first body of citizens able to make
a real impression upon the local paving situation.
They secured an expert to watch the paving as it went

down to be sure that their half of the paving money was well expended. In the belief that property values would be thus enhanced, the common aim brought together the more prosperous people of the vicinity, somewhat as the Hull-House Coöperative Coal Association brought together the poorer ones.

I remember that during the second campaign against our alderman, Governor Pingree of Michigan came to visit at Hull-House. He said that the stronghold of such a man was not the place in which to start municipal regeneration; that good aldermen should be elected from the promising wards first, until a majority of honest men in the city council should make politics unprofitable for corrupt men. We replied that it was difficult to divide Chicago into good and bad wards, but that a new organization called the Municipal Voters' League was attempting to give to the well-meaning voter in each ward throughout the city accurate information concerning the candidates and their relation, past and present, to vital issues. One of our trustees who was most active in inaugurating this League always said that his nineteenth-ward experience had convinced him of the unity of city politics, and that he constantly used our campaign as a challenge to the unaroused citizens living in wards less conspicuously corrupt.

Certainly the need for civic coöperation was obvious in many directions, and in none more strikingly than in that organized effort which must be carried on unceasingly if young people are to be protected from the darker and coarser dangers of the city. The coöperation between Hull-House and the Juvenile Protective Association came about gradually, and it seems now almost inevitably. From our earliest days we saw many boys constantly arrested, and I had a number of most enlightening experiences in the police station with an Irish lad whose mother upon her deathbed had begged me "to look after him." We were distressed by the gangs of very little boys who would sally forth with an enterprising leader in search of old brass and iron, sometimes breaking into empty houses for the sake of the faucets or lead pipe which they would sell for a good price to a junk dealer. With the money thus obtained they would buy cigarettes and beer or even candy, which could be conspicuously consumed in the alleys where they might enjoy the excitement of being seen and suspected by the "coppers." From the third year of Hull-House, one of the residents held a semiofficial position in the nearest police station; at least, the sergeant agreed to give her provisional charge of every boy and girl under arrest for a trivial offense.

Mrs. Stevens, who performed this work for several years, became the first probation officer of the Juvenile Court when it was established in Cook County in 1899. She was the sole probation officer at first, but at the time of her death, which occurred at Hull-House in 1900, she was the senior officer of a corps of six. Her entire experience had fitted her to deal wisely with wayward children. She had gone into a New England cotton mill at the age of thirteen, where she had promptly lost the index finger of her right hand, through "carelessness" she was told, and no one then seemed to understand that freedom from care was the prerogative of childhood. Later she became a typesetter and was one of the first women in America to become a member of the typographical union, retaining her "card" through all the later years of editorial work. As the Juvenile Court developed, the committee of public-spirited citizens who first supplied only Mrs. Stevens' salary later maintained a corps of twenty-two such officers; several of these were Hull-House residents who brought to the house for many years a sad little procession of children struggling against all sorts of handicaps. When legislation was secured which placed the probation officers upon the payroll of the county, it was a challenge to the efficiency of the civil service method of appointment to obtain by examination men and women fitted for this delicate human task. As one of five people asked by the civil service commission to conduct this first examination for probation officers, I became convinced that we were but at the beginning of the nonpolitical method of selecting public servants, but even stiff and unbending as the examination may be, it is still our hope of political salvation.

In 1907 the Juvenile Court was housed in a model court building of its own, containing a detention home and equipped with a competent staff. The committee of citizens largely responsible for this result thereupon turned their attention to the conditions which the records of the court indicated had led to the alarming amount of juvenile delinquency and crime. They organized the Juvenile Protective Association, whose twenty-two officers meet weekly at Hull-House with their executive committee to report what they have found and to discuss city conditions affecting the lives of children and young people.

The association discovers that there are certain temptations into which children so habitually fall that it is evident that the average child cannot withstand them. An overwhelming mass of data is accumulated showing the need of enforcing existing legislation and of securing new legislation, but it also indicates a hundred other directions in which the young people who so gaily walk our streets, often to their own destruction, need safeguarding and protection.

The effort of the association to treat the youth of the city with consideration and understanding has rallied the most unexpected forces to its standard. Quite as the basic needs of life are supplied solely by those who make money out of the business, so the modern city has assumed that the craving for pleasure must be ministered to only by the sordid. This assumption, however, in a large measure broke down as soon as the Juvenile Protective Association courageously put it to the test. After persistent prosecutions, but also after many friendly interviews, the Druggists' Association itself prosecutes those of its members who sell indecent postal cards; the Saloon Keepers' Protective Association not only declines to protect members who sell liquor to minors, but now takes drastic action to prevent such sales; the Retail Grocers' Association forbids the selling of tobacco to minors; the Association of Department Store Managers not only increased the vigilance in their waiting rooms by supplying more matrons, but as a body they have become regular contributors to the association; the special watchmen in all the railroad yards agree not to arrest trespassing boys but to report them to the association; the firms manufacturing moving picture films not only submit their films to a volunteer inspection committee, but ask for suggestions in regard to new matter; and the Five-Cent Theaters arrange for "stunts" which shall deal with the subject of public health and morals, when the lecturers provided are entertaining as well as instructive.

It is not difficult to arouse the impulse of protection for the young, which would doubtless dictate the daily acts of many a bartender and poolroom keeper if they could only indulge it without giving their rivals an advantage. When this difficulty is removed by an even-handed enforcement of the law, that simple kindliness which the innocent always evoke goes from one to another like a slowly spreading flame of good will. Doubtless the most rewarding experience in any such undertaking as that of the Juvenile Protective Association is the warm and intelligent coöperation coming from unexpected sources—official and commercial as well as philanthropic. Upon the suggestion of the association, social centers have been opened in various parts of the city, disused buildings turned into recreation rooms, vacant lots made into gardens, hiking parties organized for country excursions, bathing beaches established on the lake front, and public schools opened for social purposes. Through the efforts of public-spirited citizens a medical clinic and a Psychopathic Institute have become associated with the Juvenile Court of Chicago, in addition to which an exhaustive study of court-records has been completed. To this carefully collected data concerning the abnormal child, the Juvenile Protective Association hopes in time to add knowledge of the normal child who lives under the most adverse city conditions.

It was not without hope that I might be able to forward in the public school system the solution of some of these problems of delinquency so dependent upon truancy and ill-adapted education that I became a member of the Chicago Board of Education in July, 1905. It is impossible to write of the situation as it became dramatized in half a dozen strong personalities, but the entire experience was so illuminating as to the difficulties and limitations of democratic government that it would be unfair in a chapter on Civic Coöperation not to attempt an outline.

Even the briefest statement, however, necessitates a review of the preceding few years. For a decade the Chicago schoolteachers, or rather a majority of them who were organized into the Teachers' Federation, had been engaged in a conflict with the Board of Education both for more adequate salaries and for more self-direction in the conduct of the schools. In pursuance of the first object, they had attacked the tax dodger along the entire line of his defense, from the curbstone to the Supreme Court. They began with an intricate investigation which uncovered the fact that in 1899, $235,000,000 of value of public utility corporations paid nothing in taxes. The Teachers' Federation brought a suit which was prosecuted through the Supreme Court of Illinois and resulted in an order entered against the State Board of Equalization, demanding that it tax the corporations mentioned in the bill. In spite of the fact that the defendant companies sought federal aid and obtained an order which restrained the payment of a portion of the tax, each year since 1900, the Chicago Board of Education has benefited to the extent of more than a quarter of a million dollars. Although this result had been attained through the unaided efforts of the teachers, to their surprise and indignation their salaries were not increased. The Teachers' Federation, therefore, brought a suit against the Board of Education for the advance which had been promised them three years earlier but never paid. The decision of the lower court was in their favor, but the Board of Education appealed the case, and this was the situation when the seven new members appointed by Mayor Dunne in 1905 took their seats. The conservative public suspected that these new members were merely representatives of the Teachers' Federation. This opinion was founded upon the fact that Judge Dunne had rendered a favorable decision in the teachers' suit and that the teachers had been very active in the campaign which had resulted in his election as mayor of the city. It seemed obvious that the teachers had entered into politics for the sake of securing their own representatives on the Board of Education. These suspicions were, of course, only confirmed when the new board voted to withdraw the suit of their predecessors from the Appellate Court and to act upon the decision of the lower court. The teachers, on the other hand, defended their long effort in the courts, the State Board of Equalization, and the Legislature against the charge of "dragging the schools into politics," and declared that the exposure of the indifference and cupidity of the politicians was a well-deserved rebuke, and that it was the politicians who had brought the schools to the verge of financial ruin; they further insisted that the levy and collection of taxes, tenure of office, and pensions to civil servants in Chicago were all entangled with the traction situation, which in their minds at least had come to be an example of the struggle between the democratic and plutocratic administration of city affairs. The new appointees to the School Board represented no concerted policy of any kind, but were for the most part adherents of the new education. The teachers, confident that their cause was identical with the principles advocated by such educators as Colonel Parker, were therefore sure that the plans of the "new education" members would of necessity coincide with the plans of the Teachers' Federation. In one sense the situation was an epitome of Mayor Dunne's entire administration, which was founded upon the belief that if those citizens representing social ideals and reform principles were but appointed to office, public welfare must be established.

During my tenure of office I many times talked to the officers of the Teachers' Federation, but I was seldom able to follow their suggestions and, although I gladly coöperated in their plans for a better pension system and other matters, only once did I try to influence the policy of the Federation. When the withheld salaries were finally paid to the representatives of the Federation who had brought suit and were divided among the members who had suffered both financially and professionally during this long legal struggle, I was most anxious that the division should voluntarily be extended to all of the teachers who had experienced a loss of salary although they were not members of the Federation. It seemed to me a striking opportunity to refute the charge that the Federation was self-seeking and to put the whole long effort in the minds of the public, exactly where it belonged, as one of devoted public service. But it was doubtless much easier for me to urge this altruistic policy than it was for those who had borne the heat and burden of the day to act upon it.

The second object of the Teachers' Federation also entailed much stress and storm. At the time of the financial stringency, and largely as a result of it, the Board had made the first substantial advance in a teacher's salary dependent upon a so-called promotional examination, half of which was upon academic subjects entailing a long and severe preparation. The teachers resented this upon two lines of argument: first, that the scheme was unprofessional in that the teacher was advanced on her capacity as a student rather than on her professional ability; and, second, that it added an intolerable and unnecessary burden to her already over-full day. The administration, on the other hand, contended with much justice that there was a constant danger in a great public school system that teachers lose pliancy and the open mind, and that many of them had obviously grown mechanical and indifferent. The conservative public approved the promotional examinations as the symbol of an advancing educational standard, and their sympathy with the superintendent was increased because they continually resented the affiliation of the Teachers' Federation with the Chicago Federation of Labor, which had taken place several years before the election of Mayor Dunne on his traction platform.

This much talked of affiliation between the teachers and the trades-unionists had been, at least in the first instance, but one more tactic in the long struggle against the tax-dodging corporations. The Teachers' Federation had won in their first skirmish against that public indifference which is generated in the accumulation of wealth and which has for its nucleus successful commercial men. When they found themselves in need of further legislation to keep the offending corporations under control, they naturally turned for political influence and votes to the organization representing workingmen. The affiliation had none of the sinister meaning so often attached to it. The Teachers' Federation never obtained a charter from the American Federation of Labor, and its main interest always centered in the legislative committee.

And yet this statement of the difference between the majority of the grade-school teachers and the Chicago School Board is totally inadequate, for the difficulties were stubborn and lay far back in the long effort of public school administration in America to free itself from the rule and exploitation of politics. In every city for many years the politician had secured positions for his friends as teachers and janitors; he had received a rake-off in the contract for every new building or coal supply or adoption of schoolbooks. In the long struggle against this political corruption, the one remedy continually advocated was the transfer of authority in all educational matters from the Board to the superintendent. The one cure for "pull" and corruption was the authority of the "expert." The rules and records of the Chicago Board of Education are full of relics of this long struggle honestly waged by honest men, who unfortunately became content with the ideals of an "efficient business administration." These businessmen established an able superintendent with a large salary, with his tenure of office secured by State law so that he would not be disturbed by the wrath of the balked politician. They instituted impersonal examinations for the teachers both as to entrance into the system and promotion, and they proceeded "to hold the superintendent responsible" for smooth-running schools. All this, however, dangerously approximated the commercialistic ideal of high salaries only for the management with the final test of a small expense account and a large output.

In this long struggle for a quarter of a century to free the public schools from political interference, in Chicago at least, the high wall of defense erected around the school system in order "to keep the rascals out" unfortunately so restricted the teachers inside the system that they had no space in which to move about freely and the more adventurous of them fairly panted for light and air. Any attempt to lower the wall for the sake of the teachers within was regarded as giving an opportunity to the politicians without, and they were often openly accused, with a show of truth, of being in league with each other. Whenever the Dunne members of the Board attempted to secure more liberty for the teachers, we were warned by tales of former difficulties with the politicians, and it seemed impossible that the struggle so long the focus of attention should recede into the dullness of the achieved and allow the energy of the Board to be free for new effort.

The whole situation between the superintendent supported by a majority of the Board and the Teachers' Federation had become an epitome of the struggle between efficiency and democracy; on one side a well-intentioned expression of the bureaucracy necessary in a large system but which under pressure had become unnecessarily self-assertive, and on the other side a fairly militant demand for self-government made in the name of freedom. Both sides inevitably exaggerated the difficulties of the situation, and both felt that they were standing by important principles.

I certainly played a most inglorious part in this unnecessary conflict; I was chairman of the School Management Committee during one year when a majority of the members seemed to me exasperatingly conservative, and during another year when they were frustratingly radical, and I was of course highly unsatisfactory to both. Certainly a plan to retain the undoubted benefit of required study for teachers in such wise as to lessen its burden, and various schemes devised to shift the emphasis from scholarship to professional work, were mostly impatiently repudiated by the Teachers' Federation, and when one badly mutilated plan finally passed the Board, it was most reluctantly administered by the superintendent.

I at least became convinced that partisans would never tolerate the use of stepping-stones. They are much too impatient to look on while their beloved scheme is unstably balanced, and they would rather see it tumble into the stream at once than to have it brought to dry land in any such half-hearted fashion. Before my School

Board experience, I thought that life had taught me at least one hard-earned lesson, that existing arrangements and the hoped for improvements must be mediated and reconciled to each other, that the new must be dovetailed into the old as it were, if it were to endure; but on the School Board I discerned that all such efforts were looked upon as compromising and unworthy, by both partisans. In the general disorder and public excitement resulting from the illegal dismissal of a majority of the "Dunne" board and their reinstatement by a court decision, I found myself belonging to neither party. During the months following the upheaval and the loss of my most vigorous colleagues, under the regime of men representing the leading Commercial Club of the city who honestly believed that they were rescuing the schools from a condition of chaos, I saw one beloved measure after another withdrawn. Although the new president scrupulously gave me the floor in the defense of each, it was impossible to consider them upon their merits in the lurid light which at the moment enveloped all the plans of the "uplifters." Thus the building of smaller schoolrooms, such as in New York mechanically avoid overcrowding, the extension of the truant rooms so successfully inaugurated, the multiplication of school playgrounds, and many another cherished plan was thrown out or at least indefinitely postponed.

The final discrediting of Mayor Dunne's appointees to the School Board affords a very interesting study in social psychology; the newspapers had so constantly reflected and intensified the ideals of a business Board, and had so persistently ridiculed various administration plans for the municipal ownership of street railways, that from the beginning any attempt the new Board made to discuss educational matters only excited their derision and contempt. Some of these discussions were lengthy and disorderly and deserved the discipline of ridicule, but others which were well conducted and in which educational problems were seriously set forth by men of authority were ridiculed quite as sharply. I recall the surprise and indignation of a University professor who had consented to speak at a meeting arranged in the Board rooms, when next morning his nonpartisan

and careful disquisition had been twisted into the most
arrant uplift nonsense and so connected with a fake
newspaper report of a trial marriage address delivered,
not by himself, but by a colleague, that a leading
clergyman of the city, having read the newspaper account, felt impelled to preach a sermon, calling upon
all decent people to rally against the doctrines which
were being taught to the children by an immoral School
Board. As the bewildered professor had lectured in response to my invitation, I endeavored to find the ani-
mus of the complication, but neither from editor in chief
nor from the reporter could I discover anything more
sinister than that the public expected a good story out
of these School Board "talk fests," and that any man who
even momentarily allied himself with a radical administration must expect to be ridiculed by those papers
which considered the traction policy of the administration both foolish and dangerous.

As I myself was treated with uniform courtesy by
the leading papers, I may perhaps here record my discouragement over this complicated difficulty of open
discussion, for democratic government is founded upon
the assumption that differing policies shall be freely
discussed and that each party shall have an opportunity
for at least a partisan presentation of its contentions.
This attitude of the newspapers was doubtless intensified because the Dunne School Board had instituted
a lawsuit challenging the validity of the lease for the
school ground occupied by a newspaper building. This
suit has since been decided in favor of the newspaper,
and it may be that in their resentment they felt justified
in doing everything possible to minimize the prosecut-
ing School Board. I am, however, inclined to think that
the newspapers but reflected an opinion honestly held
by many people, and that their constant and partisan
presentation of this opinion clearly demonstrates one
of the greatest difficulties of governmental administration in a city grown too large for verbal discussions of
public affairs.

It is difficult to close this chapter without a reference to the efforts made in Chicago to secure the municipal franchise for women. During two long periods

of agitation for a new city charter, a representative body of women appealed to the public, to the charter convention, and to the Illinois legislature for this very reasonable provision. During the campaign when I acted as chairman of the federation of a hundred women's organizations, nothing impressed me so forcibly as the fact that the response came from bodies of women representing the most varied traditions. We were joined by a church society of hundreds of Lutheran women, because Scandinavian women had exercised the municipal franchise since the seventeenth century and had found American cities strangely conservative; by organizations of working women who had keenly felt the need of the municipal franchise in order to secure for their workshops the most rudimentary sanitation and the consideration which the vote alone obtains for workingmen; by federations of mothers' meetings, who were interested in clean milk and the extension of kindergartens; by property-owning women, who had been powerless to protest against unjust taxation; by organizations of professional women, of university students, and of collegiate alumnæ; and by women's clubs interested in municipal reforms. There was a complete absence of the traditional women's rights clamor, but much impressive testimony from busy and useful women that they had reached the place where they needed the franchise in order to carry on their own affairs. A striking witness as to the need of the ballot, even for the women who are restricted to the most primitive and traditional activities, occurred when some Russian women waited upon me to ask whether under the new charter they could vote for covered markets and so get rid of the shocking Chicago grime upon all their food; and when some neighboring Italian women sent me word that they would certainly vote for public washhouses if they ever had the chance to vote at all. It was all so human, so spontaneous, and so direct that it really seemed as if the time must be ripe for political expression of that public concern on the part of women which had so long been forced to seek indirection. None of these busy women wished to take the place of men nor to influence them in the direction of men's affairs, but they did seek an opportunity to coöperate directly in civic life through the use of the ballot in regard to their own affairs.

A Municipal Museum which was established in the Chicago public library building several years ago, largely through the activity of a group of women who had served as jurors in the departments of social economy, of education, and of sanitation in the World's Fair at St. Louis, showed nothing more clearly than that it is impossible to divide any of these departments from the political life of the modern city which is constantly forced to enlarge the boundary of its activity.

Chapter 15

THE VALUE OF
SOCIAL CLUBS

FROM the early days at Hull-House, social clubs composed of English-speaking American-born young people grew apace. So eager were they for social life that no mistakes in management could drive them away. I remember one enthusiastic leader who read aloud to a club a translation of "Antigone," which she had selected because she believed that the great themes of the Greek poets were best suited to young people. She came into the club room one evening in time to hear the president call the restive members to order with the statement, "You might just as well keep quiet for she is bound to finish it, and the quicker she gets to reading, the longer time we'll have for dancing." And yet the same club leader had the pleasure of lending four copies of the drama to four of the members, and one young man almost literally committed the entire play to memory.

On the whole we were much impressed by the great desire for self-improvement, for study and debate, exhibited by many of the young men. This very tendency, in fact, brought one of the most promising of our earlier clubs to an untimely end. The young men in the club, twenty in number, had grown much irritated by the frivolity of the girls during their long debates, and had finally proposed that three of the most "frivolous" be expelled. Pending a final vote, the three culprits appealed to certain of their friends who were members of the Hull-House Men's Club, between whom and the debating young men the incident became the cause of a quarrel so bitter that at length it led to a shooting. Fortunately the shot missed fire, or it may have been true that it was "only intended for a scare," but at any rate, we were all thoroughly frightened by this manifestation of the hot blood which the defense of woman has so often evoked. After many efforts to bring about a reconciliation, the debating club of twenty young men and the seventeen young women, who either were or pretended to be sober minded, rented a hall a mile west of Hull-House, severing their connection with us because their ambitious and right-minded efforts had been unappreciated, basing this on the ground that we had not urged the expulsion of the so-called "tough" members of the Men's Club, who had been involved in the difficulty. The seceding club invited me to the first meeting in their new quarters that I might present to them my version of the situation and set forth the incident from the standpoint of Hull-House. The discussion I had with the young people that evening has always remained with me as one of the moments of illumination which life in a Settlement so often affords. In response to my position that a desire to avoid all that was "tough" meant to walk only in the paths of smug self-seeking and personal improvement leading straight into the pit of self-righteousness and petty achievement and was exactly what the Settlement did not stand for, they contended with much justice that ambitious young people were obliged for their own reputation, if not for their own morals, to avoid all connection with that which bordered on the tough, and that it was quite another matter for the Hull-House residents who could afford a more generous judgment. It was in vain I urged that life teaches us nothing more inevitably than that right and wrong are most confusingly confounded; that the blackest wrong may be within our own motives, and that at the best, right will not dazzle us by its radiant shining and can only be found by exerting patience and discrimination. They

THE VALUE OF SOCIAL CLUBS

still maintained their wholesome bourgeois position, which I am now quite ready to admit was most reasonable.

Of course there were many disappointments connected with these clubs when the rewards of political and commercial life easily drew the members away from the principles advocated in club meetings. One of the young men who had been a shining light in the advocacy of municipal reform deserted in the middle of a reform campaign because he had been offered a lucrative office in the city hall; another even after a course of lectures on business morality, "worked" the club itself to secure orders for custom-made clothing from samples of cloth he displayed, although the orders were filled by ready-made suits slightly refitted and delivered at double their original price. But nevertheless, there was much to cheer us as we gradually became acquainted with the daily living of the vigorous young men and women who filled to overflowing all the social clubs.

We have been much impressed during our twenty years by the ready adaptation of city young people to the prosperity arising from their own increased wages or from the commercial success of their families. This quick adaptability is the great gift of the city child, his one reward for the hurried changing life which he has always led. The working girl has a distinct advantage in the task of transforming her whole family into the ways and connections of the prosperous when she works downtown and becomes conversant with the manners and conditions of a cosmopolitan community. Therefore having lived in a Settlement twenty years, I see scores of young people who have successfully established themselves in life, and in my travels in the city and outside, I am constantly cheered by greetings from the rising young lawyer, the scholarly rabbi, the successful teacher, the prosperous young matron buying clothes for blooming children. "Don't you remember me? I used to belong to a Hull-House club." I once asked one of these young people, a man who held a good position on a Chicago daily, what special thing Hull-House had meant to him, and he promptly replied, "It was the first house I had ever been in where books and magazines just lay around as if there were plenty of them in the world. Don't you remember how much I used to read at that little round table at the back of the library? To have people regard reading as a reasonable occupation changed the whole aspect of life to me, and I began to have confidence in what I could do."

Among the young men of the social clubs a large proportion of the Jewish ones at least obtain the advantages of a higher education. The parents make every sacrifice to help them through the high school, after which the young men attend universities and professional schools, largely through their own efforts. From time to time they come back to us with their honors thick upon them; I remember one who returned with the prize in oratory from a contest between several western State universities, proudly testifying that he had obtained his confidence in our Henry Clay Club; another came back with a degree from Harvard University, saying that he had made up his mind to go there the summer I read Royce's *Aspects of Modern Philosophy* with a group of young men who had challenged my scathing remark that Herbert Spencer was not the only man who had ventured a solution of the riddles of the universe. Occasionally one of these learned young folk does not like to be reminded he once lived in our vicinity, but that happens rarely, and for the most part they are loyal to us in much the same spirit as they are to their own families and traditions. Sometimes they go further and tell us that the standards of tastes and code of manners which Hull-House has enabled them to form have made a very great difference in their perceptions and estimates of the larger world as well as in their own reception there. Five out of one club of twenty-five young men who had held together for eleven years entered the University of Chicago, but although the rest of the Club called them the "intellectuals," the old friendships still held.

In addition to these rising young people given to debate and dramatics, and to the members of the public school alumni associations which meet in our rooms, there are hundreds of others who for years have come to Hull-House frankly in search of that pleasure and recreation which all young things crave and which those who have spent long hours in a factory or shop demand as a right. For these young people, all sorts of pleasure clubs have been cherished and large dancing classes have been organized. One supreme gaiety has come to be an annual event of such importance that it is talked of from year to year. For six weeks before St. Patrick's day, a small group of residents put their best powers of invention and construction into preparation for a cotillion which is like a pageant in its gaiety and vigor. The parents sit in the gallery, and the mothers appreciate more than anyone else perhaps, the value of this ball to which an invitation is so highly prized; although their standards of manners may differ widely from the conventional, they know full well when the companionship of the young people is safe and unsullied.

As an illustration of this difference in standard, I may instance an early Hull-House picnic arranged by a club of young people, who found at the last moment that the club director could not go and accepted the offer of the mother of one of the club members to take charge of them. When they trooped back in the evening, tired and happy, they displayed a photograph of the group wherein each man's arm was carefully placed about a girl; no feminine waist lacked an arm save that of the proud chaperon, who sat in the middle smiling upon all. Seeing that the photograph somewhat surprised us, the chaperon stoutly explained, "This may look queer to you, but there wasn't one thing about that picnic that wasn't nice," and her statement was a perfectly truthful one.

Although more conventional customs are carefully enforced at our many parties and festivities, and while the dancing classes are as highly prized for the opportunity they afford for enforcing standards as for their ostensible aim, the residents at Hull-House, in their efforts to provide opportunities for clean recreation, receive the most valued help from the experienced wisdom of the older women of the neighborhood. Bowen Hall is constantly used for dancing parties with soft drinks established in its foyer. The parties given by the Hull-House clubs are by invitation, and the young people themselves carefully maintain their standard of entrance so that the most cautious mother may feel safe when her daughter goes to one of our parties. No club festivity is permitted without the presence of a director; no young man under the influence of liquor is allowed; certain types of dancing often innocently started are strictly prohibited; and above all, early closing is insisted upon. This standardizing of pleasure has always seemed an obligation to the residents of Hull-House, but we are, I hope, saved from that priggishness which young people so heartily resent by the Mardi Gras dance and other festivities which the residents themselves arrange and successfully carry out.

In spite of our belief that the standards of a ball may be almost as valuable to those without as to those within, the residents are constantly concerned for those many young people in the neighborhood who are too hedonistic to submit to the discipline of a dancing class or even to the claim of a pleasure club, but who go about in freebooter fashion to find pleasure wherever it may be cheaply on sale.

Such young people, well meaning but impatient of control, become the easy victims of the worst type of public dance halls and of even darker places, whose purposes are hidden under music and dancing. We were thoroughly frightened when we learned that during the year which ended last December, more than twenty-five thousand young people under the age of twenty-five passed through the Juvenile and Municipal Courts of Chicago—approximately one out of every eighty of the entire population, or one out of every fifty-two of those under twenty-five years of age. One's heart aches for these young people caught by the outside glitter of city gaiety, who make such a feverish attempt to snatch it for themselves. The young people in our clubs are comparatively safe, but many instances come to the knowledge of Hull-House residents which make us long for the time when the city, through more small parks, municipal gymnasiums, and schoolrooms open for recreation, can guard from disaster these young people who walk so carelessly on the edge of the pit.

The heedless girls believe that if they lived in big houses and possessed pianos and jewelry, the coveted social life would come to them. I know a Bohemian girl who surreptitiously saved her overtime wages until she had enough money to hire for a week a room with a piano in it where young men might come to call, as they could not do in her crowded untidy home. Of course she had no way of knowing the sort of young men who quickly discover an unprotected girl.

Another girl of American parentage who had come to Chicago to seek her fortune found at the end of a year that sorting shipping receipts in a dark corner of a warehouse not only failed to accumulate riches but did not even bring the "attentions" which her quiet country home afforded. By dint of long sacrifice she had saved fifteen dollars; with five she bought an imitation sapphire necklace, and the balance she changed into a ten dollar bill. The evening her pathetic little snare was set, she walked home with one of the clerks in the establishment, told him that she had come into a fortune, and was obliged to wear the heirloom necklace to insure its safety, permitted him to see that she carried ten dollars in her glove for carfare, and conducted him to a handsome Prairie Avenue residence. There she gaily bade him good-by and ran up the steps shutting herself in the vestibule from which she did not emerge until the dazzled and bewildered young man had vanished down the street.

Then there is the ever-recurring difficulty about dress; the insistence of the young to be gaily bedecked to the utter consternation of the hardworking parents who are paying for a house and lot. The Polish girl who stole five dollars from her employer's till with which to buy a white dress for a church picnic was turned away from home by her indignant father who replaced the money to save the family honor, but would harbor no "thief" in a household of growing children who, in spite of the sister's revolt, continued to be dressed in dark heavy clothes through all the hot summer. There are a multitude of working girls who for hours carry hair ribbons and jewelry in their pockets or stockings, for they can wear them only during the journey to and from work. Sometimes this desire to taste pleasure, to escape into a world of congenial companionship, takes more elaborate forms and often ends disastrously. I recall a charming young girl, the oldest daughter of a respectable German family, whom I first saw one spring afternoon issuing from a tall factory. She wore a blue print gown which so deepened the blue of her eyes that Wordsworth's line fairly sung itself:

The pliant harebell swinging in the breeze
On some gray rock.

I was grimly reminded of that moment a year later when I heard the tale of this seventeen-year-old girl, who had worked steadily in the same factory for four years before she resolved "to see life." In order not to arouse her parents' suspicions, she borrowed thirty dollars from one of those loan sharks who require no security from a pretty girl, so that she might start from home every morning as if to go to work. For three weeks she spent the first part of each dearly bought day in a department store where she lunched and unfortunately made some dubious acquaintances; in the afternoon she established herself in a theater and sat contentedly hour after hour watching the endless vaudeville until the usual time for returning home. At the end of each week she gave her parents her usual wage, but when her thirty dollars was exhausted it seemed unendurable that she should return to the monotony of the factory. In the light of her newly acquired experience she had learned that possibility which the city ever holds open to the restless girl.

That more such girls do not come to grief is due to those mothers who understand the insatiable demand for a good time, and if all of the mothers did understand, those pathetic statistics which show that four fifths of all prostitutes are under twenty years of age would be marvelously changed. We are told that "the will to live" is aroused in each baby by his mother's irresistible desire to play with him, the physiological value of joy that a child is born, and that the high death rate in institutions is increased by "the discontented babies" whom no one persuades into living. Something of the same sort is necessary in that second birth at adolescence. The young people need affection and understanding each one for himself, if they are to be induced to live in an inheritance of decorum and safety and to understand the foundations upon which this orderly world rests. No one comprehends their needs so sympathetically as those mothers who iron the flimsy starched finery of their grown-up daughters late into the night, and who pay for a red velvet parlor set on the installment plan, although the younger children may sadly need new shoes. These mothers apparently understand the sharp demand for social pleasure and do their best to respond to it, although at the same time they constantly minister to all the physical needs of an exigent family of little children. We often come to a realization of the truth of Walt Whitman's statement, that one of the surest sources of wisdom is the mother of a large family.

It is but natural, perhaps, that the members of the Hull-House Woman's Club whose prosperity has given them some leisure and a chance to remove their own families to neighborhoods less full of temptations should have offered their assistance in our attempt to provide recreation for these restless young people. In many instances their experience in the club itself has enabled them to perceive these needs. One day a Juvenile Court officer told me that a woman's club member, who has a large family of her own and one boy sufficiently difficult, had undertaken to care for a ward of the Juvenile Court who lived only a block from her house, and that she had kept him in the path of rectitude for six months. In reply to my congratulations upon this successful bit of reform to the club woman herself, she said that she was quite ashamed that she had not undertaken the task earlier for she had for years known the boy's mother who scrubbed a downtown office building, leaving home every evening at five and returning at eleven during the very time the boy could most easily find opportunities for wrongdoing. She said that her obligation toward this boy had not occurred to her until one day when the club members were making pillowcases for the Detention Home of the Juvenile Court, it suddenly seemed perfectly obvious that her share in the salvation of wayward children was to care for this particular boy, and she had asked the Juvenile Court officer to commit him to her. She invited the boy to her house to supper every day that she might know just where he was at the crucial moment of twilight, and she adroitly managed to keep him under her own roof for the evening if she did not approve of the plans he had made. She concluded with the remark that it was queer that the sight of the boy himself hadn't appealed to her, but that the suggestion had come to her in such a roundabout way.

She was, of course, reflecting upon a common trait in human nature—that we much more easily see the duty at hand when we see it in relation to the social duty of which it is a part. When she knew that an effort was being made throughout all the large cities in the United States to reclaim the wayward boy, to provide him with reasonable amusement, to give him his chance for growth and development, and when she became ready to take her share in that movement, she suddenly saw the concrete case which she had not recognized before.

We are slowly learning that social advance depends quite as much upon an increase in moral sensibility as it does upon a sense of duty, and of this one could cite many illustrations. I was at one time chairman of the Child Labor Committee in the General Federation of Woman's Clubs, which sent out a schedule asking each club in the United States to report as nearly as possible all the working children under fourteen living in its vicinity. A Florida club filled out the schedule with an astonishing number of Cuban children who were at work in sugar mills, and the club members registered a complaint that our committee had sent the schedule too late, for if they had realized the conditions earlier, they might have presented a bill to the legislature which had now adjourned. Of course the children had been working in the sugar mills for years, and had probably gone back and forth under the very eyes of the club women, but the women had never seen them, much less felt any obligation to protect them, until they joined a club, and the club joined a Federation, and the Federation appointed a Child Labor Committee who sent them a schedule. With their quickened perceptions they then saw the rescue of these familiar children in the light of a social obligation. Through some such experiences the members of the Hull-House Woman's Club have obtained the power of seeing the concrete through the general and have entered into various undertakings.

Very early in its history the club formed what was called "A Social Extension Committee." Once a month this committee gives parties to people in the neighborhood who for any reason seem forlorn and without much social pleasure. One evening they invited only

Italian women, thereby crossing a distinct social "gulf," for there certainly exists as great a sense of social difference between the prosperous Irish-American women and the South-Italian peasants as between any two sets of people in the city of Chicago. The Italian women, who were almost eastern in their habits, all stayed at home and sent their husbands, and the social extension committee entered the drawing room to find it occupied by rows of Italian workingmen, who seemed to prefer to sit in chairs along the wall. They were quite ready to be "socially extended," but plainly puzzled as to what it was all about. The evening finally developed into a very successful party, not so much because the committee were equal to it, as because the Italian men rose to the occasion.

Untiring pairs of them danced the tarantella; they sang Neapolitan songs; one of them performed some of those wonderful sleight-of-hand tricks so often seen on the streets of Naples; they explained the coral finger of St. Januarius which they wore; they politely ate the strange American refreshments; and when the evening was over, one of the committee said to me, "Do you know I am ashamed of the way I have always talked about 'dagoes.' They are quite like other people, only one must take a little more pains with them. I have been nagging my husband to move off M Street because they are moving in, but I am going to try staying awhile and see if I can make a real acquaintance with some of them." To my mind at that moment the speaker had passed from the region of the uncultivated person into the possibilities of the cultivated person. The former is bounded by a narrow outlook on life, unable to overcome differences of dress and habit, and his interests are slowly contracting within a circumscribed area; while the latter constantly tends to be more a citizen of the world because of his growing understanding of all kinds of people with their varying experiences. We send our young people to Europe that they may lose their provincialism and be able to judge their fellows by a more universal test, as we send them to college that they may attain the cultural background and a larger outlook; all of these it is possible to acquire in other ways, as this member of the woman's club had discovered for herself.

This social extension committee under the leadership of an ex-president of the Club, a Hull-House resident with a wide acquaintance, also discovers many of those lonely people of which every city contains so large a number. We are only slowly apprehending the very real danger to the individual who fails to establish some sort of genuine relation with the people who surround him. We are all more or less familiar with the results of isolation in rural districts; the Brontë sisters have portrayed the hideous immorality and savagery of the remote dwellers on the bleak moorlands of northern England; Miss Wilkins has written of the overdeveloped will of the solitary New Englander; but tales still wait to be told of the isolated city dweller. In addition to the lonely young man recently come to town, and the country family who have not yet made their connections, are many other people who, because of temperament or from an estimate of themselves which will not permit them to make friends with the "people around here," or who, because they are victims to a combination of circumstances, lead a life as lonely and untouched by the city about them as if they were in remote country districts. The very fact that it requires an effort to preserve isolation from the tenement-house life which flows all about them makes the character stiffer and harsher than mere country solitude could do.

Many instances of this come into my mind: the faded, ladylike hairdresser, who came and went to her work for twenty years, carefully concealing her dwelling place from the "other people in the shop," moving whenever they seemed too curious about it, and priding herself that no neighbor had ever "stepped inside her door," and yet when discovered through an asthma which forced her to crave friendly offices, she was most responsive and even gay in a social atmosphere. Another woman made a long effort to conceal the poverty resulting from her husband's inveterate gambling and to secure for her children the educational advantages to which her family had always been accustomed. Her five children, who are now university graduates, do not realize how hard and solitary was her early married life when we first knew her, and she was beginning to regret the isolation in which her children were being reared, for she saw that their lack of early companionship would always cripple their power to make friends. She was glad to avail herself of the social resources of Hull-House for them, and at last even for herself.

The leader of the social extension committee has also been able, through her connection with the vacant lot garden movement in Chicago, to maintain a most flourishing "friendly club" largely composed of people who cultivate these garden plots. During the club evening at least, they regain something of the ease of the man who is being estimated by the bushels per acre of potatoes he has raised, and not by that flimsy city judgment so often based upon store clothes. Their jollity and enthusiasm are unbounded, expressing itself in clog dances and rousing old songs often in sharp contrast to the overworked, worn aspects of the members.

Of course there are surprising possibilities discovered through other clubs, in one of Greek women or in the "circolo Italiano," for a social club often affords a sheltered space in which the gentler social usages may be exercised, as the more vigorous clubs afford a point of departure into larger social concerns.

The experiences of the Hull-House Woman's Club constantly react upon the family life of the members. Their husbands come with them to the annual midwinter reception, to club concerts and entertainments; the little children come to the May party, with its dancing and games; the older children, to the day in June when prizes are given to those sons and daughters of the members who present a good school record as graduates either from the eighth grade or from a high school.

It seemed, therefore, but a fit recognition of their efforts when the president of the club erected a building planned especially for their needs, with their own library and a hall large enough for their various social undertakings, although of course Bowen Hall is constantly put to many other uses.

It was under the leadership of this same able president that the club achieved its wider purposes and took its place with the other forces for city betterment. The club had begun, as nearly all women's clubs do, upon the basis of self-improvement, although the foundations for this later development had been laid by one of their earliest presidents, who was the first probation officer of the Juvenile Court and who had so shared her experi-

Facade of Bowen Hall

ences with the club that each member felt the truth as well as the pathos of the lines inscribed on her memorial tablet erected in their club library:

> As more exposed to suffering and distress
> Thence also more alive to tenderness.

Each woman had discovered opportunities in her own experience for this same tender understanding, and under its succeeding president, Mrs. Pelham, in its determination to be of use to the needy and distressed, the club developed many philanthropic undertakings from the humble beginnings of a linen chest kept constantly filled with clothing for the sick and poor. It required, however, an adequate knowledge of adverse city conditions so productive of juvenile delinquency and a sympathy which could enkindle itself in many others of divers faiths and training, to arouse the club to its finest public spirit. This was done by a later president, Mrs. Bowen, who, as head of the Juvenile Protective Association, had learned that the moralized energy of a group is best fitted to cope with the complicated problems of a city; but it required ability of an unusual order to evoke a sense of social obligation from the very knowledge of adverse city conditions which the club members possessed, and to connect it with the many civic and philanthropic organizations of the city in such wise as to make it socially useful. This financial and representative connection with outside organizations is valuable to the club only as it expresses its sympathy and kindliness at the same time in concrete form. A group of members who lunch with Mrs. Bowen each week at Hull-House discuss, not only topics of public interest, sometimes with experts whom they have long known through their mutual undertakings, but also their own club affairs in the light of this larger knowledge.

Thus the value of social clubs broadens out in one's mind to an instrument of companionship through which many may be led from a sense of isolation to one of civic responsibility, even as another type of club provides recreational facilities for those who have had only meaningless excitements, or, as a third type, opens new and interesting vistas of life to those who are ambitious.

The entire organization of the social life at Hull-House, while it has been fostered and directed by residents and others, has been largely pushed and vitalized from within by the club members themselves. Sir Walter Besant once told me that Hull-House stood in his mind more nearly for the ideal of the "Palace of Delight" than did the "London People's Palace" because we had depended upon the social resources of the people using it. He begged me not to allow Hull-House to become too educational. He believed it much easier to develop a polytechnic institute than a large recreational center, but he doubted whether the former was as useful.

The social clubs form a basis of acquaintanceship for many people living in other parts of the city. Through friendly relations with individuals, which is perhaps the sanest method of approach, they are thus brought into contact, many of them for the first time, with the industrial and social problems challenging the moral resources of our contemporary life. During our twenty years hundreds of these nonresidents have directed clubs and classes, and have increased the number of Chicago citizens who are conversant with adverse social conditions and conscious that only by the unceasing devotion of each, according to his strength, shall the compulsions and hardships, the stupidities and cruelties of life be overcome. The number of people thus informed is constantly increasing in all our American cities, and they may in time remove the reproach of social neglect and indifference which has so long rested upon the citizens of the new world. I recall the experience of an Englishman who, not only because he was a member of the Queen's Cabinet and bore a title, but also because he was an able statesman, was entertained with great enthusiasm by the leading citizens of Chicago. At a large dinner party he asked the lady sitting next to him what our tenement-house legislation was in regard to the cubic feet of air required for each occupant of a tenement bedroom; upon her disclaiming any knowledge of the subject, the inquiry was put to all the diners at the long table, all of whom showed surprise that they should be expected to possess this information. In telling me the incident afterward, the English guest said that such indifference could not have been found among the leading citizens of London, whose public spirit had been aroused to provide such housing conditions as should protect tenement dwellers at least from wanton loss of vitality and lowered industrial efficiency. When I met the same Englishman in London five years afterward, he immediately asked me whether Chicago citizens were still so indifferent to the conditions of the poor that they took no interest in their proper housing. I was quick with that defense which an American is obliged to use so often in Europe, that our very democracy so long presupposed that each citizen could care for himself that we are slow to develop a sense of social obligation. He smiled at the familiar phrases and was still inclined to attribute our indifference to sheer ignorance of social conditions.

The entire social development of Hull-House is so unlike what I predicted twenty years ago that I venture to quote from that ancient writing as an end to this chapter.

The social organism has broken down through large districts of our great cities. Many of the people living there are very poor, the majority of them without leisure or energy for anything but the gain of subsistence.

They live for the moment side by side, many of them without knowledge of each other, without fellowship, without local tradition or public spirit, without social organization of any kind. Practically nothing is done to remedy this. The people who might do it, who have the social tact and training, the large houses, and the traditions and customs of hospitality, live in other parts of the city. The club houses, libraries, galleries, and semipublic conveniences for social life are also blocks away. We find workingmen organized into armies of producers because men of executive ability and business sagacity have found it to their interests thus to organize them. But these workingmen are not organized socially; although lodging in crowded tenement houses, they are living without a corresponding social contact. The chaos is as great as it would be were they working in huge factories without foreman or superintendent. Their ideas and resources are cramped, and the desire for higher social pleasure becomes extinct. They have no share in the traditions and social energy which make for progress. Too often their only place of meeting is a saloon, their only host a bartender; a local demagogue forms their public opinion. Men of ability and refinement, of social power and university cultivation, stay away from them. Personally, I believe the men who lose most are those who thus stay away. But the paradox is here: when cultivated people do stay away from a certain portion of the population, when all social advantages are persistently withheld, it may be for years, the result itself is pointed to as a reason and is used as an argument for the continued withholding.

It is constantly said that because the masses have never had social advantages, they do not want them, that they

are heavy and dull, and that it will take political or philanthropic machinery to change them. This divides a city into
rich and poor; into the favored, who express their sense of
the social obligation by gifts of money, and into the un-
favored, who express it by clamoring for a "share"—both of
them actuated by a vague sense of justice. This division of
the city would be more justifiable, however, if the people
who thus isolate themselves on certain streets and use their
social ability for each other gained enough thereby and added sufficient to the sum total of social progress to justify the
withholding of the pleasures and results of that progress
from so many people who ought to have them. But they
cannot accomplish this for the social spirit discharges itself
in many forms, and no one form is adequate to its total
expression.

Chapter 16

ARTS AT HULL-HOUSE

THE first building erected for Hull-House contained
an art gallery well lighted for day and evening use, and
our first exhibit of loaned pictures was opened in June,
1891, by Mr. and Mrs. Barnett of London. It is always
pleasant to associate their hearty sympathy with that
first exhibit and thus to connect it with their pioneer
efforts at Toynbee Hall to secure for working people
the opportunity to know the best art, and with their establishment of the first permanent art gallery in an industrial quarter.

We took pride in the fact that our first exhibit contained some of the best pictures Chicago afforded, and
we conscientiously insured them against fire and carefully guarded them by night and day.

We had five of these exhibits during two years, after
the gallery was completed: two of oil paintings, one of
old engravings and etchings, one of water colors, and
one of pictures especially selected for use in the public
schools. These exhibits were surprisingly well attended
and thousands of votes were cast for the most popular
pictures. Their value to the neighborhood of course had
to be determined by each one of us according to the

value he attached to beauty and the escape it offers
from dreary reality into the realm of the imagination
Miss Starr always insisted that the arts should receive
adequate recognition at Hull-House and urged that one
must always remember "the hungry individual soul
which without art will have passed unsolaced and unfed
followed by other souls who lack the impulse his should
have given."

The exhibits afforded pathetic evidence that the older
immigrants do not expect the solace of art in this country; an Italian expressed great surprise when he found
that we, although Americans, still liked pictures, and
said quite naïvely that he didn't know that Americans
cared for anything but dollars—that looking at pictures
was something people only did in Italy.

The extreme isolation of the Italian colony was demonstrated by the fact that he did not know that there
was a public art gallery in the city nor any houses in
which pictures were regarded as treasures.

A Greek was much surprised to see a photograph of
the Acropolis at Hull-House, because he had lived in
Chicago for thirteen years and had never before met
any Americans who knew about this foremost glory of
the world. Before he left Greece he had imagined that
Americans would be most eager to see pictures of Athens, and as he was a graduate of a school of technolo-
gy, he had prepared a book of colored drawings and had
made a collection of photographs which he was sure
Americans would enjoy. But although from his fruit
stand near one of the large railroad stations he had con-
versed with many Americans and had often tried to
lead the conversation back to ancient Greece, no one
had responded, and he had at last concluded that "the
people of Chicago knew nothing of ancient times."

The loan exhibits were continued until the Chicago
Art Institute was opened free to the public on Sunday
afternoons and parties were arranged at Hull-House
and conducted there by a guide. In time even these
parties were discontinued as the galleries became better
known in all parts of the city and the Art Institute management did much to make pictures popular.

From the first a studio was maintained at Hull-House

which has developed through the changing years under the direction of Miss Benedict, one of the residents who is a member of the faculty in the Art Institute. Buildings on the Hull-House quadrangle furnish studios for artists who find something of the same spirit in the contiguous Italian colony that the French artist is traditionally supposed to discover in his beloved Latin Quarter. These artists uncover something of the picturesque in the foreign colonies, which they have reproduced in painting, etching, and lithography. They find their classes filled not only by young people possessing facility and sometimes talent, but also by older people to whom the studio affords the one opportunity of escape from dreariness; a widow with four children who supplemented a very inadequate income by teaching the piano, for six years never missed her weekly painting lesson because it was "her one pleasure"; another wom-

In the Hull-House Studio, from a Photograph
by Lewis W. Hine

an, whose youth and strength had gone into the care of an invalid father, poured into her afternoon in the studio once a week all of the longing for self-expression which she habitually suppressed.

Perhaps the most satisfactory results of the studio have been obtained through the classes of young men who are engaged in the commercial arts, and who are glad to have an opportunity to work out their own ideas. This is true of young engravers and lithographers; of the men who have to do with posters and illustrations in various ways. The little pile of stones and the lithographer's handpress in a corner of the studio have been used in many an experiment, as has a set of beautiful type loaned to Hull-House by a bibliophile.

The work of the studio almost imperceptibly merged into the crafts, and well within the first decade a shop was opened at Hull-House under the direction of several residents who were also members of the Chicago Arts and Crafts Society. This shop is not merely a school where people are taught and then sent forth to use their teaching in art according to their individual initiative and opportunity, but where those who have already been carefully trained may express the best they can in wood or metal. The Settlement soon discovers how difficult it is to put a fringe of art on the end of a day spent in a factory. We constantly see young people doing overhurried work. Wrapping bars of soap in pieces of paper might at least give the pleasure of accuracy and repetition if it could be done at a normal pace, but when paid for by the piece, speed becomes the sole requirement and the last suggestion of human interest is taken away. In contrast to this the Hull-House shop affords many examples of the restorative power in the exercise of a genuine craft; a young Russian who, like too many of his countrymen, had made a desperate effort to fit himself for a learned profession, and who had almost finished his course in a night law school, used to watch constantly the work being done in the metal shop at Hull-House. One evening in a moment of sudden resolve, he took off his coat sat down at one of the benches, and began to work obviously as a very clever silversmith. He had long concealed his craft because he thought it would hurt his efforts as a lawyer and because he imagined an office more honorable and "more American" than a shop. As he worked on during his two leisure evenings each week, his entire bearing and conversation registered the relief of one who abandons the effort he is not fitted for and becomes a man on his own feet, expressing himself through a familiar and delicate technique.

Miss Starr at length found herself quite impatient with her role of lecturer on the arts, while all the handicraft about her was untouched by beauty and did not even reflect the interest of the workman. She took a training in bookbinding in London under Mr. Cobden-Sanderson and established her bindery at Hull-House in which design and workmanship, beauty and thoroughness, are taught to a small number of apprentices.

From the very first winter, concerts which are still continued were given every Sunday afternoon in the Hull-House drawing room and later, as the audiences increased, in the larger halls. For these we are indebted to musicians from every part of the city. Mr. William Tomlins early trained large choruses of adults as his assistants did of children, and the response to all of these showed that while the number of people in our vicinity caring for the best music was not large, they constituted a steady and appreciative group. It was in connection with these first choruses that a public-spirited citizen of Chicago offered a prize for the best labor song, competition to be open to the entire country. The responses to the offer literally filled three large barrels and speaking at least for myself as one of the bewildered judges, we were more disheartened by their quality than even by their overwhelming bulk. Apparently the workers of America are not yet ready to sing, although I recall a creditable chorus trained at Hull-House for a large meeting in sympathy with the anthracite coal strike in which the swinging lines

> Who was it made the coal?
> Our God as well as theirs.

seemed to relieve the tension of the moment. Miss Eleanor Smith, the head of the Hull-House Music School, who had put the words to music, performed the same office for the "Sweatshop" of the Yiddish poet, the translation of which presents so graphically the bewilderment and tedium of the New York shop that it might be applied to almost any other machinery industry as the first verse indicates:

> The roaring of the wheels has filled my ears,
> The clashing and the clamor shut me in,
> Myself, my soul, in chaos disappears,
> I cannot think or feel amid the din.

It may be that this plaint explains the lack of labor songs in this period of industrial maladjustment when the worker is overmastered by his very tools. In addition to sharing with our neighborhood the best music we could procure, we have conscientiously provided careful musical instruction that at least a few young people might understand those old usages of art; that they might master its trade secrets, for after all it is only through a careful technique that artistic ability can express itself and be preserved.

From the beginning we had classes in music, and the Hull-House Music School, which is housed in quarters of its own in our quieter court, was opened in 1893. The school is designed to give a thorough musical instruction to a limited number of children. From the first lessons they are taught to compose and to reduce to order the musical suggestions which may come to them, and in this wise the school has sometimes been able to recover the songs of the immigrants through their children. Some of these folk songs have never been committed to paper, but have survived through the centuries because of a touch of undying poetry which the world has always cherished; as in the song of a Russian who is digging a post hole and finds his task dull and difficult until he strikes a stratum of red sand, which in addition to making digging easy, reminds him of the red hair of his sweetheart, and all goes merrily as the song lifts into a joyous melody. I recall again the almost hilarious enjoyment of the adult audience to whom it was sung by the children who had revived it, as well as the more sober appreciation of the hymns taken from the lips of the cantor, whose father before him had officiated in the synagogue.

Exterior, Hull-House Music School

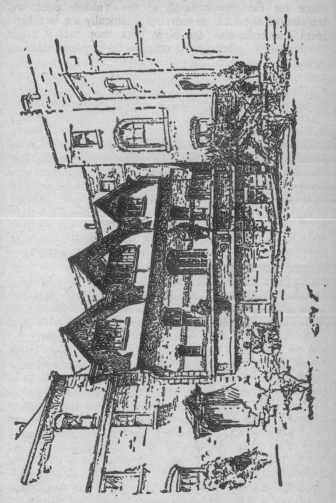

The recitals and concerts given by the school are attended by large and appreciative audiences. On the Sunday before Christmas the program of Christmas songs draws together people of the most diverging faiths. In the deep tones of the memorial organ erected at Hull-House, we realize that music is perhaps the most potent agent for making the universal appeal and inducing men to forget their differences.

Some of the pupils in the music school have developed during the years into trained musicians and are supporting themselves in their chosen profession. On the other hand, we constantly see the most promising musical ability extinguished when the young people enter industries which so sap their vitality that they cannot carry on serious study in the scanty hours outside of factory work. Many cases indisputably illustrate this: a Bohemian girl, who, in order to earn money for pressing family needs, first ruined her voice in a six months' constant vaudeville engagement, returned to her trade working overtime in a vain effort to continue the vaudeville income; another young girl whom Hull-House had sent to the high school so long as her parents consented, because we realized that a beautiful voice is often unavailable through lack of the informing mind, later extinguished her promise in a tobacco factory; a third girl who had supported her little sisters since she was fourteen, eagerly used her fine voice for earning money at entertainments held late after her day's work, until exposure and fatigue ruined her health as well as a musician's future; a young man whose music-loving family gave him every possible opportunity, and who produced some charming and even joyous songs during the long struggle with tuberculosis which preceded his death, had made a brave beginning, not only as a teacher of music but as a composer. In the little service held at Hull-House in his memory, when the children sang his composition, "How Sweet is the Shepherd's Sweet Lot," it was hard to realize that such an interpretive pastoral could have been produced by one whose childhood had been passed in a crowded city quarter.

Even that bitter experience did not prepare us for the sorrowful year when six promising pupils out of a class of fifteen developed tuberculosis. It required but little penetration to see that during the eight years the class of fifteen schoolchildren had come together to the music school, they had approximately an even chance, but as soon as they reached the legal working age only a scanty moiety of those who became self-supporting could endure the strain of long hours and bad air. Thus the average human youth, "With all the sweetness of the common dawn," is flung into the vortex of industrial life wherein the everyday tragedy escapes us save when one of them becomes conspicuously unfortunate. Twice in one year we were compelled

> To find the inheritance of this poor child
> His little kingdom of a forced grave.

It has been pointed out many times that Art lives by devouring her own offspring and the world has come to justify even that sacrifice, but we are unfortified and unsolaced when we see the children of Art devoured, not by her, but by the uncouth stranger, Modern Industry, who, needlessly ruthless and brutal to her own children, is quickly fatal to the offspring of the gentler mother. And so schools in art for those who go to work at the age when more fortunate young people are still sheltered and educated constantly epitomize one of the haunting problems of life: why do we permit the waste of this most precious human faculty, this consummate possession of civilization? When we fail to provide the vessel in which it may be treasured, it runs out upon the ground and is irretrievably lost.

The universal desire for the portrayal of life lying quite outside of personal experience evinces itself in many forms. One of the conspicuous features of our neighborhood, as of all industrial quarters, is the persistency with which the entire population attends the theater. The very first day I saw Halsted Street a long line of young men and boys stood outside the gallery entrance of the Bijou Theater, waiting for the Sunday matinée to begin at two o'clock, although it was only high noon. This waiting crowd might have been seen every Sunday afternoon during the twenty years which have elapsed since then. Our first Sunday evening in Hull-House, when a group of small boys sat on our piazza and told us "about things around here," their talk was all of the theater and of the astonishing things they had seen that afternoon.

But quite as it was difficult to discover the habits and purposes of this group of boys because they much preferred talking about the theater to contemplating their own lives, so it was all along the line; the young men told us their ambitions in the phrases of stage heroes, and the girls, so far as their romantic dreams could be shyly put into words, possessed no others but those soiled by long use in the melodrama. All of these young people looked upon an afternoon a week in the gallery of a Halsted Street theater as their one opportunity to see life. The sort of melodrama they see there has recently been described as "the ten commandments written in red fire." Certainly the villain always comes to a violent end, and the young and handsome hero is rewarded by marriage with a beautiful girl, usually the daughter of a millionaire, but after all that is not a portrayal of the morality of the ten commandments any more than of life itself.

Nevertheless the theater, such as it was, appeared to be the one agency which freed the boys and girls from that destructive isolation of those who drag themselves up to maturity by themselves, and it gave them a glimpse of that order and beauty into which even the poorest drama endeavors to restore the bewildering facts of life. The most prosaic young people bear testimony to this overmastering desire. A striking illustration of this came to us during our second year's residence on Halsted Street through an incident in the Italian colony, where the men have always boasted that they were able to guard their daughters from the dangers of city life, and until evil Italians entered the business of the "white slave traffic," their boast was well founded. The first Italian girl to go astray known to the residents of Hull-House was so fascinated by the stage that on her way home from work she always loitered outside a theater before the enticing posters. Three months after her elopement with an actor, her distracted mother received a picture of her dressed in the men's clothes in which she appeared in vaudeville. Her family mourned her as dead and her name was never mentioned among them nor in the entire colony. In further illustration of an overmastering desire to see life as portrayed on the stage are two young girls whose sober parents did not approve of the theater and would allow no money for such foolish purposes. In sheer desperation the sisters evolved a plot that one of them would feign a toothache, and while she was having her tooth pulled by a neighboring dentist the other would steal the gold crowns from his table, and with the money thus procured they could attend the vaudeville theater every night on their way home from work. Apparently the pain and wrongdoing did not weigh for a moment against the anticipated pleasure. The plan was carried out to the point of selling the gold crowns to a pawn-broker, when the disappointed girls were arrested.

All this effort to see the play took place in the years before the five-cent theaters had become a feature of every crowded city thoroughfare and before their popularity had induced the attendance of two and a quarter million people in the United States every twenty-four hours. The eagerness of the penniless children to get into these magic spaces is responsible for an entire crop of petty crimes made more easy because two children are admitted for one nickel at the last performance when the hour is late and the theater nearly deserted. The Hull-House residents were aghast at the early popularity of these mimic shows, and in the days before the inspection of films and the present regulations for the five-cent theaters, we established at Hull-House a moving picture show. Although its success justified its existence, it was so obviously but one in the midst of hundreds that it seemed much more advisable to turn our attention to the improvement of all of them or rather to assist as best we could the successful efforts in this direction by the Juvenile Protective Association.

However, long before the five-cent theater was even heard of, we had accumulated much testimony as to the power of the drama, and we would have been dull indeed if we had not availed ourselves of the use of the play at Hull-House, not only as an agent of recreation and education, but as a vehicle of self-expression for the teeming young life all about us.

Long before the Hull-House theater was built we had many plays, first in the drawing room and later in the gymnasium. The young people's clubs never tired of rehearsing and preparing for these dramatic occasions, and we also discovered that older people were almost equally ready and talented. We quickly learned that no celebration at Thanksgiving was so popular as a graphic portrayal on the stage of the Pilgrim Fathers, and we were often put to it to reduce to dramatic effects the great days of patriotism and religion.

At one of our early Christmas celebrations Longfellow's "Golden Legend" was given, the actors portraying it with the touch of the miracle play spirit which it reflects. I remember an old blind man, who took the part of a shepherd, said, at the end of the last performance, "Kind Heart," a name by which he always addressed me, "it seems to me that I have been waiting all my life to hear some of these things said. I am glad we had so many performances, for I think I can remember them to the end. It is getting hard for me to listen to reading, but the different voices and all made this very plain." Had he not perhaps made a legitimate demand upon the drama, that it shall express for us that which we have not been able to formulate for ourselves, that it shall warm us with a sense of companionship with the experiences of others? Does not every genuine drama present our relations to each other and to the world in which we find ourselves in such wise as may fortify us to the end of the journey?

The immigrants in the neighborhood of Hull-House have utilized our little stage in an endeavor to reproduce the past of their own nations through those immortal dramas which have escaped from the restraining bond of one country into the land of the universal.

A large colony of Greeks near Hull-House, who often feel that their history and classic background are completely ignored by Americans, and that they are easily confused with the more ignorant immigrants from other parts of southeastern Europe, welcome an occasion to present Greek plays in the ancient text. With expert help in the difficulties of staging and rehearsing a classic play, they reproduced the Ajax of Sophocles upon the Hull-House stage. It was a genuine triumph to the actors who felt that they were "showing forth the glory of Greece" to "ignorant Americans." The scholar who came with a copy of Sophocles in hand and followed the play with real enjoyment did not in the least realize that the revelation of the love of Greek poets was mutual between the audience and the actors. The Greeks have quite recently assisted an enthusiast in producing "Electra," while the Lithuanians, the Poles, and other Russian subjects often use the Hull-House stage to present plays in their own tongue, which shall at one and the same time keep alive their sense of participation in the great Russian revolution and relieve their feelings in regard to it. There is something still more appealing in the yearning efforts the immigrants sometimes make to formulate their situation in America. I recall a play, written by an Italian playwright of our neighborhood, which depicted the insolent break between Americanized sons and old country parents so touchingly that it moved to tears all the older Italians in the audience. Did the tears of each express relief in finding that others had had the same experience as himself, and did the knowledge free each one from a sense of isolation and an injured belief that his children were the worst of all?

This effort to understand life through its dramatic portrayal, to see one's own participation intelligibly set forth, becomes difficult when one enters the field of social development, but even here it is not impossible if a Settlement group is constantly searching for new material.

A labor story appearing in the *Atlantic Monthly* was kindly dramatized for us by the author who also superintended its presentation upon the Hull-House stage. The little drama presented the untutored effort of a trades-union man to secure for his side the beauty of self-sacrifice, the glamour of martyrdom, which so often seems to belong solely to the nonunion forces. The presentation of the play was attended by an audience of trades-unionists and employers and those other people who are supposed to make public opinion. Together they felt the moral beauty of the man's conclusion that "it's the side that suffers most that will win out in this war— the saints is the only ones that has got the world under their feet—we've got to do the way they done if the unions is to stand," so completely that it seemed quite natural that he should forfeit his life upon the truth of this statement.

The dramatic arts have gradually been developed at Hull-House through amateur companies, one of which has held together for more than fifteen years. The members were originally selected from the young people who had evinced talent in the plays the social clubs were always giving, but the association now adds to itself only as a vacancy occurs. Some of them have developed almost a professional ability, although contrary to all predictions and in spite of several offers, none of them have taken to a stage career. They present all sorts of plays from melodrama and comedy to those of Shaw, Ibsen, and Galsworthy. The latter are surprisingly popular, perhaps because of their sincere attempt to expose the shams and pretenses of contemporary life and to penetrate into some of its perplexing social and domestic situations. Through such plays the stage may become a pioneer teacher of social righteousness.

I have come to believe, however, that the stage may do more than teach, that much of our current moral instruction will not endure the test of being cast into a lifelike mold, and when presented in dramatic form will reveal itself as platitudinous and effete. That which may have sounded like righteous teaching when it was remote and wordy will be challenged afresh when it is obliged to simulate life itself.

This function of the stage, as a reconstructing and reorganizing agent of accepted moral truths, came to me with overwhelming force as I listened to the Passion Play at Oberammergau one beautiful summer's day in 1900. The peasants who portrayed exactly the successive scenes of the wonderful Life, who used only the very words found in the accepted version of the Gospels, yet curiously modernized and reorientated the message. They made clear that the opposition to the young Teacher sprang from the merchants whose traffic in the temple He had disturbed and from the Pharisees who were dependent upon them for support. Their query was curiously familiar, as they demanded the antecedents of the Radical who dared to touch vested interests, who presumed to dictate the morality of trade, and who insulted the marts of honest merchants by calling them "a den of thieves." As the play developed, it became clear that this powerful opposition had friends in Church and State, that they controlled influences which ramified in all directions. They obviously believed in their statement of the case and their very wealth and position in the community gave their words such weight that finally all of their hearers were convinced that the young Agitator must be done away with in order that the highest interests of society might be conserved. These simple peasants made it clear that it was the money power which induced one of the Agitator's closest friends to betray him, and the villain of the piece, Judas himself, was only a man who was so dazzled by money, so under the domination of all it represented, that he was perpetually blind to the spiritual vision unrolling before him. As I sat through the long summer day, seeing the shadows on the beautiful mountain back of the open stage shift from one side to the other and finally grow long and pointed in the soft evening light, my mind was filled with perplexing questions. Did the dramatization of the life of Jesus set forth its meaning more clearly and conclusively than talking and preaching could possibly do as a shadowy following of the command "to do the will"?

The peasant actors whom I had seen returning from mass that morning had prayed only to portray the life as He had lived it and, behold, out of their simplicity and piety arose this modern version which even Harnack was only then venturing to suggest to his advanced colleagues in Berlin. Yet the Oberammergau folk were very like thousands of immigrant men and women of Chicago, both in their experiences and in their familiarity with the hard facts of life, and throughout that day as my mind dwelt on my faraway neighbors, I was reproached with the sense of an ungarnered harvest.

Of course such a generally uplifted state comes only at rare moments, while the development of the little theater at Hull-House has not depended upon the moods of anyone, but upon the genuine enthusiasm and sustained effort of a group of residents, several of them artists who have ungrudgingly given their time to it year after year. This group has long fostered junior dramatic associations, through which it seems possible to give a training in manners and morals more directly than through any other medium. They have learned to determine very cleverly the ages at which various types of the drama are most congruous and expressive of the sentiments of the little troupes, from the fairy plays such as "Snow-White" and "Puss-in-Boots" which appeal to the youngest children, to the heroic plays of "William Tell," "King John," and "Wat Tyler" for the older lads, and to the romances and comedies which set forth in stately fashion the elaborated life which so many young people admire. A group of Jewish boys gave a dramatic version of the story of Joseph and his brethren and again of Queen Esther. They had almost a sense of proprietorship in the fine old lines and were pleased to bring from home bits of Talmudic lore for the stage setting. The same club of boys at one time will buoyantly give a roaring comedy and five years later will solemnly demand a drama dealing with modern industrial conditions. The Hull-House theater is also rented from time to time to members of the Young People's Socialist League who give plays both in Yiddish and English which reduce their propaganda to conversation. Through such humble experiments as the Hull-House stage, as well as through the more ambitious reforms which are attempted in various parts of the country, the theater may at last be restored to its rightful place in the community.

There have been times when our little stage was able to serve the *théatre libre*. A Chicago troupe, finding it difficult to break into a trust theater, used it one winter twice a week for the presentation of Ibsen and old French comedy. A visit from the Irish poet Yeats inspired us to do our share toward freeing the stage from its slavery to expensive scene setting, and a forest of stiff conventional trees against a gilt sky still remains with us as a reminder of an attempt not wholly unsuccessful in this direction.

This group of Hull-House artists have filled our little foyer with a series of charming playbills and by dint of painting their own scenery and making their own costumes have obtained beguiling results in stage setting.

Sometimes all the artistic resources of the House unite in a Wagnerian combination; thus, the text of the "Troll's Holiday" was written by one resident, set to music by another, sung by the Music School, and placed upon the stage under the careful direction and training of the dramatic committee; and the little brown trolls could never have tumbled about so gracefully in their gleaming caves unless they had been taught in the gymnasium.

Some such synthesis takes place every year at the Hull-House annual exhibition, when an effort is made to bring together in a spirit of holiday the nine thousand people who come to the House every week during duller times. Curiously enough the central feature at the annual exhibition seems to be the brass band of the boys' club which apparently dominates the situation by sheer size and noise, but perhaps their fresh boyish enthusiasm expresses that which the older people take more soberly.

As the stage of our little theater had attempted to portray the heroes of many lands, so we planned one early spring seven years ago to carry out a scheme of mural decoration upon the walls of the theater itself, which should portray those cosmopolitan heroes who have become great through identification with the common lot, in preference to the heroes of mere achievement. In addition to the group of artists living at Hull-House several others were in temporary residence, and they all threw themselves enthusiastically into the plan. The series began with Tolstoy plowing his field, which was painted by an artist of the Glasgow school, and the next was of the young Lincoln pushing his flatboat down the Mississippi River at the moment he received his first impression of the "great iniquity." This was done by a promising young artist of Chicago, and the wall spaces nearest to the two selected heroes were quickly filled with their immortal sayings.

A spirited discussion thereupon ensued in regard to the heroes for the two remaining large wall spaces, when to the surprise of all of us the group of twenty-five residents, who had lived in unbroken harmony for more than ten years, suddenly broke up into cults and even camps of hero worship. Each cult exhibited drawings of its own hero in his most heroic moment, and of course

each drawing received enthusiastic backing from th
neighborhood, each according to the nationality of th
hero. Thus Phidias standing high on his scaffold as h
finished the heroic head of Athene; the young Davi
dreamily playing his harp as he tended his father's shee
at Bethlehem; St. Francis washing the feet of the lepe
the young slave Patrick guiding his master through th
bogs of Ireland, which he later rid of their danger
the poet Hans Sachs cobbling shoes; Jeanne d'Arc dro
ping her spindle in startled wonder before the heaven
visitants, naturally all obtained such enthusiastic fo
lowing from our cosmopolitan neighborhood that it wa
certain to give offense if any two were selected. The
there was the cult of residents who wished to keep th
series contemporaneous with the two heroes alread
painted, and they advocated William Morris at h
loom, Walt Whitman tramping the open road, Pas
teur in his laboratory, or Florence Nightingale seekin
the wounded on the field of battle. But beyond th
socialists, few of the neighbors had heard of Willia
Morris, and the fame of Walt Whitman was still mor
apocryphal; Pasteur was considered merely a clever sc
entist without the romance which evokes popular affec
tion and in the provisional drawing submitted for vote
gentle Florence Nightingale was said "to look more a
if she were robbing the dead than succoring the wound
ed." The remark shows how high the feeling ran, an
then, as something must be done quickly, we tried t
unite upon strictly local heroes such as the famous fir
marshal who had lived for many years in our neigh
borhood—but why prolong this description which dem
onstrates once more that art, if not always the handmai
of religion, yet insists upon serving those deeper senti
ments for which we unexpectedly find ourselves read
to fight. When we were all fatigued and hopeless c
compromise, we took refuge in a series of landscape
connected with our two heroes by a quotation fror
Wordsworth slightly distorted to meet our dire nee
but still stating his impassioned belief in the efficaciou
spirit capable of companionship with men which reside
in "particular spots." Certainly peace emanates fror
the particular folding of the hills in one of our treasure

mural landscapes, yet occasionally when a guest with a bewildered air looks from one side of the theater to the other, we are forced to conclude that the connection is not convincing.

In spite of its stormy career this attempt at mural decoration connects itself quite naturally with the spirit of our earlier efforts to make Hull-House as beautiful as we could, which had in it a desire to embody in the outward aspect of the House something of the reminiscence and aspiration of the neighborhood life.

As the House enlarged for new needs and mellowed through slow-growing associations, we endeavored to fashion it from without, as it were, as well as from within. A tiny wall fountain modeled in classic pattern for us penetrates into the world of the past, but for the Italian immigrant it may defy distance and barriers as he dimly responds to that typical beauty in which Italy has ever written its message, even as classic art knew no region of the gods which was not also sensuous, and as the art of Dante mysteriously blended the material and the spiritual.

Perhaps the early devotion of the Hull-House residents to the pre-Raphaelites recognized that they, above all English-speaking poets and painters, reveal "the sense of the expressiveness of outward things" which is at once the glory and the limitation of the arts.

Chapter 17

ECHOES OF THE
RUSSIAN REVOLUTION

THE residents of Hull-House have always seen man
evidences of the Russian Revolution; a forlorn family (
little children whose parents have been massacred a
Kishinev are received and supported by their relative
in our Chicago neighborhood; or a Russian woma:
her face streaming with tears of indignation and pit
asks you to look at the scarred back of her sister,
young girl, who has escaped with her life from th
whips of the Cossack soldiers; or a studious youn
woman suddenly disappears from the Hull-House clas:
es because she has returned to Kiev to be near he
brother while he is in prison, that she may earn mone
for the nourishing food which alone will keep hi
from contracting tuberculosis; or we attend a protes
meeting against the newest outrages of the Russia
government in which the speeches are interrupted b
the groans of those whose sons have been sacrificed an
by the hisses of others who cannot repress their indigna
tion. At such moments an American is acutely consciou
of our ignorance of this greatest tragedy of moder
times and at our indifference to the waste of perhaps th

South Halsted Street

noblest human material among our contemporaries. Certain it is, as the distinguished Russian revolutionists have come to Chicago, they have impressed me, as no one else ever has done, as belonging to that noble company of martyrs who have ever and again poured forth blood that human progress might be advanced. Sometimes these men and women have addressed audiences gathered quite outside the Russian colony and have filled to overflowing Chicago's largest halls with American citizens deeply touched by this message of martyrdom. One significant meeting was addressed by a member of the Russian Duma and by one of Russia's oldest and sanest revolutionists; another by Madame Breshkovsky, who later languished a prisoner in the fortress of St. Peter and St. Paul.

In this wonderful procession of revolutionists, Prince Kropotkin, or, as he prefers to be called, Peter Kropotkin, was doubtless the most distinguished. When he came to America to lecture, he was heard throughout the country with great interest and respect; that he was a guest of Hull-House during his stay in Chicago attracted little attention at the time, but two years later, when the assassination of President McKinley occurred, the visit of this kindly scholar, who had always called himself an "anarchist" and had certainly written fiery tracts in his younger manhood, was made the basis of an attack upon Hull-House by a daily newspaper, which ignored the fact that while Prince Kropotkin had addressed the Chicago Arts and Crafts Society at Hull-House, giving a digest of his remarkable book on "Fields, Factories, and Workshops," he had also spoken at the State Universities of Illinois and Wisconsin and before the leading literary and scientific societies of Chicago. These institutions and societies were not, therefore, called anarchistic. Hull-House had doubtless laid itself open to this attack through an incident connected with the imprisonment of the editor of an anarchistic paper, who was arrested in Chicago immediately after the assassination of President McKinley. In the excitement following the national calamity and the avowal by the assassin of the influence of the anarchistic lecture to which he had listened, arrests were made in Chicago of every one suspected of anarchy, in the belief that a widespread plot would be uncovered. The editor's house was searched for incriminating literature, his wife and daughter taken to a police station, and his son and himself, with several other suspected anarchists, were placed in the disused cells in the basement of the city hall.

It is impossible to overstate the public excitement of the moment and the unfathomable sense of horror with which the community regarded an attack upon the chief executive of the nation as a crime against government itself which compels an instinctive recoil from all law-abiding citizens. Doubtless both the horror and recoil have their roots deep down in human experience; the earliest forms of government implied a group which offered competent resistance to outsiders, but assuming no protection was necessary between any two of its own members, promptly punished with death the traitor who had assaulted anyone within. An anarchistic attack against an official thus furnishes an accredited basis both for unreasoning hatred and for prompt punishment. Both the hatred and the determination to punish reached the highest pitch in Chicago after the assassination of President McKinley, and the group of wretched men detained in the old-fashioned, scarcely habitable cells had not the least idea of their ultimate fate. They were not allowed to see an attorney and were kept "in communicado" as their excited friends called it. I had seen the editor and his family only during Prince Kropotkin's stay at Hull-House, when they had come to visit him several times. The editor had impressed me as a quiet, scholarly man, challenging the social order by the philosophic touchstone of Bakunin and of Herbert Spencer, somewhat startled by the radicalism of his fiery young son and much comforted by the German domesticity of his wife and daughter. Perhaps it was but my hysterical symptom of the universal excitement, but it certainly seemed to me more than I could bear when a group of his individualistic friends, who had come to ask for help, said: "You see what becomes of your boasted law; the authorities won't even allow an attorney, nor will they accept bail for these men, against whom nothing can be proved, although the veriest criminals are not denied such a right." Challenged by an anarchist, one is always sensitive for the honor of legally constituted society, and I replied that of course the men could have an attorney, that the assassin himself would eventually be furnished with one, that the fact that a man was an anarchist had nothing to do with his rights before the law! I was met with the retort that that might do for a theory, but that the fact still remained that these men had been absolutely isolated, seeing no one but policemen, who constantly frightened them with tales of public clamor and threatened lynching.

This conversation took place on Saturday night and, as the final police authority rests in the mayor, with a friend who was equally disturbed over the situation, I repaired to his house on Sunday morning to appeal to him in the interest of a law and order that should not yield to panic. We contended that to the anarchist above all men it must be demonstrated that law is impartial and stands the test of every strain. The mayor heard us through with the ready sympathy of the successful politician. He insisted, however, that the men thus far had merely been properly protected against lynching, but that it might now be safe to allow them to see some one; he would not yet, however, take the responsibility of permitting an attorney, but if I myself chose to see them on the humanitarian errand of an assurance of fair play, he would write me a permit at once. I promptly fell into the trap, if trap it was, and within half an hour was in a corridor in the city hall basement, talking to the distracted editor and surrounded by a cordon of police, who assured me that it was not safe to permit him out of his cell. The editor, who had grown thin and haggard under his suspense, asked immediately as to the whereabouts of his wife and daughter, concerning whom he had heard not a word since he had seen them arrested. Gradually he became composed as he learned, not that his testimony had been believed to the effect that he had never seen the assassin but once and had then considered him a foolish half-witted creature, but that the most thoroughgoing "dragnet" investigations on the part of the united police of

he country had failed to discover a plot and that the
ublic was gradually becoming convinced that the das-
ardly act was that of a solitary man with no political
or social affiliations.

The entire conversation was simple and did not seem
to me unlike, in motive or character, interviews I had
had with many another forlorn man who had fallen
into prison. I had scarce returned to Hull-House, however, before it was filled with reporters, and I at once
discovered that whether or not I had helped a brother
out of a pit, I had fallen into a deep one myself. A
period of sharp public opprobrium followed, traces of
which, I suppose, will always remain. And yet in the
midst of the letters of protest and accusation which made
my mail a horror every morning came a few letters of
another sort, one from a federal judge whom I had
never seen and another from a distinguished professor
in constitutional law, who congratulated me on what
they termed a sane attempt to uphold the law in time
of panic.

Although one or two ardent young people rushed into
print to defend me from the charge of "abetting anarchy," it seemed to me at the time that mere words
would not avail. I had felt that the protection of the
law itself extended to the most unpopular citizen was
the only reply to the anarchistic argument, to the effect
that this moment of panic revealed the truth of their
theory of government; that the custodians of law and
order have become the government itself quite as the
armed men hired by the medieval guilds to protect them
in the peaceful pursuit of their avocations through sheer
possession of arms finally made themselves rulers of
the city. At that moment I was firmly convinced that
the public could only be convicted of the blindness of
its course, when a body of people with a hundredfold
of the moral energy possessed by a Settlement group
should make clear that there is no method by which any
community can be guarded against sporadic efforts on
the part of half-crazed, discouraged men, save by a sense
of mutual rights and securities which will include the
veriest outcast.

It seemed to me then that in the millions of words

uttered and written at that time, no one adequately urged that public-spirited citizens set themselves the task of patiently discovering how these sporadic acts of violence against government may be understood and averted. We do not know whether they occur among the discouraged and unassimilated immigrants who might be cared for in such a way as enormously to lessen the probability of these acts, or whether they are the result of anarchistic teaching. By hastily concluding that the latter is the sole explanation for them, we make no attempt to heal and cure the situation. Failure to make a proper diagnosis may mean treatment of a disease which does not exist, or it may furthermore mean that the dire malady from which the patient is suffering be permitted to develop unchecked. And yet as the details of the meager life of the President's assassin were disclosed, they were a challenge to the forces for social betterment in American cities. Was it not an indictment to all those whose business it is to interpret and solace the wretched, that a boy should have grown up in an American city so uncared for, so untouched by higher issues, his wounds of life so unhealed by religion that the first talk he ever heard dealing with life's wrongs, although anarchistic and violent, should yet appear to point a way of relief?

The conviction that a sense of fellowship is the only implement which will break into the locked purpose of a half-crazed creature bent upon destruction in the name of justice came to me through an experience recited to me at this time by an old anarchist.

He was a German cobbler who, through all the changes in the manufacturing of shoes, had steadily clung to his little shop on a Chicago thoroughfare, partly as an expression of his individualism and partly because he preferred bitter poverty in a place of his own to good wages under a disciplinary foreman. The assassin of President McKinley on his way through Chicago only a few days before he committed his dastardly deed had visited all the anarchists whom he could find in the city, asking them for "the password" as he called it. They, of course, possessed no such thing, and had turned him away, some with disgust and all with a certain degree of impatience, as a type of the ill-balanced man who, as they put it, was always "hanging around the movement, without the slightest conception of its meaning." Among other people, he visited the German cobbler, who treated him much as the others had done, but who, after the event had made clear the identity of his visitor, was filled with the most bitter remorse that he had failed to utilize his chance meeting with the assassin to deter him from his purpose. He knew as well as any psychologist who has read the history of such solitary men that the only possible way to break down such a persistent and secretive purpose was by the kindliness which might have induced confession, which might have restored the future assassin into fellowship with normal men.

In the midst of his remorse, the cobbler told me a tale of his own youth; that years before, when an ardent young fellow in Germany, newly converted to the philosophy of anarchism, as he called it, he had made up his mind that the Church, as much as the State, was responsible for human oppression, and that this fact could best be set forth "in the deed" by the public destruction of a clergyman or priest; that he had carried firearms for a year with this purpose in mind, but that one pleasant summer evening, in a moment of weakness, he had confided his intention to a friend, and that from that moment he not only lost all desire to carry it out, but it seemed to him the most preposterous thing imaginable. In concluding the story he said: "That poor fellow sat just beside me on my bench; if I had only put my hand on his shoulder and said, 'Now, look here, brother, what is on your mind? What makes you talk such nonsense? Tell me. I have seen much of life, and understand all kinds of men. I have been young and hot-headed and foolish myself, if he had told me of his purpose then and there, he would never have carried it out. The whole nation would have been spared this horror." As he concluded he shook his gray head and sighed as if the whole incident were more than he could bear—one of those terrible sins of omission; one of the things he "ought to have done," the memory of which is so hard to endure.

The attempt a Settlement makes to interpret Ameri
can institutions to those who are bewildered concernin
them either because of their personal experiences, o
because of preconceived theories, would seem to lie i
the direct path of its public obligation, and yet it i
apparently impossible for the overwrought communit
to distinguish between the excitement the Settlement
are endeavoring to understand and to allay and the at
titude of the Settlement itself. At times of public panic
fervid denunciation is held to be the duty of every goo
citizen, and if a Settlement is convinced that the inci
dent should be used to vindicate the law and does no
at the moment give its strength to denunciation, its at
titude is at once taken to imply a championship o
anarchy itself.

The public mind at such a moment falls into the ol
medieval confusion—he who feeds or shelters a here
tic is upon *prima facie* evidence a heretic himself—he
who knows intimately people among whom anarchist
arise is therefore an anarchist. I personally am con
vinced that anarchy as a philosophy is dying down, no
only in Chicago, but everywhere; that their leadin
organs have discontinued publication, and that thei
most eminent men in America have deserted them. Even
those groups which have continued to meet are divid
ing, and the major half in almost every instance call
itself socialist-anarchists, an apparent contradiction o
terms, whose members insist that the socialistic organiza
tion of society must be the next stage of social develop
ment and must be gone through with, so to speak, before
the ideal state of society can be reached, so nearly beg
ging the question that some orthodox socialists are will
ing to recognize them. It is certainly true that just because
anarchy questions the very foundations of society, the
most elemental sense of protection demands that the
method of meeting the challenge should be intelligently
considered.

Whether or not Hull-House has accomplished any
thing by its method of meeting such a situation, or at
least attempting to treat it in a way which will not de
stroy confidence in the American institutions so adored

by refugees from foreign governmental oppression, it is of course impossible for me to say.

And yet it was in connection with an effort to pursue an intelligent policy in regard to a so-called "foreign anarchist" that Hull-House again became associated with that creed six years later. This again was an echo of the Russian revolution, but in connection with one of its humblest representatives. A young Russian Jew named Averbuch appeared in the early morning at the house of the Chicago chief of police upon an obscure errand. It was a moment of panic everywhere in regard to anarchists because of a recent murder in Denver which had been charged to an Italian anarchist, and the chief of police, assuming that the dark young man standing in his hallway was an anarchist bent upon his assassination, hastily called for help. In a panic born of fear and self-defense, young Averbuch was shot to death. The members of the Russian-Jewish colony on the west side of Chicago were thrown into a state of intense excitement as soon as the nationality of the young man became known. They were filled with dark forebodings from a swift prescience of what it would mean to them were the odium of anarchy rightly or wrongly attached to one of their members. It seemed to the residents of Hull-House most important that every effort should be made to ascertain just what did happen, that every means of securing information should be exhausted before a final opinion should be formed and this odium fastened upon a colony of law-abiding citizens. The police might be right or wrong in their assertion that the man was an anarchist. It was, to our minds, also most unfortunate that the Chicago police in the determination to uncover an anarchistic plot should have utilized the most drastic methods of search within the Russian-Jewish colony composed of families only too familiar with the methods of the Russian police. Therefore, when the Chicago police ransacked all the printing offices they could locate in the colony, when they raided a restaurant which they regarded as suspicious because it had been supplying food at cost to the unemployed, when they searched through private houses for papers and photographs of revolutionaries, when they seized the library of the Edelstadt group and carried the books, including Shakespeare and Herbert Spencer, to the city hall, when they arrested two friends of young Averbuch and kept them in the police station forty-eight hours, when they mercilessly "sweated" the sister, Olga, that she might be startled into a confession —all these things so poignantly reminded them of Russian methods that indignation, fed both by old memory and bitter disappointment in America, swept over the entire colony. The older men asked whether constitutional rights gave no guarantee against such violent aggression of police power, and the hot-headed younger ones cried out at once that the only way to deal with the police was to defy them, which was true of police the world over. It was said many times that those who are without influence and protection in a strange country fare exactly as hard as do the poor in Europe; that all the talk of guaranteed protection through political institutions is nonsense.

Every Settlement has classes in citizenship in which the principles of American institutions are expounded, and of these the community, as a whole, approves. But the Settlements know better than anyone else that while these classes and lectures are useful, nothing can possibly give lessons in citizenship so effectively and make so clear the constitutional basis of a self-governing community as the current event itself. The treatment at a given moment of that foreign colony which feels itself outraged and misunderstood either makes its constitutional rights clear to it, or forever confuses it on the subject.

The only method by which a reasonable and loyal conception of government may be substituted for the one formed upon Russian experiences is that the actual experience of refugees with government in America shall gradually demonstrate what a very different thing government means here. Such an event as the Averbuch affair affords an unprecedented opportunity to make clear this difference and to demonstrate beyond the possibility of misunderstanding that the guarantee of constitutional rights implies that officialism shall be restrained and guarded at every point, that the official represents, not the will of a small administrative body, but the will of the entire people, and that methods therefore have been constituted by which official aggression may be restrained. The Averbuch incident gave an opportunity to demonstrate this to that very body of people who need it most; to those who have lived in Russia where autocratic officers represent autocratic power and where government is officialism. It seemed to the residents in the Settlements nearest the Russian-Jewish colony that it was an obvious piece of public spirit to try out all the legal value involved, to insist that American institutions were stout enough to break down in times of stress and public panic.

The belief of many Russians that the Averbuch incident would be made a prelude to the constant use of the extradition treaty for the sake of terrorizing revolutionists both at home and abroad received a certain corroboration when an attempt was made in 1908 to extradite a Russian revolutionist named Rudovitz who was living in Chicago. The first hearing before a United States Commissioner gave a verdict favorable to the Russian Government, although this was afterward reversed by the Department of State in Washington. Partly to educate American sentiment, partly to express sympathy with the Russian refugees in their dire need, a series of public meetings was arranged in which the operations of the extradition treaty were discussed by many of us who had spoken at a meeting held in protest against its ratification fifteen years before. It is impossible for anyone unacquainted with the Russian colony to realize the consternation produced by this attempted extradition. I acted as treasurer of the fund collected to defray the expenses of halls and printing in the campaign against the policy of extradition and had many opportunities to talk with members of the colony. One old man, tearing his hair and beard as he spoke, declared that all his sons and grandsons might thus be sent back to Russia; in fact, all of the younger men in the colony might be extradited, for every high-spirited young Russian was, in a sense, a revolutionist.

Would it not provoke to ironic laughter that very nemesis which presides over the destinies of nations, if the most autocratic government yet remaining in civilization should succeed in utilizing for its own autocratic methods the youngest and most daring experiment in democratic government which the world has ever seen? Stranger results have followed a course of stupidity and injustice resulting from blindness and panic!

It is certainly true that if the decision of the federal office in Chicago had not been reversed by the Department of State in Washington, the United States government would have been committed to return thousands of spirited young refugees to the punishments of the Russian autocracy.

It was perhaps significant of our need of what Napoleon called a "revival of civic morals" that the public appeal against such a reversal of our traditions had to be based largely upon the contributions to American progress made from other revolutions; the Puritans from the English, Lafayette from the French, Carl Schurz and many another able man from the German upheavals in the middle of the century.

A distinguished German scholar writing at the end of his long life a description of his friends of 1848 who made a gallant although premature effort to unite the German states and to secure a constitutional government, thus concludes: "But not a few saw the whole of their lives wrecked, either in prison or poverty, though they had done no wrong, and in many cases were the finest characters it has been my good fortune to know. They were before their time; the fruit was not ripe, as it was in 1871, and Germany but lost her best sons in those miserable years." When the time is ripe in Russia, when she finally yields to those great forces which are molding and renovating contemporary life, when her Cavour and her Bismarck finally throw into the first governmental forms all that yearning for juster human relations which the idealistic Russian revolutionists embody, we may look back upon these "miserable years" with a sense of chagrin at our lack of sympathy and understanding.

Again it is far from easy to comprehend the great Russian struggle. I recall a visit from the famous revolutionist Gershuni, who had escaped from Siberia in a barrel of cabbage rolled under the very fortress of the commandant himself, had made his way through Manchuria and China to San Francisco, and on his way back to Russia had stopped in Chicago for a few days. Three months later we heard of his death, and whenever I recall the conversation held with him, I find it invested with that dignity which last words imply. Upon the request of a comrade, Gershuni had repeated the substance of the famous speech he had made to the court which sentenced him to Siberia. As representing the government against which he had rebelled, he told the court that he might in time be able to forgive all of their outrages and injustices save one; the unforgivable outrage would remain that hundreds of men like himself, who were vegetarians because they were not willing to participate in the destruction of living creatures, who had never struck a child even in punishment, who were so consumed with tenderness for the outcast and oppressed that they had lived for weeks among starving peasants only that they might cheer and solace them—that these men should have been driven into terrorism, until impelled to "execute," as they call it—"assassinate" the Anglo-Saxon would term it—public officials, was something for which he would never forgive the Russian government. It was, perhaps, the heat of the argument, as much as conviction, which led me to reply that it would be equally difficult for society to forgive these very revolutionists for one thing they had done, their institution of the use of force in such wise that it would inevitably be imitated by men of less scruple and restraint; that to have revived such a method in civilization, to have justified it by their disinterestedness of purpose and nobility of character, was perhaps the gravest responsibility that any group of men could assume. With a smile of indulgent pity such as one might grant to a mistaken child, he replied that such Tolstoyan principles were as fitted to Russia as "these toilettes," pointing to the thin summer gowns of his listeners, "were fitted to a Siberian winter." And yet I held the belief then, as I certainly do now, that when the sense of justice seeks to express itself quite outside the regular channels of established government, it has set forth on a dangerous journey inevitably ending in disaster, and that this is true in spite of the fact that the adventure may have been inspired by noble motives.

Still more perplexing than the use of force by the revolutionists is the employment of the *agent-provocateur* on the part of the Russian government. The visit of Vladimir Bourtzeff to Chicago just after his exposure of the famous secret agent, Azeff, filled one with perplexity in regard to a government which would connive at the violent death of a faithful official and that of a member of the royal household for the sake of bringing opprobrium and punishment to the revolutionists and credit to the secret police.

The Settlement has also suffered through its effort to secure open discussion of the methods of the Russian government. During the excitement connected with the visit of Gorki to this country, three different committees of Russians came to Hull-House begging that I would secure a statement in at least one of the Chicago dailies of their own view, that the agents of the Czar had cleverly centered public attention upon Gorki's private life and had fomented a scandal so successfully that the object of Gorki's visit to America had been foiled; he who had known intimately the most wretched of the Czar's subjects, who was best able to sympathetically portray their wretchedness, not only failed to get a hearing before an American audience, but could scarcely find the shelter of a roof. I told two of the Russian committees that it was hopeless to undertake any explanation of the bitter attack until public excitement had somewhat subsided; but one Sunday afternoon when a third committee arrived, I said that I would endeavor to have reprinted in a Chicago daily the few scattered articles written for the magazines which tried to explain the situation, one by the head professor in political economy of a leading university, and others by publicists well informed as to Russian affairs.

I hoped that a cosmopolitan newspaper might feel an obligation to recognize the desire for fair play on the part of thousands of its readers among the Russians, Poles, and Finns, at least to the extent of reproducing these magazine articles under a noncommittal caption.

That same Sunday evening, in company with one of the residents, I visited a newspaper office only to hear its representative say that my plan was quite out of the question, as the whole subject was what newspaper men called "a sacred cow." He said, however, that he would willingly print an article which I myself should write and sign. I declined this offer with the statement that one who had my opportunities to see the struggles of poor women in securing support for their children found it impossible to write anything which would however remotely justify the loosening of marriage bonds, even if the defense of Gorki made by the Russian committees was sound. We left the newspaper office somewhat discouraged with what we thought one more unsuccessful effort to procure a hearing for the immigrants.

I had considered the incident closed, when to my horror and surprise several months afterward it was made the basis of a story with every possible vicious interpretation. One of the Chicago newspapers had been indicted by Mayor Dunne for what he considered an actionable attack upon his appointees to the Chicago School Board of whom I was one, and the incident enlarged and coarsened was submitted as evidence to the Grand Jury in regard to my views and influence. Although the evidence was thrown out, an attempt was again made to revive this story by the managers of Mayor Dunne's second campaign, this time to show how "the protector of the oppressed" was traduced. The incident is related here as an example of the clever use of that old device which throws upon the radical in religion, in education, and in social reform the odium of encouraging "harlots and sinners" and of defending their doctrines.

If the underdog were always right, one might quite easily try to defend him. The trouble is that very often he is but obscurely right, sometimes only partially right, and often quite wrong; but perhaps he is never so altogether wrong and pig-headed and utterly reprehensible as he is represented to be by those who add the possession of prejudices to the other almost insuperable difficulties of understanding him. It was, perhaps, not surprising that with these excellent opportunities for misjudging Hull-House, we should have suffered attack from time to time whenever any untoward event gave an opening, as when an Italian immigrant murdered a priest in Denver, Colorado. Although the wretched man had never been in Chicago, much less at Hull-House, a Chicago ecclesiastic asserted that he had learned hatred of the Church as a member of the Giordano Bruno Club, an Italian Club, one of whose members lived at Hull-House, and which had occasionally met there, although it had long maintained clubrooms of its own. This club had its origin in the old struggles of united Italy against the temporal power of the Pope, one of the European echoes with which Chicago resounds. The Italian resident, as the editor of a paper representing new Italy, had come in sharp conflict with the Chicago ecclesiastic, first in regard to naming a public school of the vicinity after Garibaldi, which was of course not tolerated by the Church, and then in regard to many another issue arising in anticlericalism, which, although a political party, is constantly involved, from the very nature of the case, in theological difficulties. The contest had been carried on with a bitterness impossible for an American to understand, but its origin and implications were so obvious that it did not occur to any of us that it could be associated with Hull-House either in its motive or direction.

The ecclesiastic himself had lived for years in Rome, and as I had often discussed the problems of Italian politics with him, I was quite sure he understood the *raison d'être* for the Giordano Bruno Club. Fortunately in the midst of the rhetorical attack, our friendly relations remained unbroken with the neighboring priests from whom we continued to receive uniform courtesy as we coöperated in cases of sorrow and need. Hundreds of devout communicants identified with the various Hull-House clubs and classes were deeply distressed by the incident, but assured us it was all a misunderstanding. Easter came soon afterwards, and it was not difficult to make a connection between the attack and the myriad of Easter cards which filled my mail.

Thus a Settlement becomes involved in the many difficulties of its neighbors as its experiences make vivid the consciousness of modern internationalism. And yet the very fact that the sense of reality is so keen and the obligation of the Settlement so obvious may perhaps in itself explain the opposition Hull-House has encountered when it expressed its sympathy with the Russian revolution. We were much entertained, although somewhat ruefully, when a Chicago woman withdrew from us a large annual subscription because Hull-House had defended a Russian refugee while she, who had seen much of the Russian aristocracy in Europe, knew from them that all the revolutionary agitation was both unreasonable and unnecessary!

It is, of course, impossible to say whether these oppositions were inevitable or whether they were indications that Hull-House had somehow bungled at its task. Many times I have been driven to the confession of the blundering Amiel: "It requires ability to make what we seem agree with what we are."

Chapter 18

SOCIALIZED EDUCATION

IN a paper written years ago I deplored at some length the fact that educational matters are more democratic in their political than in their social aspect, and I quote the following extract from it as throwing some light upon the earlier educational undertakings at Hull-House:

> Teaching in a Settlement requires distinct methods, for it is true of people who have been allowed to remain undeveloped and whose facilities are inert and sterile that they cannot take their learning heavily. It has to be diffused in a social atmosphere, information must be held in solution, in a medium of fellowship and good will.
>
> Intellectual life requires for its expansion and manifestation the influences and assimilation of the interests and affections of others. Mazzini, that greatest of all democrats, who broke his heart over the condition of the South European peasantry, said: "Education is not merely a necessity of true life by which the individual renews his vital force in the vital force of humanity; it is a Holy Communion with generations dead and living, by which he fecundates all his faculties. When he withheld from this Communion for generations, as the Italian peasant has been, we say, 'He is like a beast of the field; he must be controlled by force.' "

Even to this it is sometimes added that it is absurd to educate him, immoral to disturb his content. We stupidly use the effect as an argument for a continuance of the cause. It is needless to say that a Settlement is a protest against a restricted view of education.

In line with this declaration, Hull-House in the very beginning opened what we called College Extension classes with a faculty finally numbering thirty-five college men and women, many of whom held their pupils for consecutive years. As these classes antedated in Chicago the University Extension and Normal Extension classes and supplied a demand for stimulating instruction, the attendance strained to their utmost capacity the spacious rooms in the old house. The relation of students and faculty to each other and to the residents was that of guest and hostess, and at the close of each term the residents gave a reception to students and faculty which was one of the chief social events of the season. Upon this comfortable social basis some very good work was done.

In connection with these classes a Hull-House summer school was instituted at Rockford College, which was most generously placed at our disposal by the trustees. For ten years one hundred women gathered there for six weeks; in addition there were always men on the faculty, and a small group of young men among the students who were lodged in the gymnasium building. The outdoor classes in bird study and botany, the serious reading of literary masterpieces, the boat excursions on the Rock River, the coöperative spirit of doing the housework together, the satirical commencements in parti-colored caps and gowns, lent themselves toward a reproduction of the comradeship which college life fosters.

As each member of the faculty, as well as the students, paid three dollars a week, and as we had little outlay beyond the actual cost of food, we easily defrayed our expenses. The undertaking was so simple and gratifying in results that it might well be reproduced in many college buildings which are set in the midst of beautiful surroundings, unused during the two months of the year when hundreds of people, able to pay only

a moderate price for lodgings in the country, can find
nothing comfortable and no mental food more satisfying
than piazza gossip.

Every Thursday evening during the first years a public
lecture came to be an expected event in the neighborhood, and Hull-House became one of the early University Extension centers, first in connection with an
independent society and later with the University of Chicago. One of the Hull-House trustees was so impressed
with the value of this orderly and continuous presentation of economic subjects that he endowed three courses
in a downtown center, in which the lectures were free
to anyone who chose to come. He was much pleased
that these lectures were largely attended by workingmen,
who ordinarily prefer that an economic subject shall be
presented by a partisan and who are supremely indifferent
to examinations and credits. They also dislike the bal-
ancing of pro and con which scholarly instruction implies, and prefer to be "inebriated on raw truth" rather
than to sip a carefully prepared draught of knowledge.

Nevertheless Bowen Hall, which seats seven hundred
and fifty people, is often none too large to hold the
audiences of men who come to Hull-House every Sunday evening during the winter to attend the illustrated
lectures provided by the faculty of the University of Chicago and others who kindly give their services. These
courses differ enormously in their popularity: one on
European capitals and their social significance was followed with the most vivid attention and sense of participation indicated by groans and hisses when the
audience was reminded of an unforgettable feud between
Austria and her Slavic subjects, or when they wildly
applauded a Polish hero endeared through his tragic
failure.

In spite of the success of these Sunday evening courses,
it has never been an easy undertaking to find ac-
ceptable lecturers. A course of lectures on astronomy
illustrated by stereopticon slides will attract a large audience the first week, who hope to hear of the wonders
of the heavens and the relation of our earth thereto,
but instead are treated to spectrum analyses of star dust,
or the latest theory concerning the milky way. The

habit of research and the desire to say the latest word upon any subject often overcomes the sympathetic understanding of his audience which the lecturer might otherwise develop, and he insensibly drops into the dull terminology of the classroom. There are, of course, notable exceptions; we had twelve gloriously popular talks on organic evolution, but the lecturer was not yet a professor—merely a university instructor—and his mind was still eager over the marvel of it all. Fortunately there is an increasing number of lecturers whose matter is so real, so definite, and so valuable, that in an attempt to give it an exact equivalence in words, they utilize the most direct forms of expression.

It sometimes seems as if the men of substantial scholarship were content to leave to the charlatan the teaching of those things which deeply concern the welfare of mankind, and that the mass of men get their intellectual food from the outcasts of scholarship, who provide millions of books, pictures, and shows, not to instruct and guide, but for the sake of their own financial profit. A Settlement soon discovers that simple people are interested in large and vital subjects, and the Hull-House residents themselves at one time, with only partial success, undertook to give a series of lectures on the history of the world, beginning with the nebular hypothesis and reaching Chicago itself in the twenty-fifth lecture! Absurd as the hasty review appears, there is no doubt that the beginner in knowledge is always eager for the general statement, as those wise old teachers of the people well knew, when they put the history of creation on the stage and the monks themselves became the actors. I recall that in planning my first European journey I had soberly hoped in two years to trace the entire pattern of human excellence as we passed from one country to another, in the shrines popular affection had consecrated to the saints, in the frequented statues erected to heroes, and in the "worn blasonry of funeral brasses"—an illustration that when we are young we all long for those mountaintops upon which we may soberly stand and dream of our own ephemeral and uncertain attempts at righteousness. I have had many other illustrations of this; a statement was recently made to me by a member of the Hull-House Boys' club, who had been unjustly arrested as an accomplice to a young thief and held in the police station for three days, that during his detention he "had remembered the way Jean Valjean behaved when he was everlastingly pursued by that policeman who was only trying to do right"; "I kept seeing the pictures in that illustrated lecture you gave about him, and I thought it would be queer if I couldn't behave well for three days when he had kept it up for years."

The power of dramatic action may unfortunately be illustrated in other ways. During the weeks when all the daily papers were full of the details of a notorious murder trial in New York and all the hideous events which preceded the crime, one evening I saw in the street a knot of working girls leaning over a newspaper, admiring the clothes, the beauty, and "sorrowful expression" of the unhappy heroine. In the midst of the trial a woman whom I had known for years came to talk to me about her daughter, shamefacedly confessing that the girl was trying to dress and look like the notorious girl in New York, and that she had even said to her mother in a moment of defiance, "Some day I shall be taken into court and then I shall dress just as Evelyn did and face my accusers as she did in innocence and beauty."

If one makes calls on a Sunday afternoon in the homes of the immigrant colonies near Hull-House, one finds the family absorbed in the Sunday edition of a sensational daily newspaper, even those who cannot read, quite easily following the comic adventures portrayed in the colored pictures of the supplement or tracing the clue of a murderer carefully depicted by a black line drawn through a plan of the houses and streets.

Sometimes lessons in the great loyalties and group affections come through life itself and yet in such a manner that one cannot but deplore it. During the teamsters' strike in Chicago several years ago when class bitterness rose to a dramatic climax, I remember going to visit a neighborhood boy who had been severely injured when he had taken the place of a union driver upon a coal wagon. As I approached the house in which he lived, a large group of boys and girls, some of them very little children, surrounded me to convey the exciting information that "Jack T. was a 'scab,'" and that I couldn't go in there. I explained to the excited children that his mother, who was a friend of mine, was in trouble, quite irrespective of the way her boy had been hurt. The crowd around me outside of the house of the "scab" constantly grew larger and I, finally abandoning my attempt at explanation, walked in only to have the mother say: "Please don't come here. You will only get hurt, too." Of course I did not get hurt, but the episode left upon my mind one of the most painful impressions I have ever received in connection with the children of the neighborhood. In addition to all else are the lessons of loyalty and comradeship to come to them as the mere reversals of class antagonism? And yet it was but a trifling incident out of the general spirit of bitterness and strife which filled the city.

Therefore the residents of Hull-House place increasing emphasis upon the great inspirations and solaces of literature and are unwilling that it should ever languish as a subject for class instruction or for reading parties. The Shakespeare club has lived a continuous existence at Hull-House for sixteen years, during which time its members have heard the leading interpreters of Shakespeare, both among scholars and players. I recall that one of its earliest members said that her mind was peopled with Shakespeare characters during her long hours of sewing in a shop, that she couldn't remember what she thought about before she joined the club, and concluded that she hadn't thought about anything at all. To feed the mind of the worker, to lift it above the monotony of his task, and to connect it with the larger world outside of his immediate surroundings, has always been the object of art, perhaps never more nobly fulfilled than by the great English bard. Miss Starr has held classes in Dante and Browning for many years, and the great lines are conned with never-failing enthusiasm. I recall Miss Lathrop's Plato club and an audience who listened to a series of lectures by Dr. John Dewey on "Social Psychology" as genuine intellectual groups consisting largely of people from the immediate neighborhood who were willing to make "that effort from which we all shrink, the effort of thought." But while we prize these classes as we do the help we are able to give to the exceptional young man or woman who reaches the college and university and leaves the neighborhood of his childhood behind him, the residents of Hull-House feel increasingly that the educational efforts of a Settlement should not be directed primarily to reproduce the college type of culture, but to work out a method and an ideal adapted to the immediate situation. They feel that they should promote a culture which will not set its possessor aside in a class with others like himself, but which will, on the contrary, connect him with all sorts of people by his ability to understand them as well as by his power to supplement their present surroundings with the historic background. Among the hundreds of immigrants who have for years attended classes at Hull-House designed primarily to teach the English language, dozens of them have struggled to express in the newly acquired tongue some of those hopes and longings which had so much to do with their emigration.

A series of plays was thus written by a young Bohemian; essays by a Russian youth, outpouring sorrows rivaling Werther himself and yet containing the precious stuff of youth's perennial revolt against accepted wrong; stories of Russian oppression and petty injustices throughout which the desire for free America became a crystallized hope; an attempt to portray the Jewish day of Atonement in such wise that even individualistic Americans may catch a glimpse of that deeper national life which has survived all transplanting and expresses itself in forms so ancient that they appear grotesque to the ignorant spectator. I remember a pathetic effort on the part of a young Russian Jewess to describe the vivid inner life of an old Talmud scholar, probably her uncle or father, as of one persistently occupied with the grave and important things of the spirit, although when brought into sharp contact with busy and overworked people, he inevitably appeared self-absorbed and slothful. Certainly no one who had read her paper could again see such an old man in his praying shawl bent over his crabbed book, without a sense of understanding.

On the other hand, one of the most pitiful periods in the drama of the much-praised young American who attempts to rise in life is the time when his educational requirements seem to have locked him up and made him rigid. He fancies himself shut off from his uneducated family and misunderstood by his friends. He is bowed down by his mental accumulations and often gets no farther than to carry them through life as a great burden, and not once does he obtain a glimpse of the delights of knowledge.

The teacher in a Settlement is constantly put upon his mettle to discover methods of instruction which shall make knowledge quickly available to his pupils, and I should like here to pay my tribute of admiration to the dean of our educational department, Miss Landsberg, and to the many men and women who every winter come regularly to Hull-House, putting untiring energy into the endless task of teaching the newly arrived immigrant the first use of a language of which he has such desperate need. Even a meager knowledge of English may mean an opportunity to work in a factory *versus* nonemployment, or it may mean a question of life or death when a sharp command must be understood in order to avoid the danger of a descending crane.

In response to a demand for an education which should be immediately available, classes have been established and grown apace in cooking, dressmaking, and millinery. A girl who attends them will often say that she "expects to marry a workingman next spring," and because she has worked in a factory so long she knows "little about a house." Sometimes classes are composed of young matrons of like factory experiences. I recall one of them whose husband had become so desperate after two years of her unskilled cooking that he had threatened to desert her and go where he could get "decent food," as she confided to me in a tearful interview, when she followed my advice to take the Hull-House courses in cooking, and at the end of six months reported a united and happy home.

Two distinct trends are found in response to these classes; the first is for domestic training, and the other is for trade teaching which shall enable the poor little milliner and dressmaker apprentices to shorten the years of errand running which is supposed to teach them their trade.

The beginning of trade instruction has been already evolved in connection with the Hull-House Boys' club. The ample Boys' club building presented to Hull-House three years ago by one of our trustees has afforded well-equipped shops for work in wood, iron, and brass; for smithing in copper and tin; for commercial photography, for printing, for telegraphy, and electrical construction. These shops have been filled with boys who are eager for that which seems to give them a clue to the industrial life all about them. These classes meet twice a week and are taught by intelligent workingmen who apparently give the boys what they want better than do the strictly professional teachers. While these classes in no sense provide a trade training, they often enable a boy to discover his aptitude and help him in the selection of what he "wants to be" by reducing the trades to embryonic forms. The factories are so complicated that the boy brought in contact with them, unless he has some preliminary preparation, is apt to become confused. In pedagogical terms, he loses his "power of orderly reaction" and is often so discouraged or so overstimulated in his very first years of factory life that his future usefulness is seriously impaired.

One of Chicago's most significant experiments in the direction of correlating the schools with actual industry was for several years carried on in a public school building situated near Hull-House, in which the brick-layers' apprentices were taught eight hours a day in special classes during the nonbricklaying season. This early public school venture anticipated the very successful arrangement later carried on in Cincinnati, in Pittsburgh and in Chicago itself, whereby a group of boys at work in a factory alternate month by month with another group who are in school and are thus intelligently conducted into the complicated processes of modern industry. But for a certain type of boy who has been demoralized by the constant change and excitement of street life, even these apprenticeship classes are too strenuous, and he has to be lured into the path of knowledge by all sorts of appeals.

It sometimes happens that boys are held in the Hull-House classes for weeks by their desire for the excitement of placing burglar alarms under the door mats. But to enable the possessor of even a little knowledge to thus play with it is to decoy his feet at least through the first steps of the long, hard road of learning, although even in this, the teacher must proceed warily. A typical street boy who was utterly absorbed in a wood carving class, abruptly left never to return when he was told to use some simple calculations in the laying out of the points. He evidently scented the approach of his old enemy, arithmetic, and fled the field. On the other hand, we have come across many cases in which boys have vainly tried to secure such opportunities for themselves. During the trial of a boy of ten recently arrested for truancy, it developed that he had spent many hours watching the electrical construction in a downtown building, and many others in the public library "reading about electricity." Another boy who was taken from school early, when his father lost both of his legs in a factory accident, tried in vain to find a place for himself "with machinery." He was declared too small for any such position, and for four years worked as an errand boy, during which time he steadily turned in his unopened pay envelope for the use of the household. At the end of the fourth year the boy disappeared, to the great distress of his invalid father and his poor mother whose day washings became the sole support of the family. He had beaten his way to Kansas City, hoping "they wouldn't be so particular there about a fellow's size." He came back at the end of six weeks because he felt sorry for his mother who, aroused at last to a realization of his unbending purpose, applied for help to the Juvenile Protective Association. They found a position for the boy in a machine shop and an opportunity for evening classes.

Out of the fifteen hundred members of the Hull-House Boys' club, hundreds seem to respond only to the opportunities for recreation, and many of the older ones apparently care only for the bowling and the billiards. And yet tournaments and match games under supervision and regulated hours are a great advance over the sensual and exhausting pleasures to be found so easily outside the club. These organized sports readily connect themselves with the Hull-House gymnasium and with all those enthusiasms which are so mysteriously aroused by athletics.

Our gymnasium has been filled with large and enthusiastic classes for eighteen years in spite of the popularity of dancing and other possible substitutes, while the Saturday evening athletic contests have become a feature of the neighborhood. The Settlement strives for that type of gymnastics which is at least partly a matter for character, for that training which presupposes abstinence and the curbing of impulse, as well as for those athletic contests in which the mind of the contestant must be vigilant to keep the body closely to the rules of the game. As one sees in rhythmic motion the slim bodies of a class of lads, "that scrupulous and uncontaminate purity of form which recommended itself even to the Greeks as befitting messengers from the gods, if such messengers should come," one offers up in awkward prosaic form the very essence of that old prayer, "Grant them with feet so light to pass through life." But while the glory stored up for Olympian winners was at most a handful of parsley, an ode, fame for family and city, on the other hand, when the men and boys from the Hull-House gymnasium bring back their cups and medals, one's mind is filled with something like foreboding in the reflection that too much success may lead the winners into the professionalism which is so associated with betting and so close to pugilism. Candor, however, compels me to state that a long acquaintance with the acrobatic folk who have to do with the circus, a large number of whom practice in our gymnasium every winter, has raised our estimate of that profession.

Young people who work long hours at sedentary occupations, factories and offices, need perhaps more than anything else the freedom and ease to be acquired from a symmetrical muscular development and are quick to respond to that fellowship which athletics apparently affords more easily than anything else. The Greek immigrants form large classes and are eager to reproduce the remnants of old methods of wrestling, and other bits of classic lore which they still possess, and when one of the Greeks won a medal in a wrestling match which represented the championship of the entire city, it was quite impossible that he should present it to the Hull-House trophy chest without a classic phrase which he recited most gravely and charmingly.

It was in connection with a large association of Greek lads that Hull-House finally lifted its long restriction against military drill. If athletic contests are the residuum of warfare first waged against the conqueror without and then against the tyrants within the State, the modern Greek youth is still in the first stage so far as his inherited attitude against the Turk is concerned. Each lad believes that at any moment he may be called home to fight this long-time enemy of Greece. With such a genuine motive at hand, it seemed mere affection to deny the use of our boys' club building and gymnasium for organized drill, although happily it forms but a small part of the activities of the Greek Educational Association.

Having thus confessed to military drill countenanced if not encouraged at Hull-House, it is perhaps only fair to relate an early experience of mine with the "Columbian Guards," an organization of the World's Fair summer. Although the Hull-House squad was organized as the others were with the motto of a clean city, it was very anxious for military drill. This request not only shocked my nonresistant principles, but seemed to afford an opportunity to find a substitute for the military tactics which were used in the boys' brigades everywhere, even in those connected with churches. As the cleaning of the filthy streets and alleys was the ostensible purpose of the Columbian guards, I suggested to the boys that we work out a drill with sewer spades, which with their long narrow blades and shortened handles were not so unlike bayoneted guns in size, weight, and general appearance, but that much of the usual military drill could be readapted. While I myself was present at the gymnasium to explain that it was nobler to drill in imitation of removing disease-breeding filth than to drill in simulation of warfare; while I distractedly readapted tales of chivalry to this modern rescuing of the endangered and distressed, the new drill went forward in some sort of fashion, but so surely as I withdrew, the drillmaster would complain that our troops would first grow self-conscious, then demoralized, and finally flatly refuse to go on. Throughout the years since the failure of this Quixotic experiment, I occasionally find one of these sewer spades in a Hull-House storeroom, too truncated to be used for its original purpose and too prosaic to serve the purpose for which it was bought. I can only look at it in the forlorn hope that it may foreshadow that piping time when the weapons of warfare shall be turned into the implements of civic salvation.

Before closing this chapter on Socialized Education, it is only fair to speak of the education accruing to the Hull-House residents themselves during their years of living in what at least purports to be a center for social and educational activity.

While a certain number of the residents are primarily interested in charitable administration and the amelioration which can be suggested only by those who know actual conditions, there are other residents identified with the House from its earlier years to whom the groups of immigrants make the historic appeal, and who use, not only their linguistic ability, but all the resource they can command of travel and reading to qualify themselves for intelligent living in the immigrant quarter of the city. I remember one resident lately returned from a visit in Sicily, who was able to interpret to a bewildered judge the ancient privilege of a jilted lover to scratch the cheek of his faithless sweetheart with the edge of a coin. Although the custom in America had degenerated into a knife slashing after the manner of foreign customs here, and although the Sicilian deserved punishment the incident was yet lifted out of the slough of mere brutal assault, and the interpretation won the gratitude of many Sicilians.

There is no doubt that residents in a Settlement too often move toward their ends "with hurried and ignoble gait," putting forth thorns in their eagerness to bear grapes. It is always easy for those in pursuit of ends which they consider of overwhelming importance to become themselves thin and impoverished in spirit and temper, to gradually develop a dark mistaken eagerness alternating with fatigue, which supersedes "the great and gracious ways" so much more congruous with worthy aims.

Partly because of this universal tendency, partly because a Settlement shares the perplexities of its times and is never too dogmatic concerning the final truth, the residents would be glad to make the daily life at the Settlement "conform to every shape and mode of excellence."

It may not be true

> That the good are always the merry
> Save by an evil chance,

but a Settlement would make clear that one need not be heartless and flippant in order to be merry, nor solemn in order to be wise. Therefore quite as Hull-House tries to redeem billiard tables from the association of gambling, and dancing from the temptations of the public dance halls, so it would associate with a life of upright purpose those more engaging qualities which in the experience of the neighborhood are too often connected with dubious aims.

Throughout the history of Hull-House many inquiries have been made concerning the religion of the residents, and the reply that they are as diversified in belief and in the ardor of the inner life as any like number of people in a college or similar group apparently does not carry conviction. I recall that after a house for men residents had been opened on Polk Street and the residential force at Hull-House numbered twenty, we made an effort to come together on Sunday evenings in a household service, hoping thus to express our moral unity in spite of the fact that we represented many creeds. But although all of us reverently knelt when the High Church resident read the evening service and bowed our heads when the evangelical resident led in prayer after his chapter, and although we sat respectfully through the twilight when a resident read her favorite passages from Plato and another from Abt Vogler, we concluded at the end of the winter that this was not religious fellowship and that we did not care for an-

other reading club. So it was reluctantly given up, an
we found that it was quite as necessary to come togethe
on the basis of the deed and our common aim inside th
household as it was in the neighborhood itself. I onc
had a conversation on the subject with the warden o
Oxford House, who kindly invited me to the evenin
service held for the residents in a little chapel on th
top floor of the Settlement. All the residents were Hig
Churchmen to whom the service was an important an
reverent part of the day. Upon my reply to a query o
the warden that the residents of Hull-House could no
come together for religious worship because there wer
among us Jews, Roman Catholics, English Churchme
Dissenters, and a few agnostics, and that we had foun
unsatisfactory the diluted form of worship which w
could carry on together, he replied that it must be mos
difficult to work with a group so diversified, for he de
pended upon the evening service to clear away an
difficulties which the day had involved and to bring th
residents to a religious consciousness of their commo
aim. I replied that this diversity of creed was part o
the situation in American Settlements, as it was ou
task to live in a neighborhood of many nationalities an
faiths, and that it might be possible that among suc
diversified people it was better that the Settlement cor
should also represent varying religious beliefs.

A wise man has told us that "men are once for a
so made that they prefer a rational world to believe i
and to live in," but that it is no easy matter to find
world rational as to its intellectual, æsthetic, moral, an
practical aspects. Certainly it is no easy matter if th
place selected is of the very sort where the four aspect
are apparently furthest from perfection, but an undertak
ing resembling this is what the Settlement gradually be
comes committed to, as its function is revealed throug
the reaction on its consciousness of its own experience
Because of this fourfold undertaking, the Settlement ha
gathered into residence people of widely diversifie
tastes and interests, and in Hull-House, at least, th
group has been surprisingly permanent. The majority o
the present corps of forty residents support themselve
by their business and professional occupations in th

city, giving only their leisure time to Settlement undertakings. This in itself tends to continuity of residence and has certain advantages. Among the present staff, of whom the larger number have been in residence for more than twelve years, there are the secretary of the City club, two practicing physicians, several attorneys, newspapermen, businessmen, teachers, scientists, artists, musicians, lecturers in the School of Civics and Philanthropy, officers in The Juvenile Protective Association and in The League for the Protection of Immigrants, a visiting nurse, a sanitary inspector, and others.

We have also worked out during our years of residence a plan of living which may be called coöperative, for the families and individuals who rent the Hull-House apartments have the use of the central kitchen and dining room so far as they care for them; many of them work for hours every week in the studios and shops; the theater and drawing rooms are available for such social organization as they care to form; the entire group of thirteen buildings is heated and lighted from a central plant. During the years, the common human experiences have gathered about the House; funeral services have been held there, marriages and christenings, and many memories hold us to each other as well as to our neighbors. Each resident, of course, carefully defrays his own expenses, and his relations to his fellow residents are not unlike those of a college professor to his colleagues. The depth and strength of his relation to the neighborhood must depend very largely upon himself and upon the genuine friendships he has been able to make. His relation to the city as a whole comes largely through his identification with those groups who are carrying forward the reforms which a Settlement neighborhood so sadly needs and with which residence has made him familiar.

Life in the Settlement discovers above all what has been called "the extraordinary pliability of human nature," and it seems impossible to set any bounds to the moral capabilities which might unfold under ideal civic and educational conditions. But in order to obtain these conditions, the Settlement recognizes the need of coöperation, both with the radical and the conservative, and from the very nature of the case the Settlement cannot limit its friends to any one political party or economic school.

The Settlement casts aside none of those things which cultivated men have come to consider reasonable and goodly, but it insists that those belong as well to that great body of people who, because of toilsome and underpaid labor, are unable to procure them for themselves. Added to this is a profound conviction that the common stock of intellectual enjoyment should not be difficult of access because of the economic position of him who would approach it, that those "best results of civilization" upon which depend the finer and freer aspects of living must be incorporated into our common life and have free mobility through all elements of society if we would have our democracy endure.

The educational activities of a Settlement, as well as its philanthropic, civic, and social undertakings, are but different manifestations of the attempt to socialize democracy, as is the very existence of the Settlement itself.

SELECTED BIBLIOGRAPHY

Other Works by Jane Addams

Philanthropy and Social Progress (with others), 1893 Essays
Hull-House Maps and Papers, 1895 Study
Democracy and Social Ethics, 1902 Essays
Newer Ideals of Peace, 1907 Essays
The Spirit of Youth and the City Streets, 1909 Study
A New Conscience and an Ancient Evil, 1912 Essays
The Long Road of Woman's Memory, 1916 Study
Peace and Bread in Time of War, 1922 Study
The Second Twenty Years at Hull-House, 1930 Autobiography
The Excellent Becomes the Permanent, 1932 Addresses
My Friend Julia Lathrop, 1935 Biography

Other Books Suggested

Addams, Jane. *A Centennial Reader.* New York: The Macmillan Company, 1960.

Breckinridge, Sophonisba Preston. *Public Welfare Administration in a Metropolitan Community.* Chicago: University of Chicago Press, 1933.

  Women in the Twentieth Century: A study of Their Political, Social and Economic Activities. New York: McGraw-Hill Book Company, Inc., 1933.

Dewey, John. *"Introduction" to Peace and Bread in Time of War,* by Jane Addams. New York: Columbia University Press; London: Oxford University Press, 1946.

Hamilton, Alice. *Exploring the Dangerous Trades: An Autobiography.* Boston: Little, Brown and Company, 1943.

Linn, James W. *Jane Addams: A Biography.* New York: D. Appleton-Century Company, Inc., 1935.

Tims, Margaret. *Jane Addams of Hull-House.* New York: The Macmillan Company; London: George Allen & Unwin, 1961.

Wald, Lillian. *The House on Henry Street.* New York: Henry Holt & Company, 1915.

Wise, Winifred E. *Jane Addams of Hull-House.* New York: Harcourt, Brace & Company, 1935.

Woods, R. A., and Kennedy, A. J. *The Settlement Horizon: A National Estimate.* New York: Russell Sage Foundation, 1922.

INDEX